IMAGES
of America

GEORGETOWN

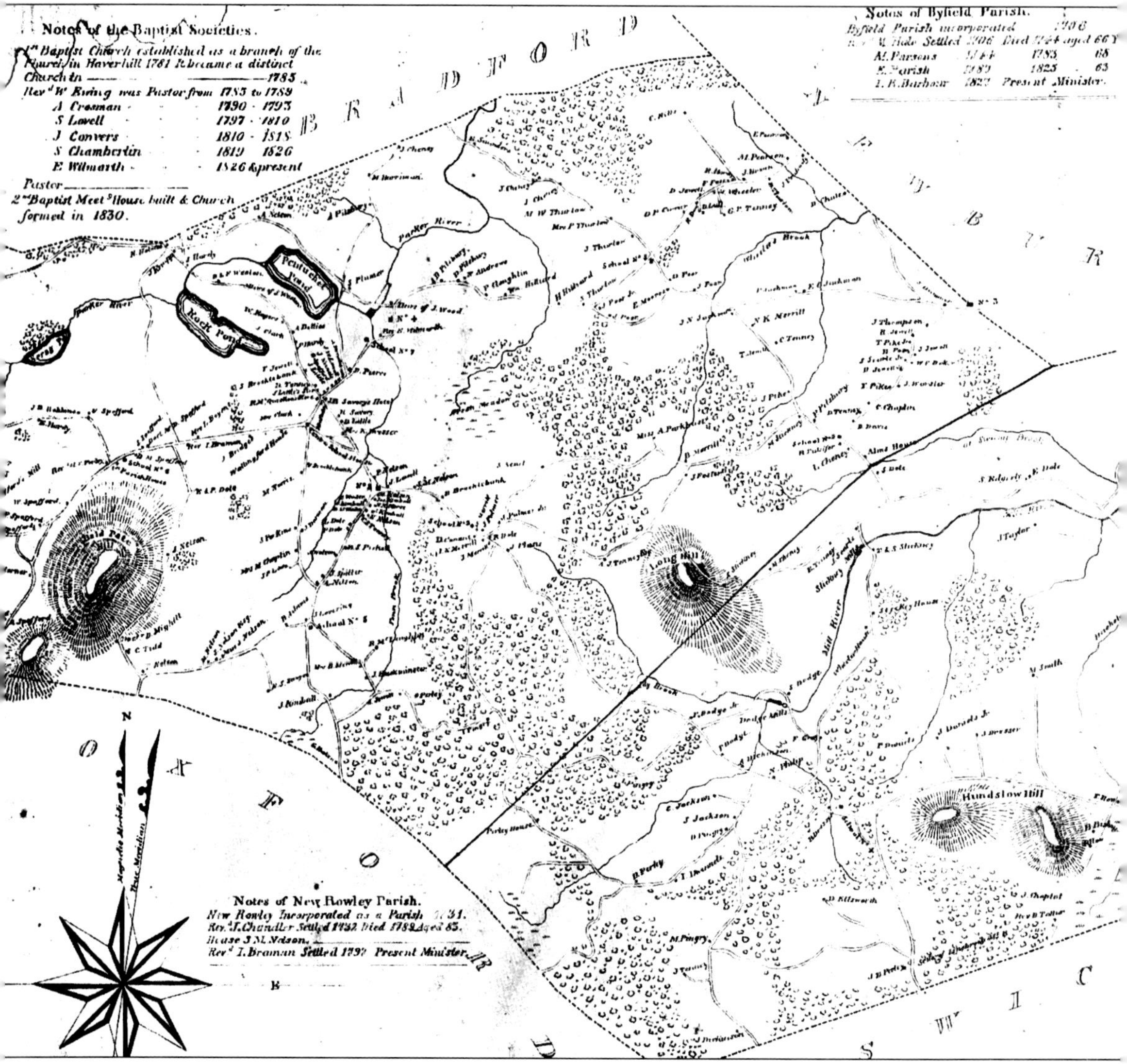

This detail of a Rowley map, surveyed and drawn in 1830 by Philander Anderson, shows New Rowley (the area incorporated as Georgetown in 1838), surrounded by the towns of Boxford, Bradford, Newbury, and Rowley. Bald Pate Hill (left) and Long Hill had heights of 320 feet and 232 feet above sea level, respectively. The three ponds—Pentucket, Rock, and Scrag Ponds—were natural features used for enjoyment, exercise, and commercial ice harvesting in the 19th and early 20th centuries. (Courtesy of the Georgetown Historical Society.)

On the cover: Photographed on June 24, 1909, in anticipation of Old Home Week, these Georgetonians rest on a bench in front of Donoghue's Grocery Store in the Phoenix Block. Seated, from left to right, are store proprietor Dennis Donoghue, William Kimball, and James Carroll. The boy with a somewhat quizzical expression is Gene Nolin, the son of the local blacksmith whose forge was behind the Phoenix Block. The canvas advertisement for Van Camp's Pork and Beans makes one wonder if a ham-and-bean supper was part of the planned festivities for visitors. (From the collection of Albert E. Meader.)

IMAGES
of America

GEORGETOWN

Anthony Mitchell Sammarco
for the Georgetown Historical Society

ARCADIA
PUBLISHING

ISBN 978-0-7385-0976-1

Published by Arcadia Publishing
Charleston, South Carolina

Printed in the United States of America

Library of Congress Control Number: 2001096790

For all general information, please contact Arcadia Publishing:
Telephone 843-853-2070
Fax 843-853-0044
E-mail sales@arcadiapublishing.com
For customer service and orders:
Toll-Free 1-888-313-2665

Visit us on the Internet at www.arcadiapublishing.com

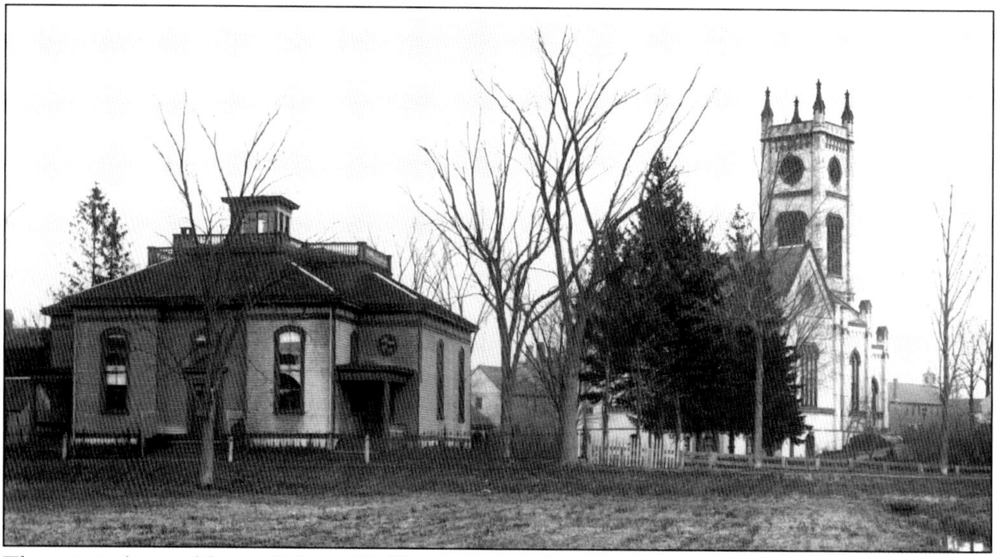

The original town library (Library Hall) was designed by the Boston architectural firm of Bryant & Gilman and built in 1868 on Library Street. Endowed by the great philanthropist George W. Peabody (1795–1869), the library building, books, and endowment fund were truly magnificent gifts to the town. This building was replaced by the present Georgetown Peabody Library, which was designed by Cooper & Bailey and built in 1905 at Lincoln Park on the corner of Park, Pleasant, and Maple Streets. On the right is the Peabody Memorial Church, which was also designed by Bryant & Gilman. Built in 1868 on East Main Street, it was the gift of George Peabody and his sister Judith Peabody Russell Daniels in memory of their mother, Judith Dodge Peabody (1770–1830). This church, which was an Orthodox Congregational society, was founded by former members of the First Congregational Church, and the cornerstone was laid in 1866. Known as Peabody Memorial Hall after 1908, it was destroyed by fire in 1920, and the site is today used as the town parking lot. (Courtesy of Homer K. Tapin.)

Contents

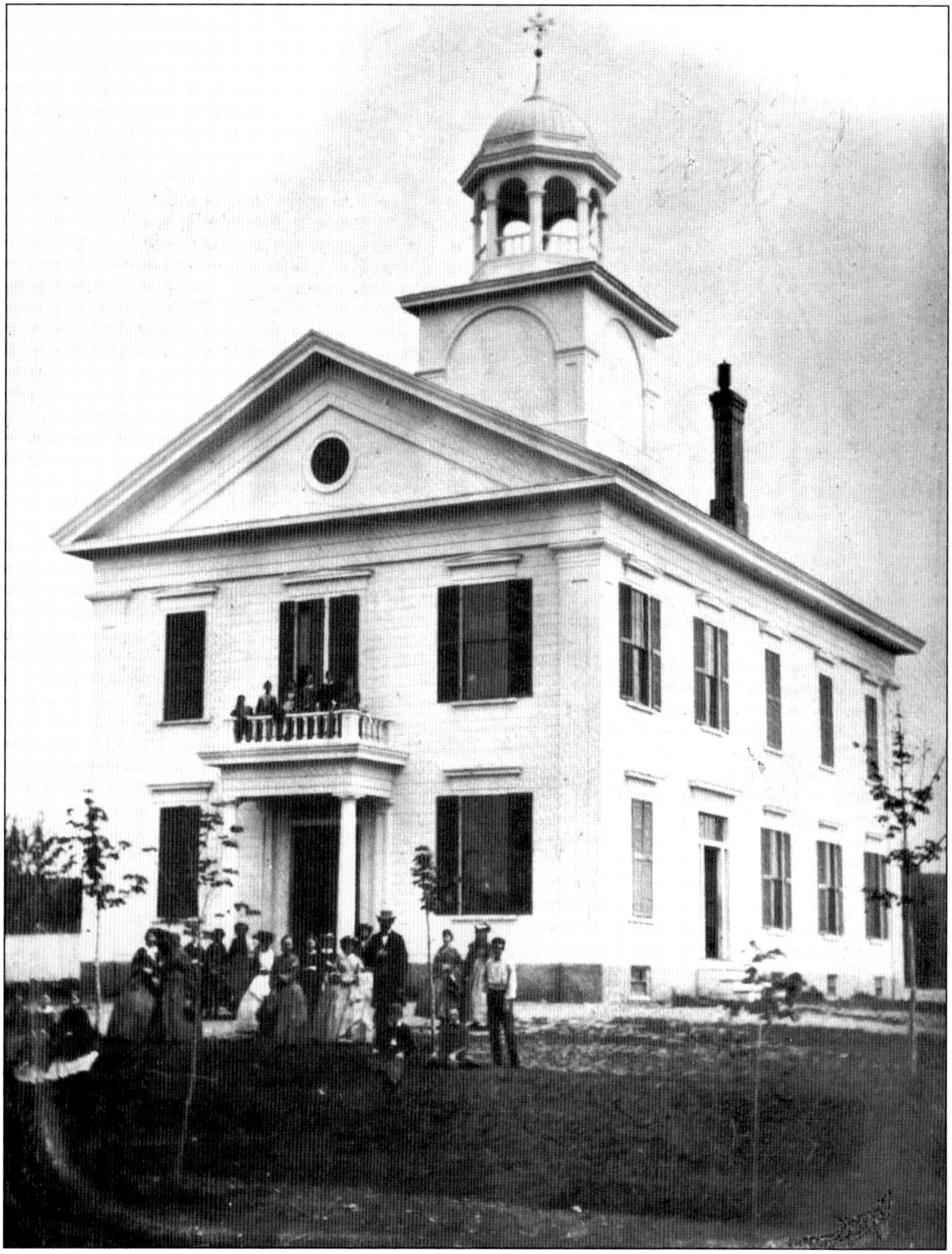

The first town house and high school in Georgetown was an impressive late–Greek Revival structure that was designed by Samuel E. Clark and built in 1856 at the corner of Library and Central Streets (the former site of the New Rowley Universalist Meeting House and the present site of the Georgetown Memorial Town Hall). Around the entrance of the wood-clapboarded building was an entablature supported by Doric columns. The octagonal cupola was surmounted by a weathervane that could be seen from most parts of the town. The building was destroyed by fire in 1898, and the Georgian Revival Central School was built in 1905 on its site. (From the collection of Albert E. Meader.)

INTRODUCTION

One of the prettiest and pleasantest of all New England towns is located about thirty miles from Boston, on the line of the Boston & Maine Railroad, and the name is Georgetown.
—The *Boston Traveler*, 1875

Georgetown was originally inhabited by the Pentucket Indians, a subtribe of the Pennacook Confederacy who spoke Algonquin and were led by Mosquenomenenet, sagamore of Agawam. The area was settled in 1639 by Rev. Ezekial Rogers, said to be "a man of marked ability and high moral worth." In 1700, the settlers paid for these lands nine pounds to Samuel and Joseph English and John Umpee, grandsons of the former sagamore of Agawam. It has been said that in "Humphrey Rainer, Thomas Mighill, Samuel and John Brockelbank, we have the pioneers who opened for settlement, the town of Georgetown." Georgetown was originally part of Rowley, once known as Mr. Rogers' Plantation, and was known as the West Parish or New Rowley until it was incorporated as an independent town in 1838. A rural town for much of its early history, it was noted for its bucolic setting—from marshland and saltgrass on the eastern side of town to the dense woods on the west.

The Rowley Meetinghouse—founded in 1638, with Rev. Ezekiel Rogers (1590–1661) serving as its first pastor—was originally located in the town center and was the only place of worship until 1731, when a meetinghouse was built in the West Parish, with Rev. James Chandler serving as the first pastor. Although Samuel Brocklebank had a small house at Pen Brook that was used during the farm season, the first permanent residents were John and Elizabeth Scott Spofford, who in 1669 received permission to lease a farm in the area that eventually came to be known as Spofford's Hill. The tranquility of the settlement was interrupted in October 1692, when Native Americans attacked and burned the Goodrich House, murdering all of the family except for one daughter, who was taken captive and ransomed the following spring. The fear of attacks by natives was omnipresent throughout the Massachusetts Bay Colony in the 17th century. To preclude surprise attacks, a watch house with a sentry was erected by the settlement. This four-sided structure was said to be so small that it had only enough room for the sentry to remain standing, which was beneficial, as he was required to remain awake during the night. This watch house is today commemorated by a granite marker on its former site in the Harmony Cemetery.

Described by John Warner Barber in his fascinating book *Historical Collections of Every Town in Massachusetts*, Georgetown was said in 1839 to have the "highest land in the county [namely] Bald Pate. From this elevation [320 feet above sea level] an extensive and delightful view may be obtained, comprehending a portion of the valley of the Merrimac, and the adjacent settlements, together with the beautiful town of Haverhill." Rowley had been named for the English town of Rowley by Puritans who had emigrated to the New World from Yorkshire, England, in 1638. The town was incorporated a year later, when it was "ordered that Mr. Ezekiel Rogers' Plantation shall be called Rowley." Originally, this plantation included present-day Rowley, Georgetown, Bradford, Groveland, and Boxford.

During the 19th century, Georgetown was noted for its widespread cultivation of fruit, with upwards of 1,000 barrels of perry (fermented pear juice) being produced annually. However, the tanning and currying of leather and the manufacture of shoes and boots represented the greatest part of the town's economy. In 1837, Georgetown's 16 tanneries produced enough leather for 32,600 pairs of boots and 300,250 pairs of shoes, at a valuation of $315,360. The boot and shoe industry was so profitable and employed so many local workers that it was an economic mainstay well into the 20th century.

The transportation options available in Georgetown in the 19th century also made it a desirable community in which to live. The Boston & Maine Railroad had depots after 1854 in Georgetown at the town center on Railroad and Moulton Streets (a new depot built in 1872) and Baldpate (South Georgetown, 1879), each of which would provide passenger service for almost a century. In 1896, the Haverhill, Georgetown & Danvers Street Railway began regular passenger service. Because the railroad commission had denied the street railway permission for the streetcars to cross the Boston & Maine Railroad tracks at West Main Street, the street railway constructed a high trestle, which allowed the streetcars to pass over the railroad tracks and continue unhindered to the square. A year later, a second streetcar line was laid out on North Street, connecting Georgetown to Newbury via South Byfield. These two streetcar lines allowed further mobility for business, shopping, and pleasure trips and were a major reason for early-20th-century development.

By the mid-20th century, Georgetown had a population of 3,756—only slightly higher than it was in the late 19th century. Many of the families could boast that their ancestors had lived here since it was known as New Rowley, but a series of changes began to reflect the changing face of Georgetown. From fires that destroyed buildings to the demolition of well-known town landmarks, the streetscape of the town further changed. However, with the building of new, modern places of worship (those of St. Mary's Roman Catholic Church on Andover Street, the Community United Methodist Church, the Church of Jesus Christ of Latter Day Saints, and the New Life Community Church), the old-line churches of the First Congregational Church, the First Baptist Church, the Byfield Parish Church, and the now defunct All Saints Episcopal Church were joined by new forms of religious worship that reflected the increasing diversity of the residents. New housing in the past three decades includes single-family residences as well as the Trestle Way residences, which were built in 1973 for senior and handicapped residents and named for the wood trestle of the old Haverhill, Georgetown & Danvers Street Railway.

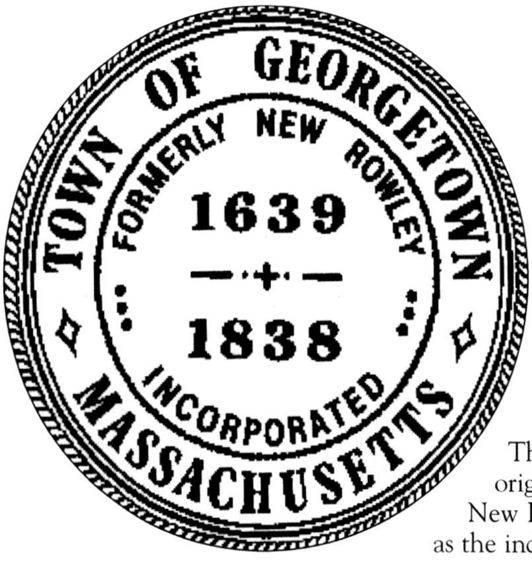

The seal of Georgetown makes mention of its origins in 1639 as part of Rowley, being known as New Rowley. In 1838, the town was incorporated as the independent town of Georgetown.

One

The Town of Georgetown

Officially named American Legion Square, Georgetown Square (or Pentucket Square, as it was known in the 19th century) is the intersection of Central, East Main, West Main, and North Streets. From the late 18th century, these corners were to see residences, stores, business blocks, and places of worship and education for the people of Georgetown.

Georgetown is 31 miles north of Boston, 16 miles to Salem, and 4 miles to East Boxford. The name Georgetown is said to have derived from the Christian name of many of the early residents, their surnames being Drew, Adams, Chaplin, Nelson, Moody, Haskell, Hale, Jewett, Daniels, Wildes, Dole, Frost, Foot, Avery, Curtis, Tenney, Boynton, and Spofford. After Georgetown was incorporated in 1838 (the first selectmen being John A. Lovering, Sewell Spofford, and Gorham P. Tenney), the population of the town was estimated at 1,500. According to Forrest P. Hull's town history, the town had "increased with great rapidity for the last ten years. Seven or eight dwelling houses have been built each year, for the last five years." By 1840, there were "225 dwelling houses, 40 shops, nine tanning houses, four mills, 226 barns and fifty-seven other buildings valued at more than twenty dollars." By the mid-19th century, the tanning of leather for use in the numerous shoe mills began to offer employment opportunities for a larger segment of the population.

Henry M. Nelson said in *The History of Essex County*, "Georgetown is a pleasant and very flourishing place. Its growth has been more rapid than that of any village in the county. The greater part of it has been built since 1827. Real estate has more than doubled in value during the last twelve years [since 1828]. More than fifty buildings, including shops, were erected in 1839."

Following the Civil War, Pentucket Square saw large commercial blocks being built, such as Little's Block, the Phoenix Block, the Union Block, the Bailey Block, and the Adams Block. These buildings had stores on the first floor, with apartments and offices above, and created the quintessential Victorian town center. The Pentucket House was in the town center with the Georgetown Savings Bank, the Georgetown National Bank, the *Georgetown Advocate* office, and numerous businesses and factories, creating a thriving town economy. However, the growth would continue in part due to the tanning and shoe industry, with new schools and firehouses being built throughout the town.

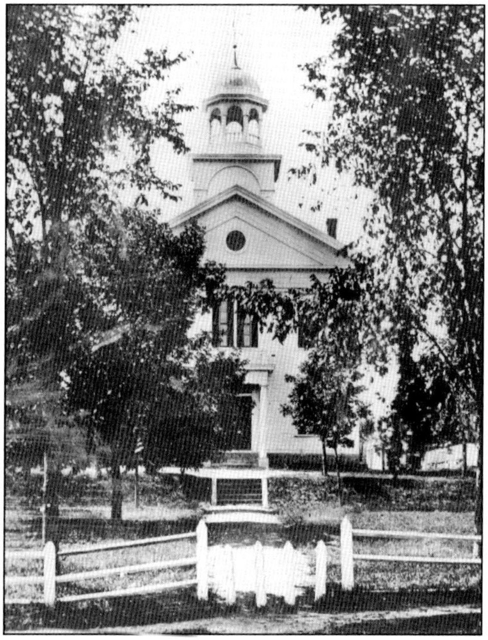

The first town house was a late–Greek Revival building designed by Samuel E. Clark and built on a knoll at the corner of Andover and Central Streets. The building also served as the first high school after it was established in 1856. The first principal was Edward S. Fickett, who served for almost 30 years, and the first teacher was William Reed. Included in the first graduating class were Nellie Yeaton, Nellie Moulton, Emma Perley, Sarah Bateman, Elizabeth Bateman, Lucy Palmer, and Ubert Killam. (Courtesy of the Georgetown Historical Society.)

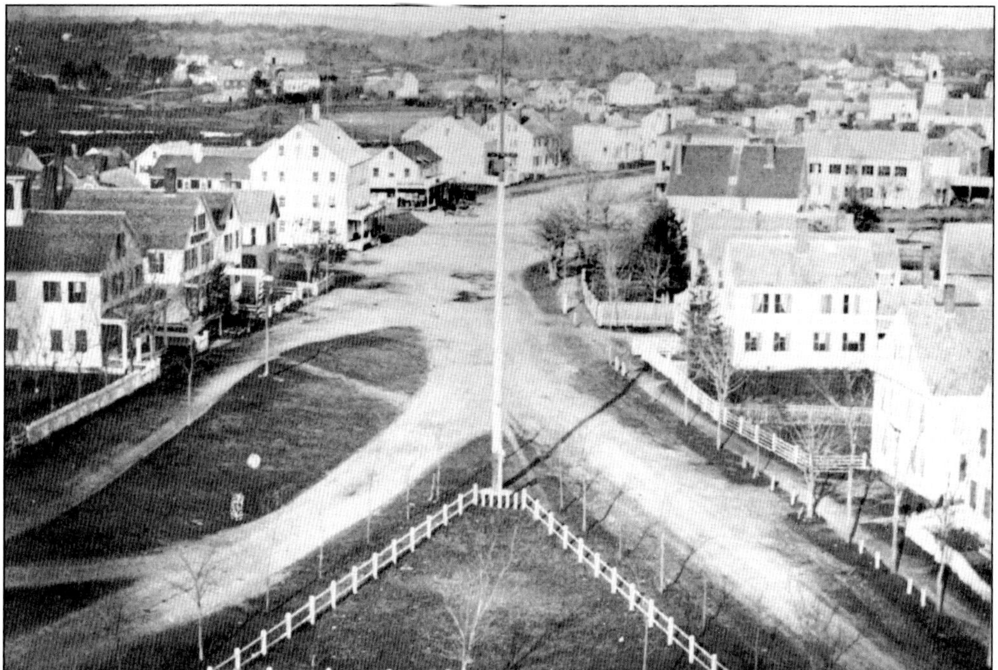

This photograph—taken in 1870 from the belfry of the town house, looking toward Pentucket Square—shows a town that had become quite built up since its founding in 1838. In the center, a flagpole rises from the green before the Civil War Soldiers' Monument was built in 1874. On the far left is the house at 21 Central Street. It was built in 1832 as the New Rowley Universalist Church, which was moved to this site in 1855 to allow for the building of the town hall. The three-story, wood-framed building in the center left is the Phoenix Block. To the upper right is the belfry of the First Baptist Church on North Street. (Courtesy of Homer K. Tapin.)

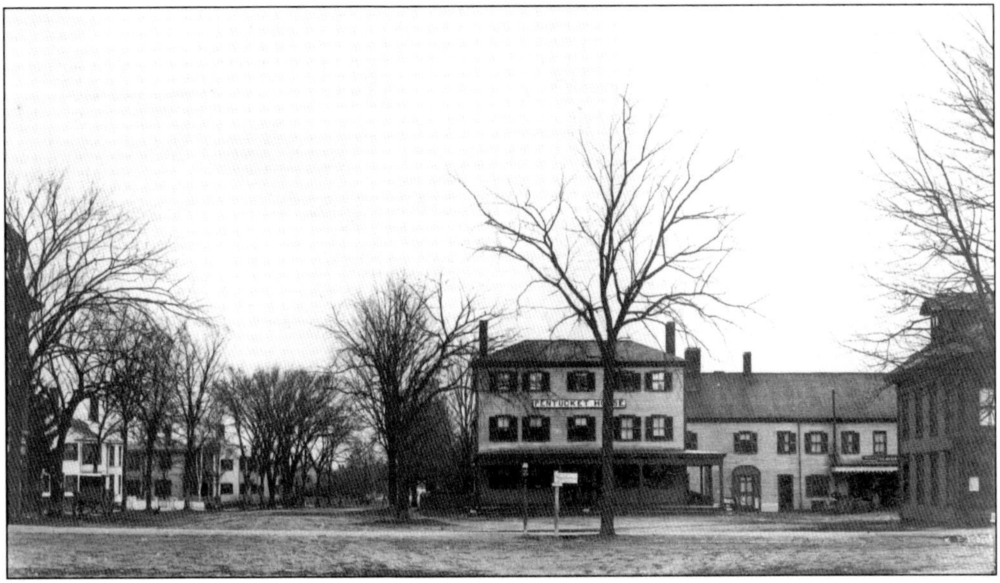

The Pentucket House, originally known as the Pillsbury Tavern, was located on the corner of North and East Main Streets. The tavern was a stop on the Newburyport-to-Lowell stagecoach route, with passengers paying a fare of $1. The driver for many years was Nathan Carter. On the right is Savory Hall, designed by Georgetown's first architect, Boss Chandler. It was owned by Col. John B. Savory and was later known as Mechanic's Hall. Town meetings were held there prior to 1856. Savory also added the third story to the Pentucket House and dubbed it Savory's Tavern during his two decades of business. On the far left is Little's Block, at the corner of North and West Main Streets. (Courtesy of the Georgetown Historical Society.)

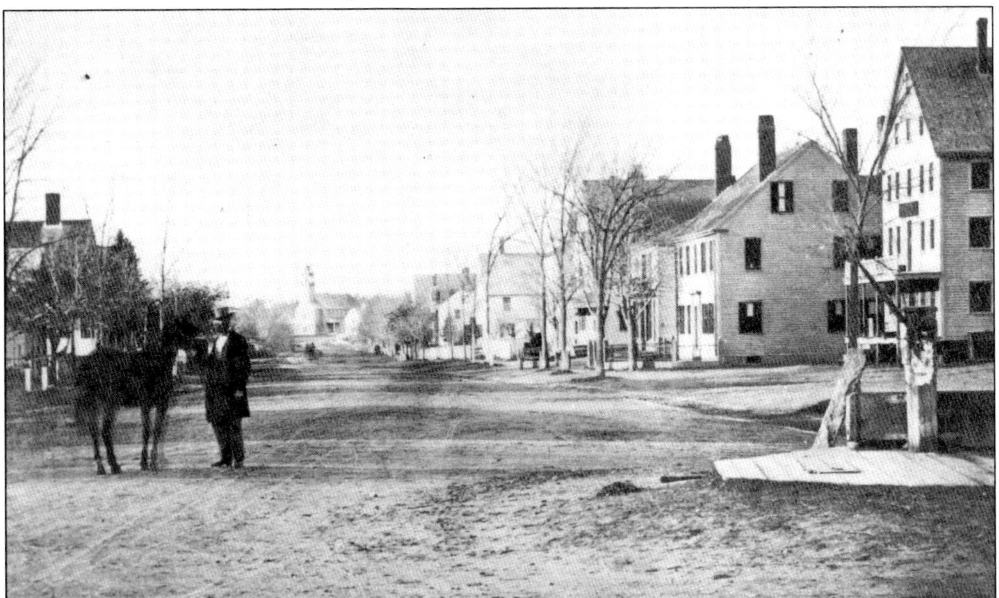

In this view, looking down East Main Street from Pentucket Square *c.* 1860, a man stops with his horse in the center of the town crossroads, once referred to as New Rowley Corners. The old town water pump can be seen on the far right. In the distance is the spire of the Old South Church, at the corner of East Main and Elm Streets. (Courtesy of Homer K. Tapin.)

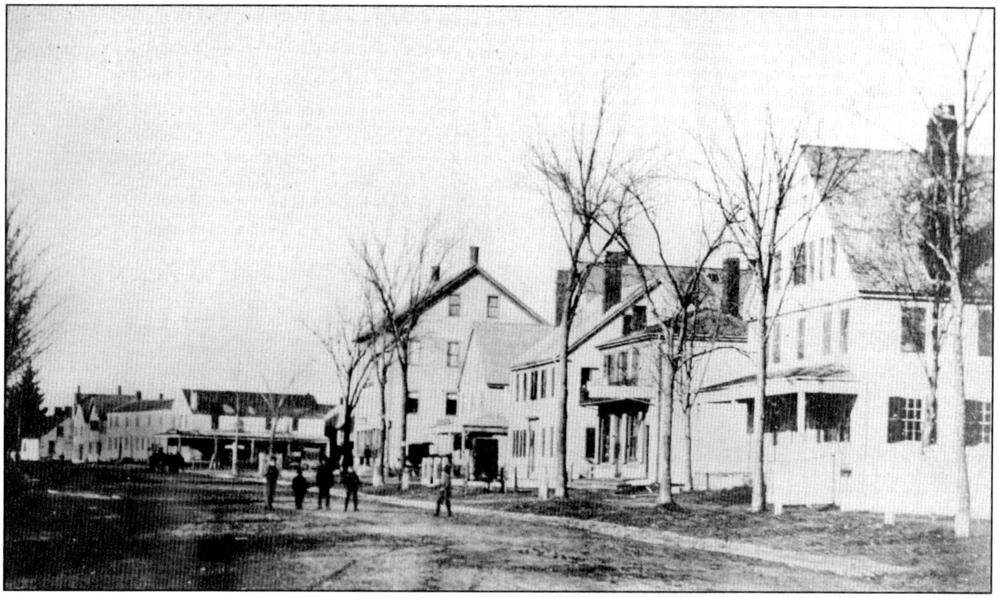

This *c.* 1865 view looks toward Georgetown Square on East Main Street. From right to left are the old Dunbar Tavern (built *c.* 1810 by James T. Dunbar and later occupied by Dr. R.C. Huse), the Dunbar Building, the home of George J. Tenney, the grocery store of William Boynton & Son, and the Masonic Block. On the left in the distance can be seen the shoe factory of Benjamin and Joseph Little, which was one of the first of a long line of boot and shoe shops in Georgetown. (Courtesy of the Georgetown Historical Society.)

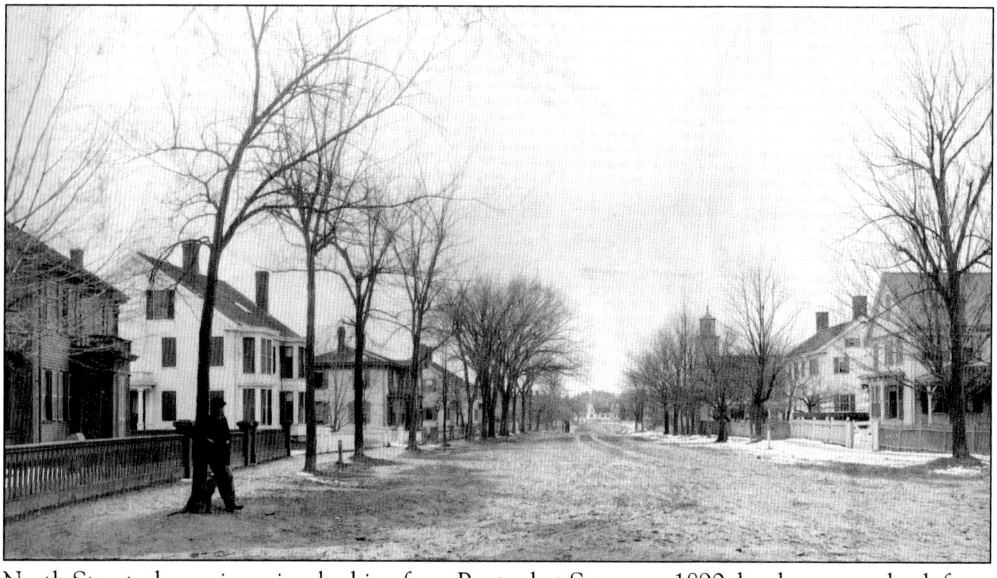

North Street, shown in a view looking from Pentucket Square *c.* 1890, has houses set back from the street, with large shade trees that seem to be the perfect place for the gentleman and his dog to rest. The First Baptist Church, built in 1829, can be seen in the center right. This streetscape is indicative of how attractive Georgetown had become by the late 19th century, with people considering it as their future home. With the Boston & Maine Railroad, the two streetcar lines, and numerous employment opportunities in town, it was to see the population increase from 1,540 in 1840 to 2,117 in 1890. (Courtesy of Louise A. Richardson.)

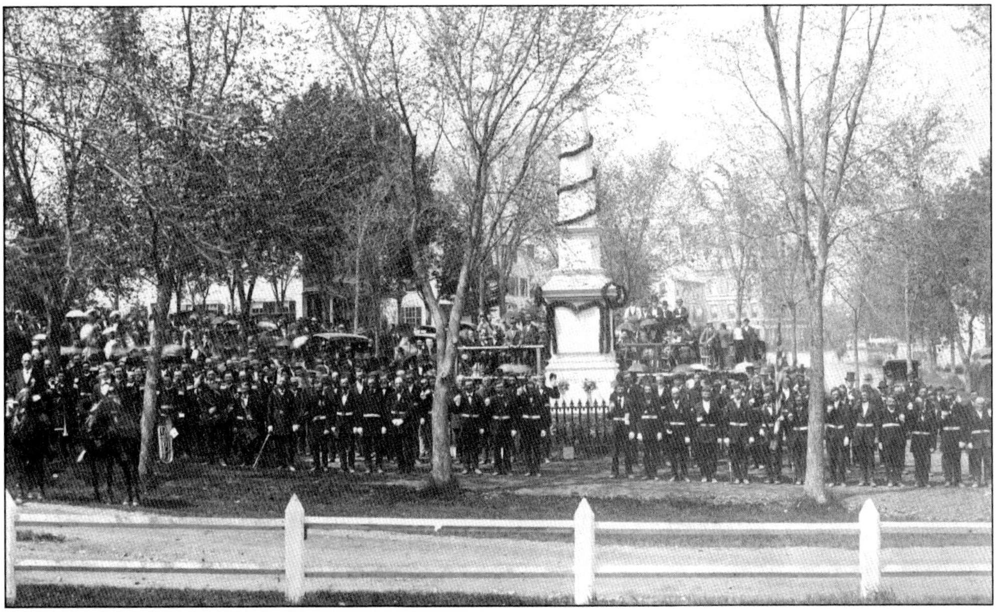

The dedication of the Civil War Soldiers' Monument, shown in a view looking toward Pentucket Square, took place at Union Park on Memorial Day 1874. Rev. W.H. Cudworth presented the address, with hundreds of participants, including the Georgetown Brass Band. Built of unpolished granite, the monument was a simple obelisk with decorative motifs of crossed swords, a soldier's cap, rifle and kit, a wheeled caisson with flanking cannonball, and the Union shield draped with flags. The use of an obelisk as a memorial monument was first used by Solomon Willard in the design of the Bunker Hill Monument, which was built of quarried granite and shipped via the first railroad in America by Gridley Bryant. (Courtesy of the Georgetown Peabody Library.)

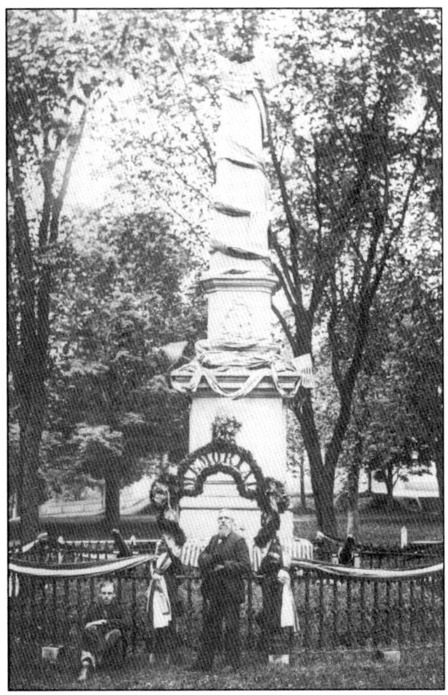

Two men pose in front of the cast-iron fence enclosing the Civil War Soldiers' Monument, which was designed by Ward Moulton Tenney. This inscription appears on the monument: "Erected by the citizens of Georgetown as a token of gratitude to those brave men who died in the service of their country during the war of the rebellion 1861–1865." The monument also lists the names of 51 soldiers from Georgetown who gave the supreme sacrifice for the retention of the union of the United States. As the inscription on the monument poignantly states, "they died that their country might live." (Courtesy of the Georgetown Historical Society.)

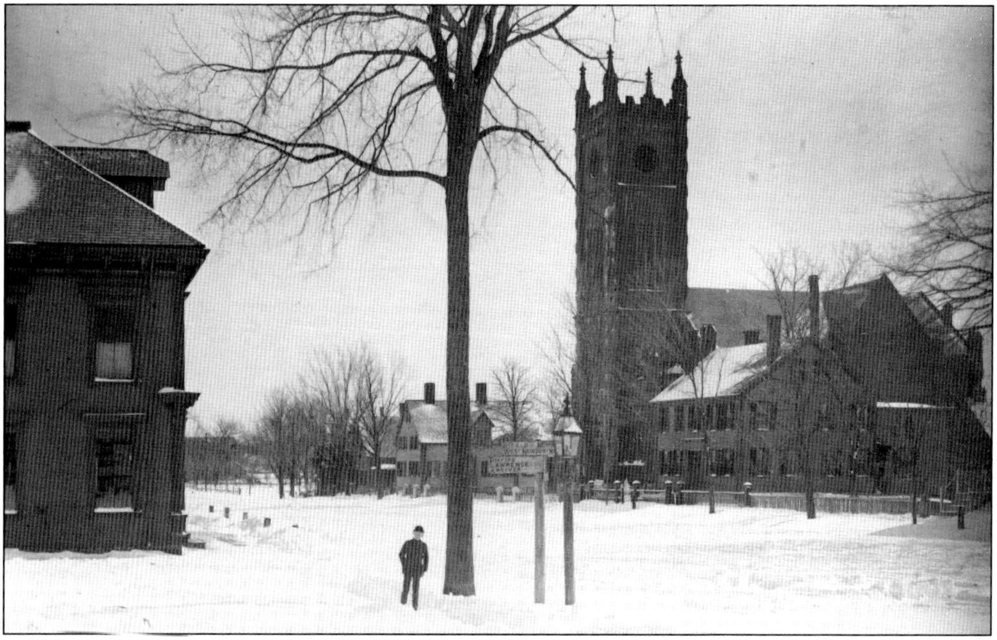

This February 1890 scene of East Main Street shows the pinnacled tower of the Peabody Memorial Church on the right and a corner of the Union Block on the left. The house to the right is the Russell House (built *c.* 1840), where Judith Peabody Russell Daniels lived and where her brother George Peabody would stay when he visited her. The house later became the parsonage for the Peabody Memorial Church. (Courtesy of Homer K. Tapin.)

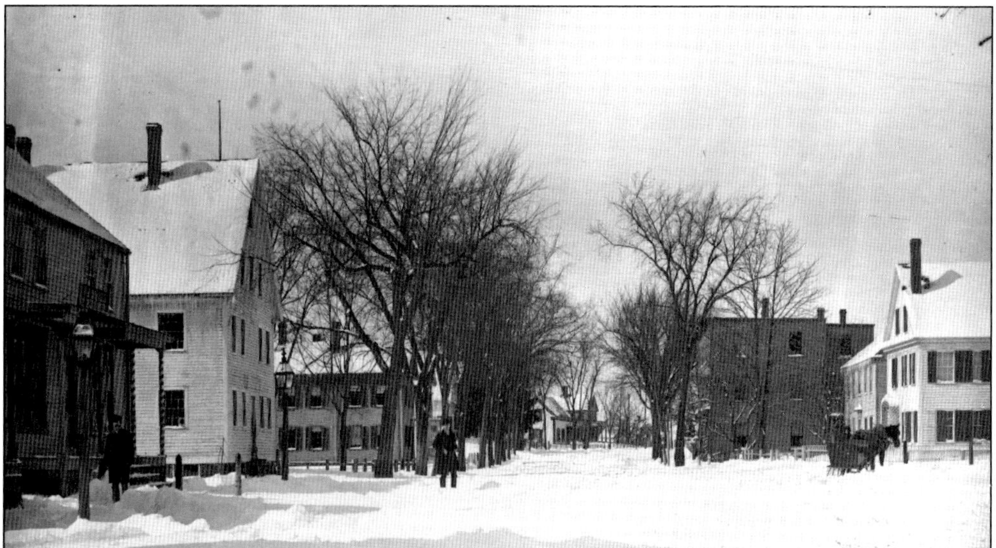

West Main Street, in this scene from February 1890, shows a horse-drawn sleigh on the right, which would be pulled by a horse over roads that had the snow rolled and flattened by a pung rather than plowed as we do today. On the left are the Thomas E. Hill Harness Shop and the C.H. Stoneman Custom Shoe Repair Shop, at 18–20 West Main Street. The Albert B. Noyes Shoe Factory is at the corner of Middle Street, where Scala's Antique Shop is today. (Courtesy of Homer K. Tapin.)

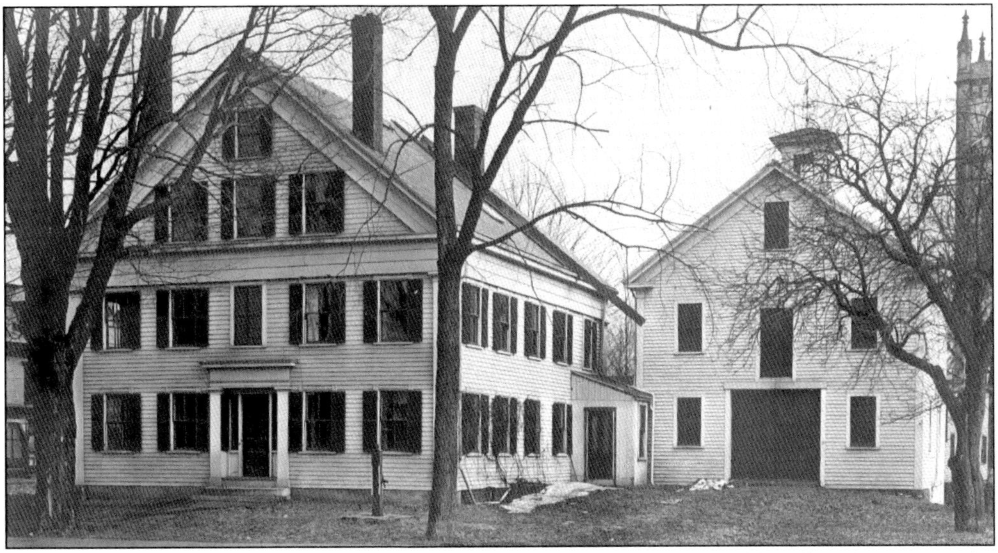

The Protection Lodge of Odd Fellows (International Order of Odd Fellows) met in the Theodore G. Elliott and Louisa Weston Elliott House at the corner of East Main and Central Streets. A large gable-fronted Greek Revival house built *c.* 1840, it once had a large barn on the right. The Odd Fellows—a fraternal organization composed of men engaged in odd trades or jobs—first began in England in the 17th century and was introduced to America in 1819, when Thomas Wildey founded the first lodge in Maryland. The pinnacled tower of the Peabody Memorial Church can be seen on the right. Today, the former lodge is the King Davis Agency. (Courtesy of the Georgetown Historical Society.)

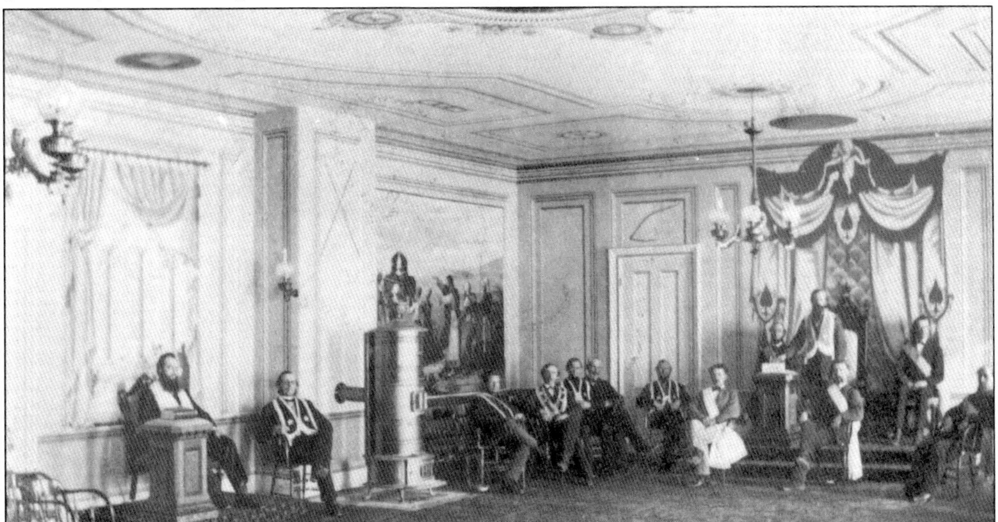

The Protection Lodge of Odd Fellows Hall had impressive wall and ceiling decorations and an elaborately festooned and draped dais, where the grand master would sit during a lodge meeting. The International Order of Odd Fellows was also known as the Three Link Fraternity, which represents friendship, love, and truth. The lodge was a fraternity of men seeking social unity and fellowship with their fellow members for mutual aid in their trades and lives. Note the elaborate stove in the center, possibly obtained from dealers John Savory or John Bailey. It was vented to a chimney behind the wall. (Courtesy of Homer K. Tapin.)

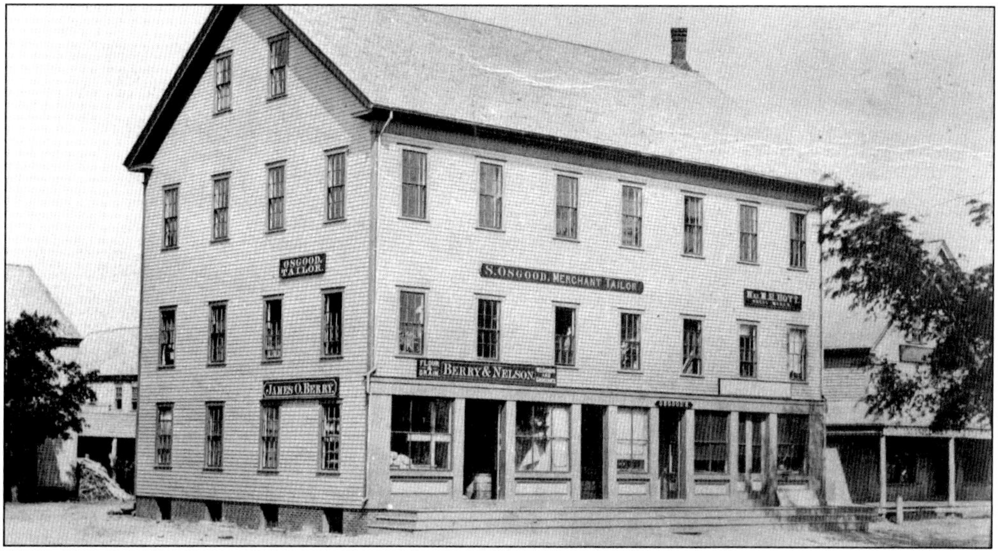

The Masonic Block was erected in 1867 as a three-story, wood-framed commercial building with businesses such as Stephen Osgood, a merchant tailor; Berry & Nelson, West Indies goods and groceries; and Miss M.E. Hoyt, dressmaker. The Charles C. Dame Lodge of Masons met upstairs, where their Masonic rooms were located until the building was destroyed by fire in 1885. The premise of the Masons is threefold: physical, intellectual, and moral. These three attributes are man's physical nature by observance of moral law, his intellectual power by studying his need, and his moral nature by doing errands of mercy. (Courtesy of the Georgetown Peabody Library.)

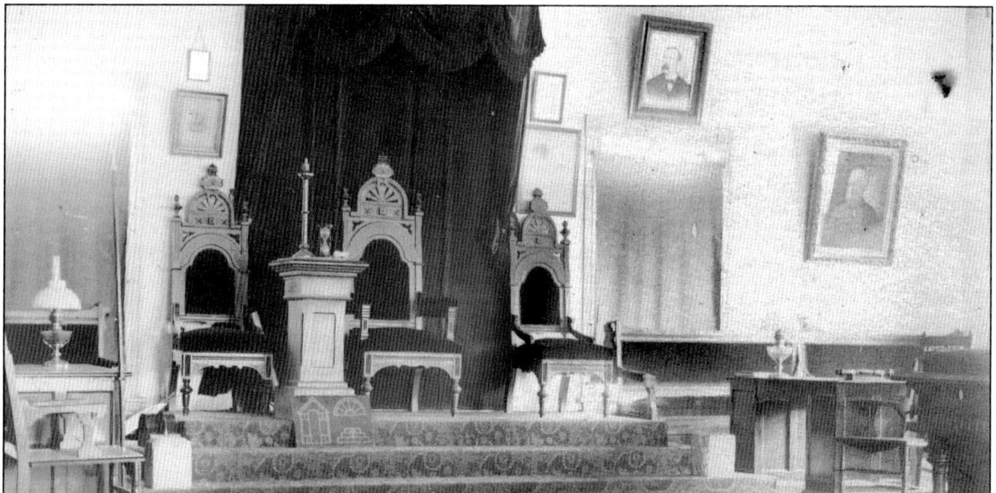

The platform of the Charles C. Dame Lodge, Ancient Free & Accepted Masons, had an elaborately draped canopy surmounting the dais, with the letter G representing God. Following the 1885 fire in the Masonic Block, the lodge received furniture from other lodges that was used in the new apartments in Little's Block—items such as maroon upholstered chairs from St. John's and St. Mark's Lodge, an altar from the Warren Lodge, and an ivory gavel from D.B. Tenney. The lodge was organized in 1867 and named for Grand Master Charles C. Dame of Newburyport. The first master was the Right Worshipful Stephen Osgood, who served from 1867 to 1869. (Courtesy of the Georgetown Historical Society.)

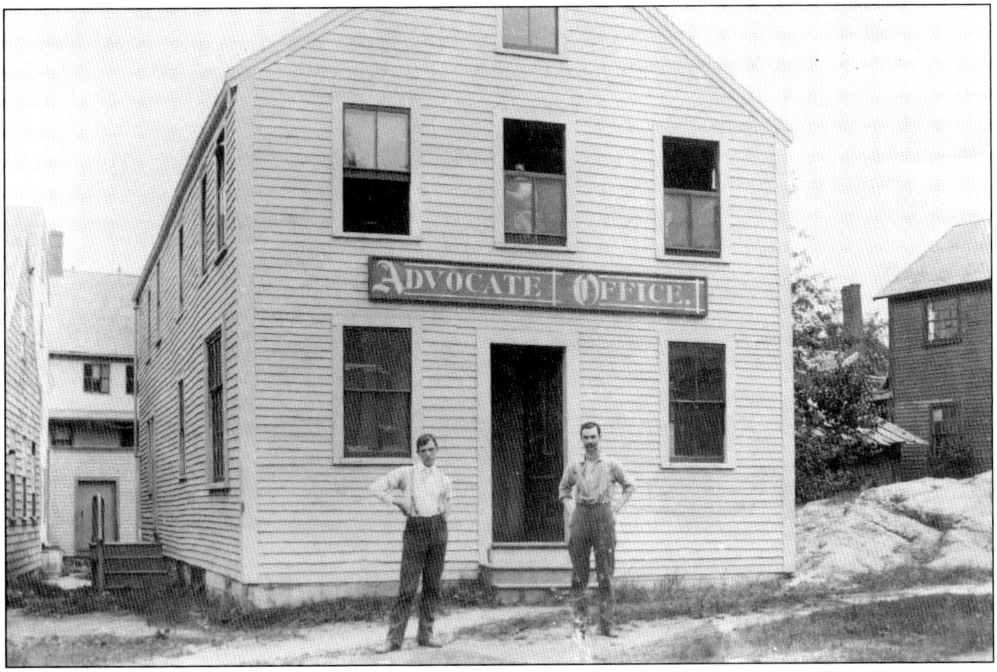

Calvin N. Pingree, on the left, and a fellow employee stand in front of the office of the *Georgetown Advocate*, the town's weekly newspaper. Note the man in the upper window. The building was the former grocery store erected by Ben Little at Little's Corner and later housed the store of A. Hamilton. It was moved in 1870 to Middle Street, opposite the Central Firehouse, where it was the site of the newspaper operation for many years. The building was demolished in the early 1960s. (Courtesy of Homer K. Tapin.)

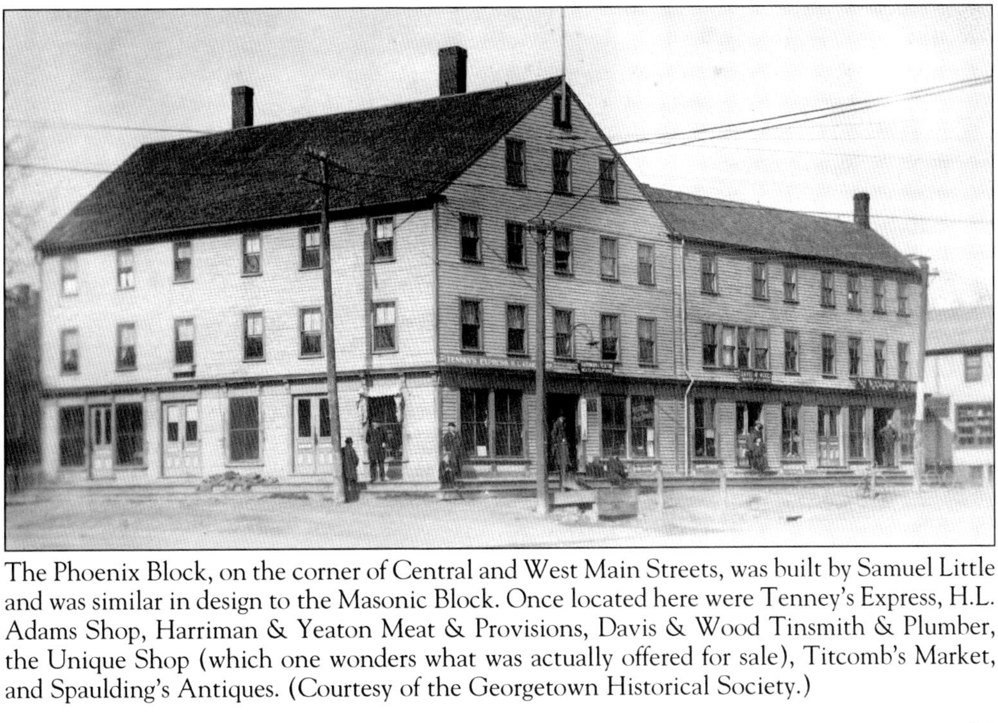

The Phoenix Block, on the corner of Central and West Main Streets, was built by Samuel Little and was similar in design to the Masonic Block. Once located here were Tenney's Express, H.L. Adams Shop, Harriman & Yeaton Meat & Provisions, Davis & Wood Tinsmith & Plumber, the Unique Shop (which one wonders what was actually offered for sale), Titcomb's Market, and Spaulding's Antiques. (Courtesy of the Georgetown Historical Society.)

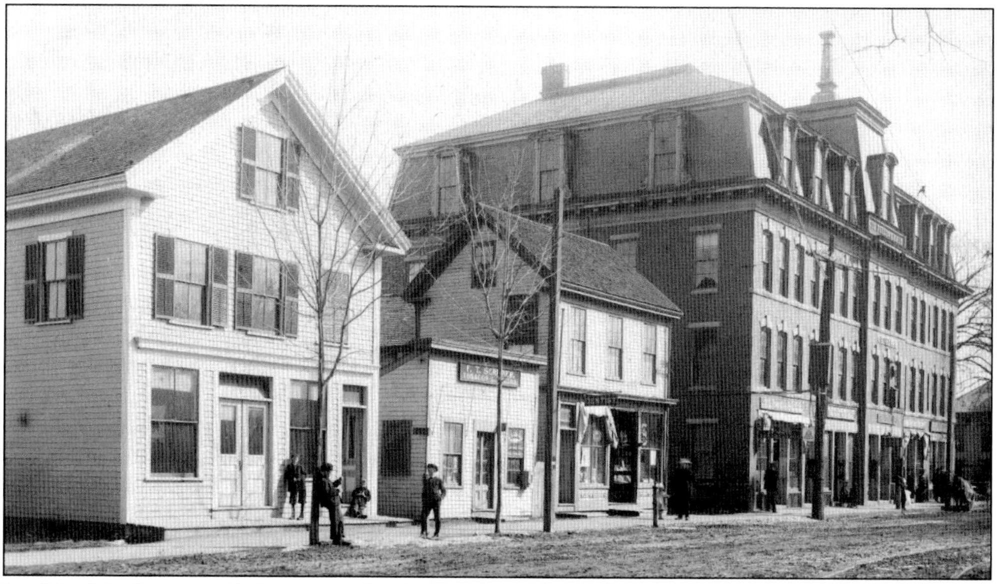

Little's Block, named for town forefathers Joseph and Benjamin Little, was an elegant brick-and-granite commercial block built by the Odd Fellows Building Association in 1870 at the corner of North and West Main Streets. Its impressive mansard roof had a projecting center section. From left to right are Justin White's Shoe Shop (which was also the location of Georgetown's first telephone exchange and office), a tobacco and cigar store, Dr. Thomas Whittle's dentist office, and the Hamilton Variety Store. (Courtesy of the Georgetown Historical Society.)

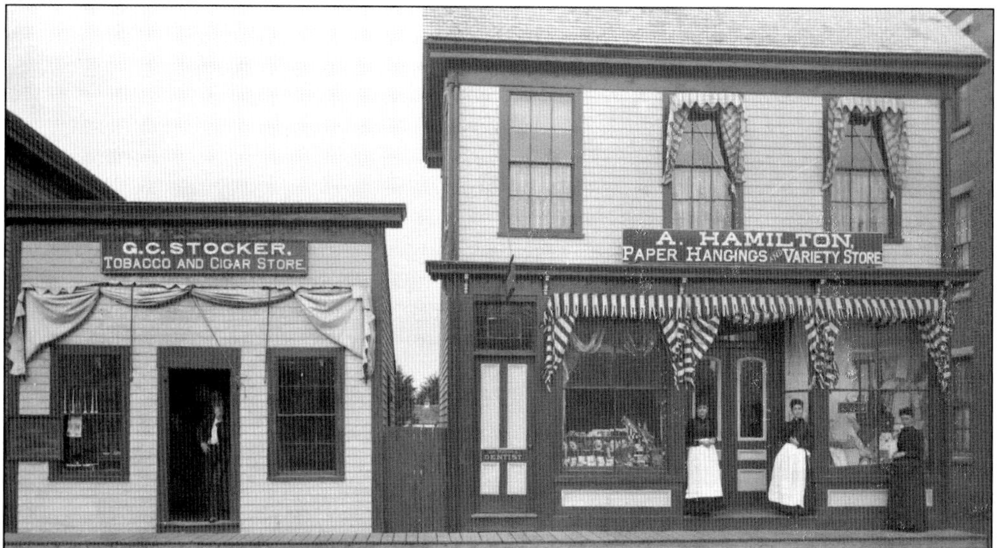

These two wood-framed buildings were between Justin White's Shop and Little's Block. Photographed in 1891, a man can be seen in the doorway of G.C. Stocker's tobacco and cigar store. On the right, saleswomen pose in front of A. Hamilton's Paper Hangings and Variety Store. On the second floor was the dentist office of Dr. Thomas Whittle, who was, according to one newspaper account, "regarded as very successful in his profession." (From the collection of Albert E. Meader.)

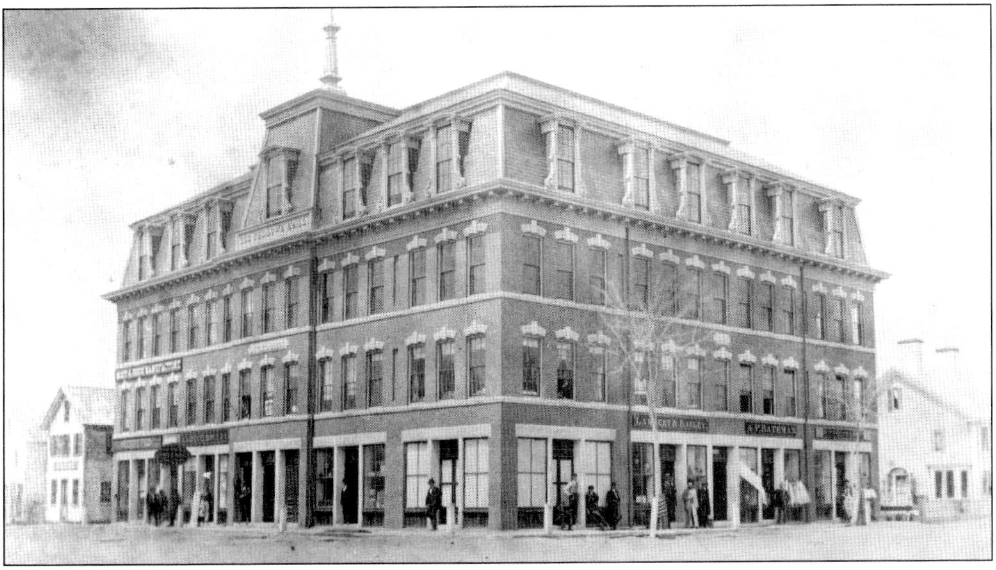

Little's Block (or Odd Fellows Hall, as was carved in the granite block in the base of the center mansard roof) was the most impressive commercial block in Georgetown. Built by the Odd Fellows Building Association in 1870, the building cost the large sum of $40,000. The Little & Tenney Boot & Shoe Manufactory is on the left, with Lambert & Bailey and A.P. Bateman on the right. (From the collection of Albert E. Meader.)

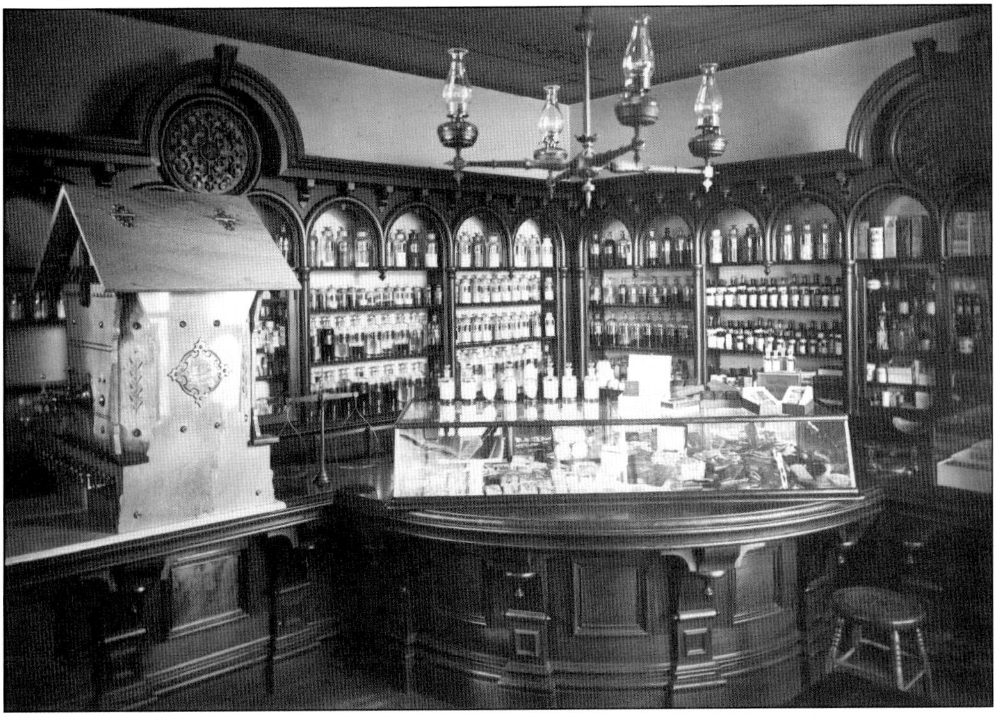

The interior of Bateman's Apothecary Shop in Little's Block was filled with glass canisters, jars, and vials of medicine and potions. In addition to drugs and chemicals, Bateman (and later his son) sold toilet and fancy articles. As a public service for those requiring it, his trade card stated that "prescriptions [were] carefully compounded at all hours." (Courtesy of Homer K. Tapin.)

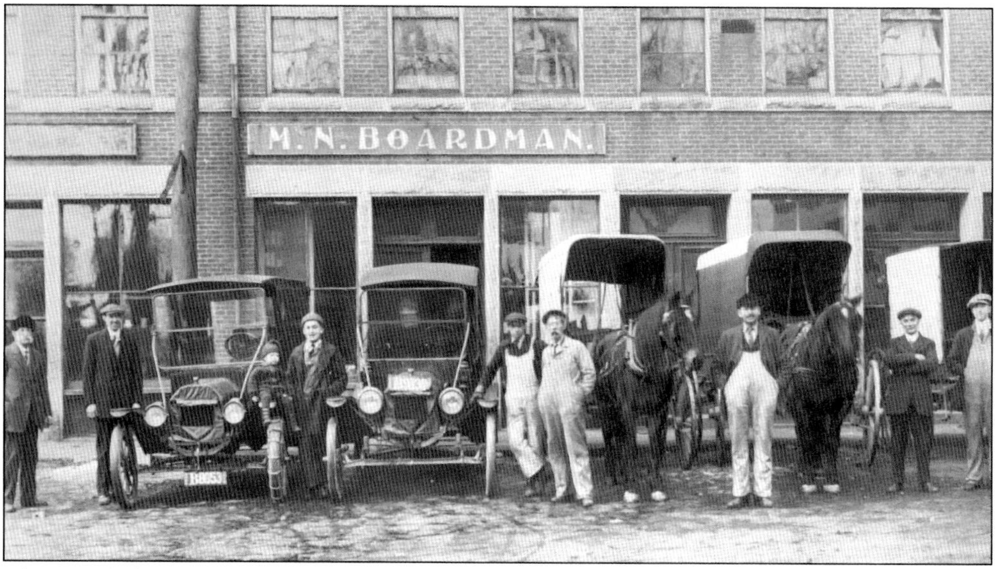

This 1915 photograph was taken in front of Moses N. Boardman's grocery store, in Little's Block. Posing beside their means of transportation for deliveries are, from left to right, Moses N. Boardman (the proprietor), unidentified, Charles Boardman (resting on the tire of the automobile), Seth Boardman (Charles's father), Punk Jones, Gene Merrill, George Hopkins, George Kelley, and Bob Adams. M.N. Boardman & Company was opened in 1873 and had been in Little's Block since 1889. Little's Block was destroyed by fire in 1923. (Courtesy of Homer K. Tapin.)

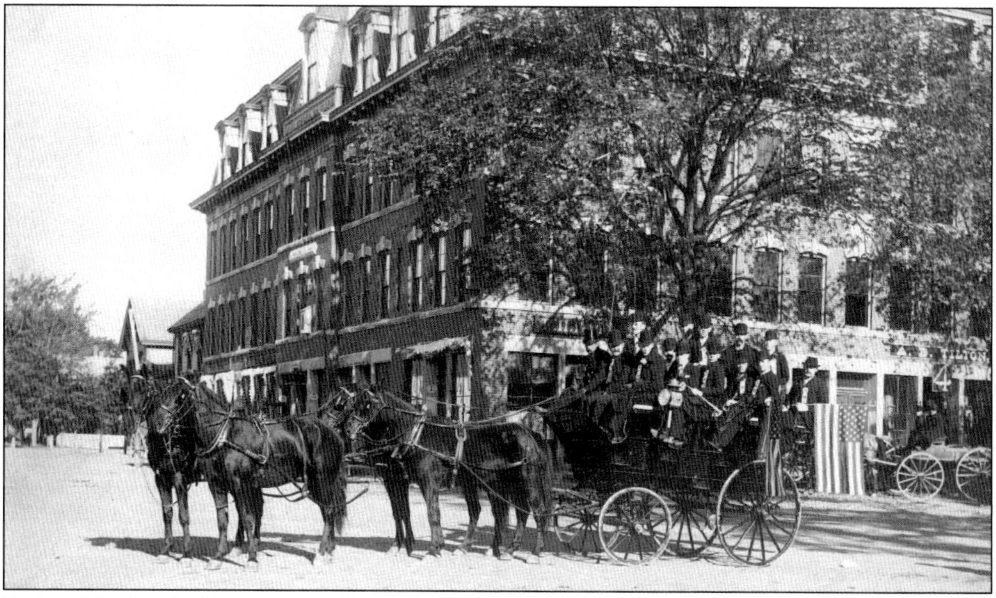

Father Matthew's Temperance Society rented the Baldpate Inn's Tally-Ho in 1892 for an afternoon outing for society members. The horse-drawn Tally-Ho stopped in front of Little's Block in Pentucket Square, as the men who had signed their names to the Total Abstinence Pledge enjoyed their outing without the consumption of alcohol. In the mid-19th century, alcohol was often perceived as evil and men were strongly encouraged to be moderate or to abstain. (From the collection of Albert E. Meader.)

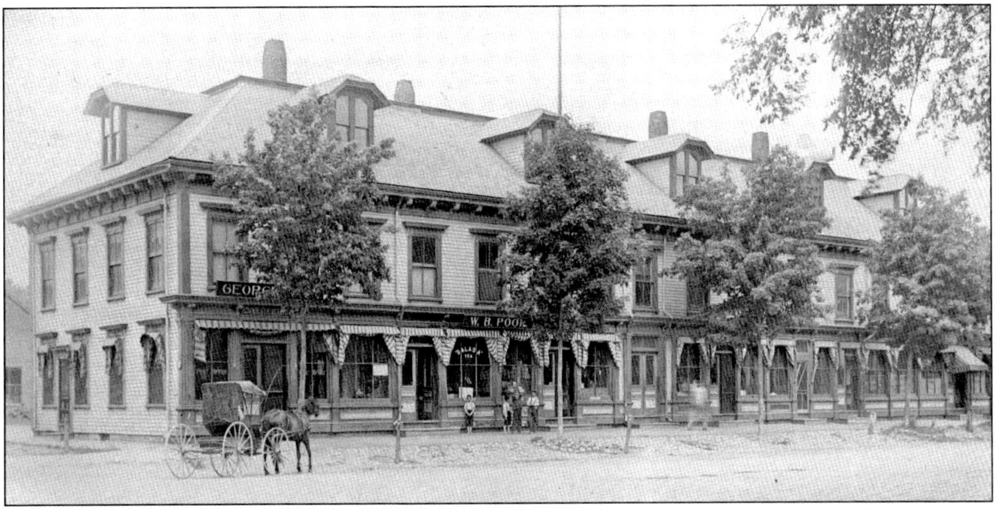

The Union Block—built in 1886 at 10–24 East Main Street between North and Park Streets—was named for the post–Civil War union of the United States. A wooden, Second Empire commercial block, it has a heavily dentiled cornice, a hip roof with large clipped-gable dormers (now removed), and shops on the first floor. It houses the post office in Donoghue's Grocery Store, A.E. Longfellow Hosiery & Fancy Goods, W.B. Poor & Company, and the John T. Connor Company. The Union Block was built a year after a disastrous fire destroyed all the buildings on and near its site. Note the healthy shade trees along the street. (Courtesy of the Georgetown Historical Society.)

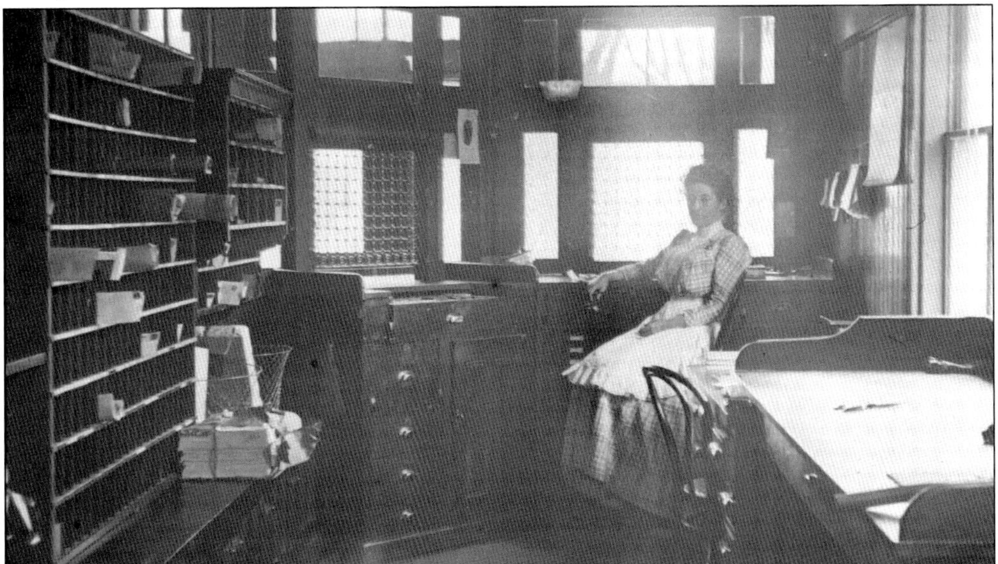

The post office was located in the Union Block from 1887 to 1926. Sylvester A. Donoghue served as postmaster from 1885 to 1892, when the post office was moved to the Union Block, where Donoghue and his son Dennis Donoghue kept a grocery store. In subsequent years, the post office was located in Little's Block and the Bailey Block on North Street before it moved to its present location on Central Street in 1958. In this c. 1900 photograph, Freda Chase Minchin sits at the desk, awaiting another postal customer. (From the collection of Albert E. Meader.)

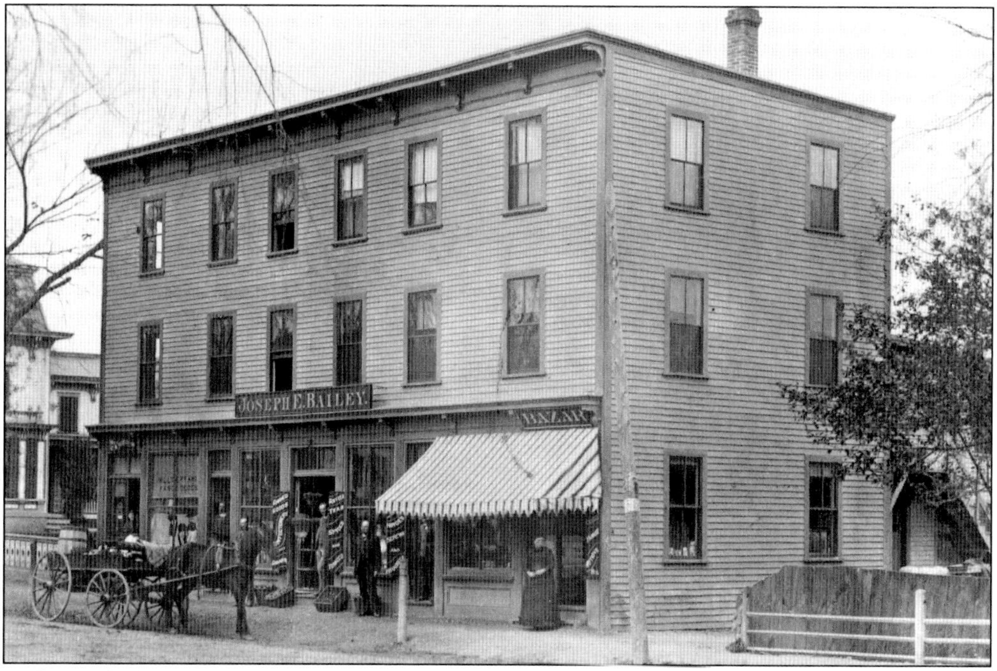

Bailey's Block was built by John W. Bailey, who kept a stove store there. It was later operated by his son Joseph E. Bailey, who sold coffee, tea, spice, tobacco, canned goods, confectioneries, and cigars. On the left, Miss Nelson sold millinery and fancy goods. The store on the right sold cloth, buttons, and fancy goods. (From the collection of Albert E. Meader.)

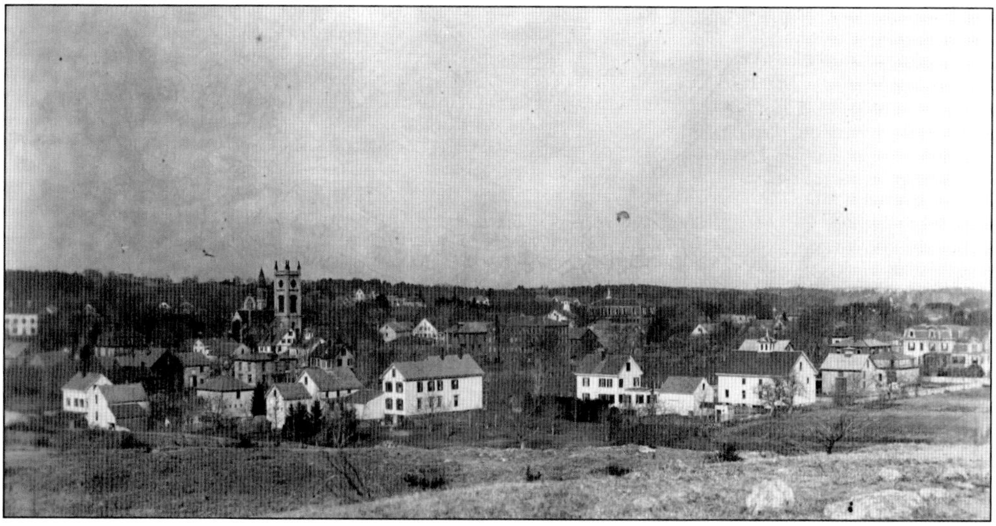

Georgetown, as seen *c.* 1890 from Scribner's or Atwood's Hill, is shown in all of its panoramic glory, with the prominently pinnacled tower of the Peabody Memorial Church rising high above the multitude of residential rooflines. The hill from which this photograph was taken was found to have an ochre pigment that was used by Moses Carter in the manufacture of red paint, which was widely used in Georgetown in the 19th century. The hill is now the site of the Georgetown High School, designed by Ellsworth Tidd of Ashton, Huntress & Pratt and built between 1958 and 1960 by his father, of Alfred E. Tidd & Son Builders. (Courtesy of Homer K. Tapin.)

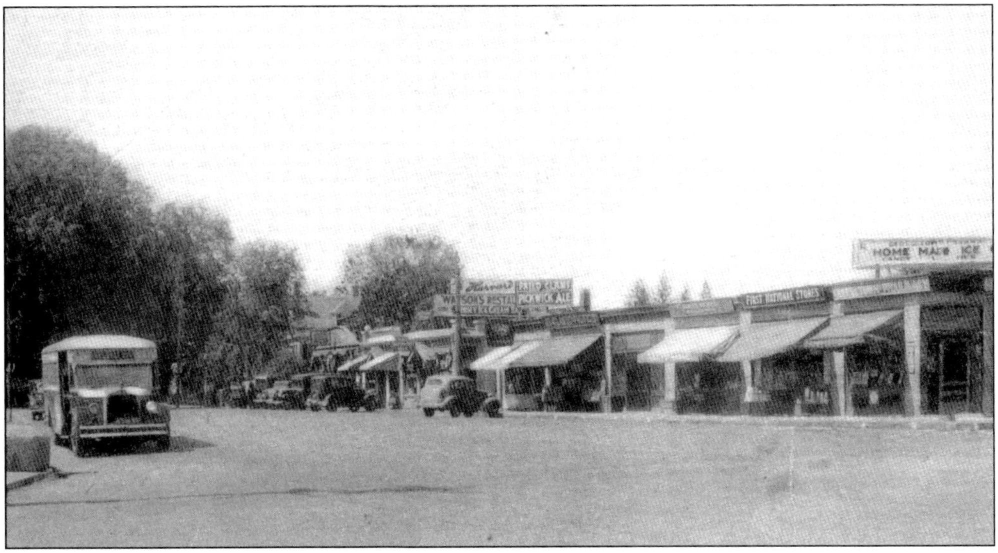

In this *c.* 1935 view, Georgetown Square shows a Haverhill-bound bus waiting for passengers on the left and a one-story commercial block on the right. On the right of the cement commercial block is the Rogers Pharmacy, which has a sign advertising homemade ice cream in addition to a full-service drugstore. From right to left are the First National store, Nally's Market, Louie's Clothing Shop, the A & P store, Molloy's Beer & Restaurant, Tom Watson's Beer & Restaurant, Boardman's Market, Annie Brown Cloth & Thread, and F.P. Andrews' Store & Newspapers. (Courtesy of Arthur Paquette.)

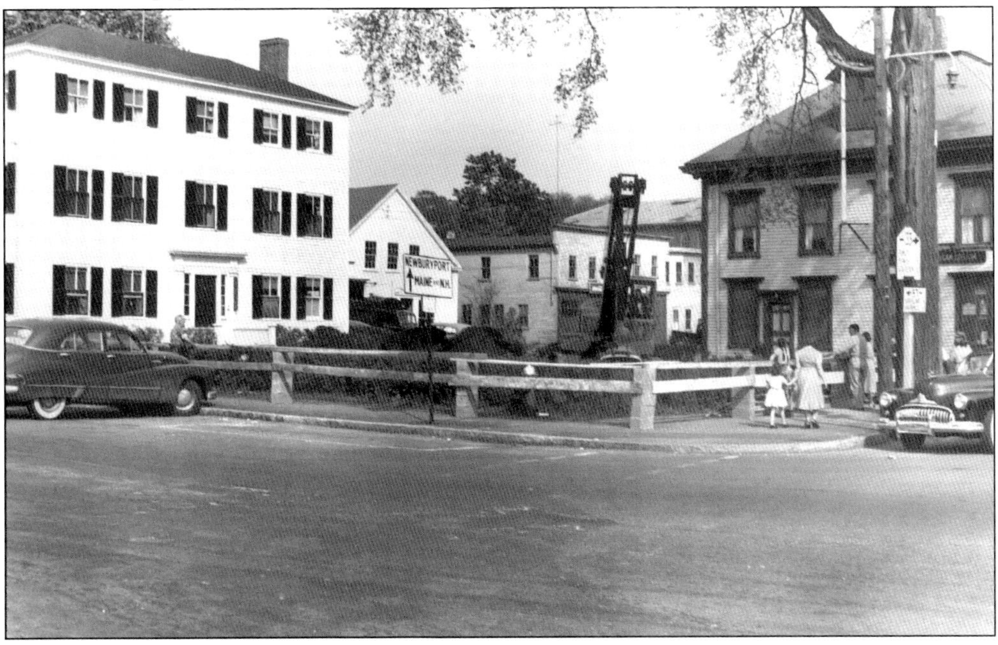

In this 1953 photograph, the site on the corner of North and East Main Streets is being excavated for the soon-to-be-built Georgetown Pharmacy and is being closely watched by curious Georgetonians. On the left is the Old Pentucket House, an attractive building then known as the Carleton Apartments. On the right is the Rene J. Gagnon Post 211, American Legion, which occupied a corner of the Union Block. (Courtesy of Louise A. Richardson.)

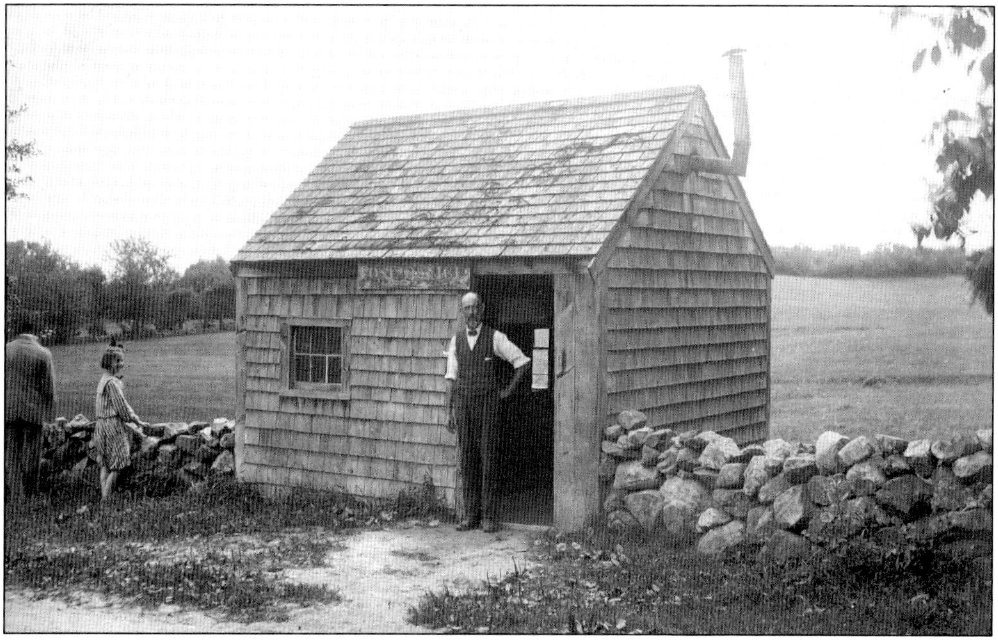

The South Byfield post office (actually a mail drop) was run by Frank Ambrose, who is seen in the doorway to the one-room post office serving this area of town. As a branch of the Georgetown post office, this station was opened under the direction of Sylvester A. Donoghue (postmaster from 1885 to 1892) and looks as if the building was a reused ten-footer shoe shop. (Courtesy of Louise A. Richardson.)

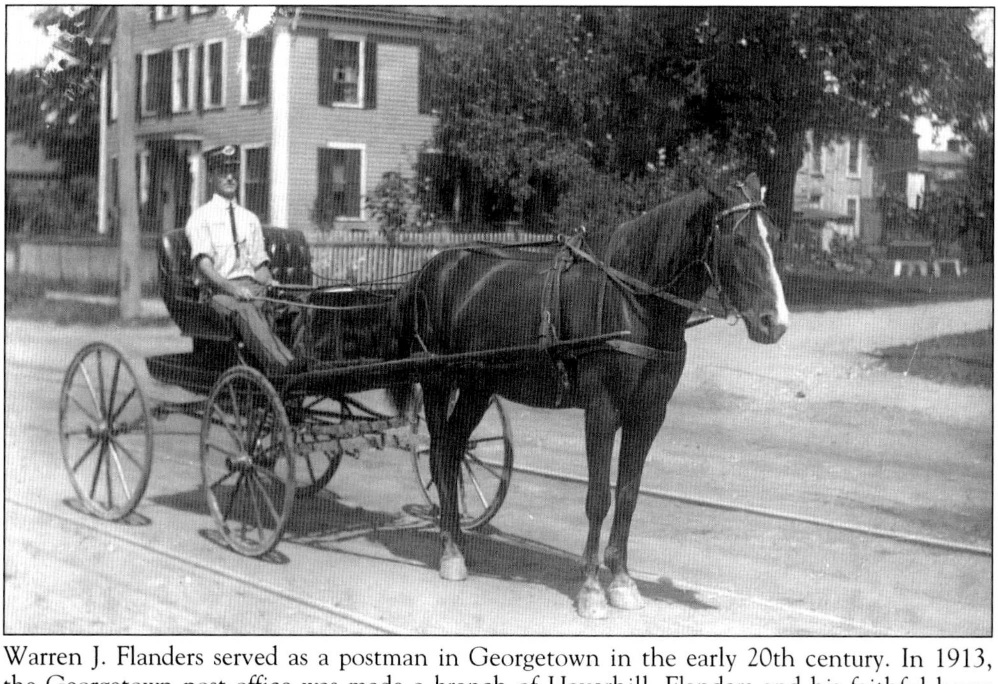

Warren J. Flanders served as a postman in Georgetown in the early 20th century. In 1913, the Georgetown post office was made a branch of Haverhill. Flanders and his faithful horse delivered the local mail in all sorts of weather until the Great Depression. (Courtesy of Ruth Flanders Tyrie.)

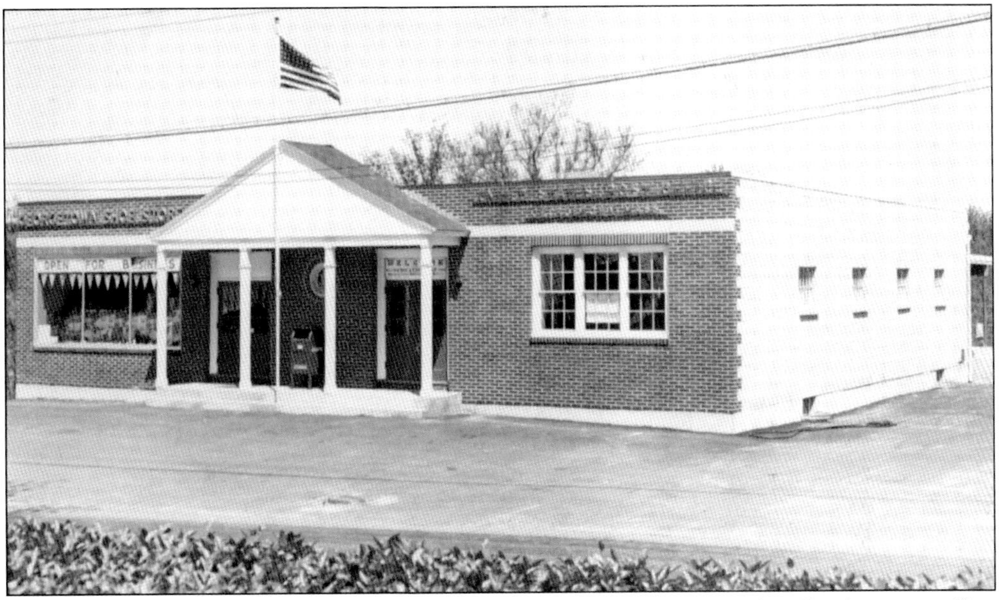

The present Georgetown post office was built on Central Street in 1958. The first post office in Georgetown was established in 1824, with Benjamin Little serving as the first postmaster for 21 years. According to one historical pamphlet, the original post office was "a wooden box 30 inches long, 12 inches wide and 12 inches deep" and was lettered the "New Rowley and Georgetown Post Office." On the left is the Georgetown Shoe Store, which shared the building with the post office for many years. (Courtesy of Homer K. Tapin.)

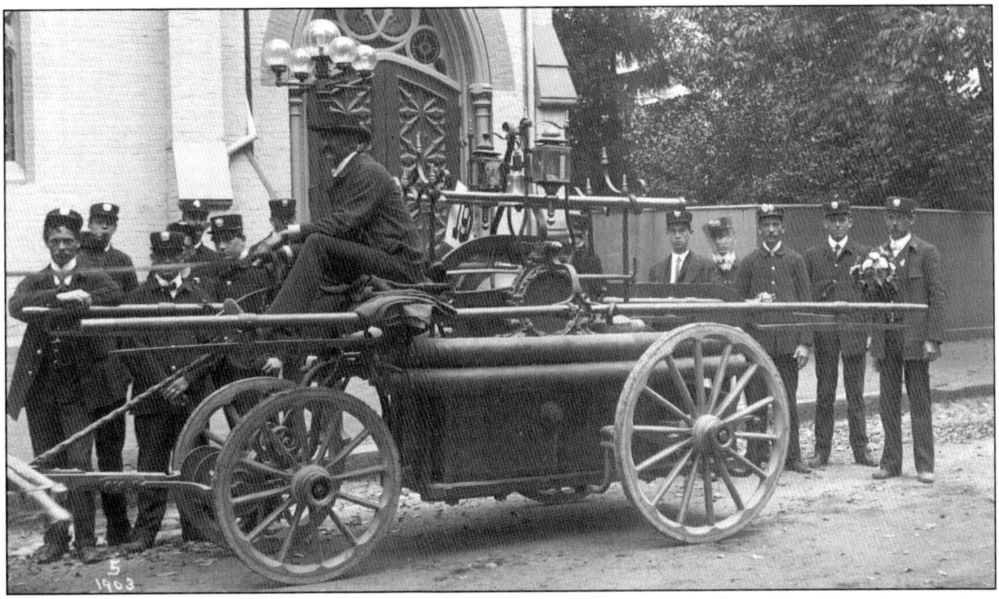

The Washington Handtub was manned by volunteer firefighters from Erie Fire Association No. 4 in Georgetown. The old pumper is shown in Newburyport in 1908 while firefighters await their entry into a parade. The Pentucket Company No. 1 was formed in 1843 as the Volunteer Association for the Protection of Property from Fire. The first engines in Georgetown were the Pentucket No. 1 and the Watchman No. 2, which were stored in the Tenney Building. (Courtesy of the Georgetown Historical Society.)

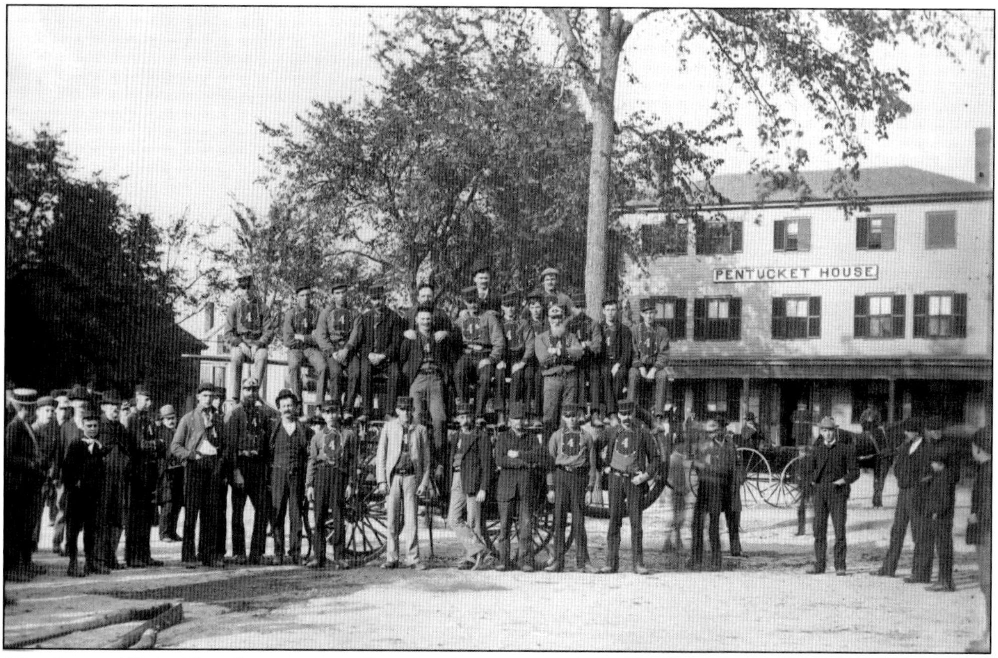

Members of Erie Fire Association No. 4—the motto of which was "Warm Hearts and Willing Hands"—pose on and around their prized engine in Pentucket Square c. 1880. Erie No. 4 was formed in 1854 with four officers and 20 volunteers who used a Hunneman Hand & Steam Fire Engine to fight fires. Today, it is the oldest privately owned volunteer firefighting company in the United States. The Hunneman engine was manufactured by Samuel Hewes Hunneman (1800–1869) in Roxbury and was among the finest available engines in the mid-19th century. (From the collection of Albert E. Meader.)

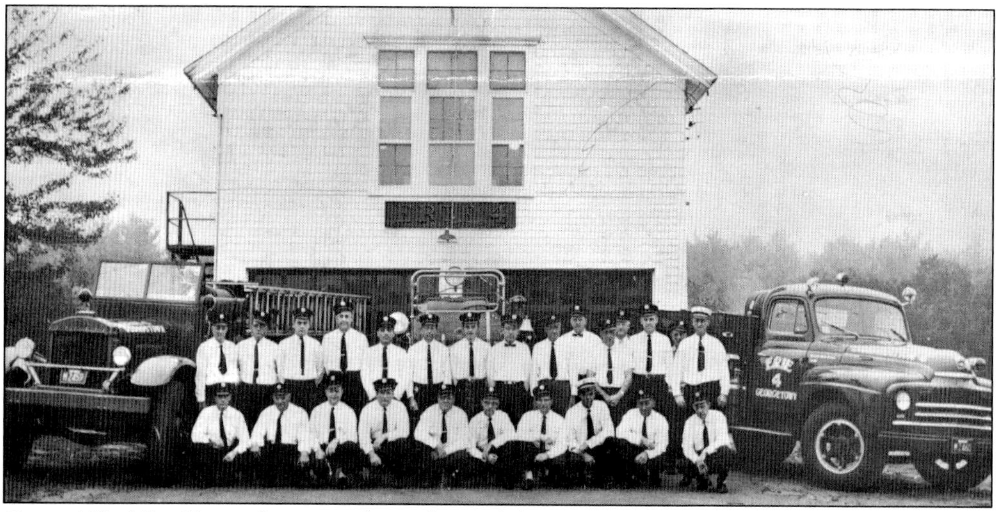

Capt. Alfred R. Chanonhouse and members of the Erie Fire Association No. 4 pose in front of their engine house at 476 North Street in 1960. Formed in 1854, this is an independent volunteer fire department, with the association owning the house, the engines, and equipment. The association maintains three fire trucks and raises funds through carnivals, suppers, fairs, and other public social activities to meet their expenses in protecting the town. (Courtesy of the Georgetown Peabody Library.)

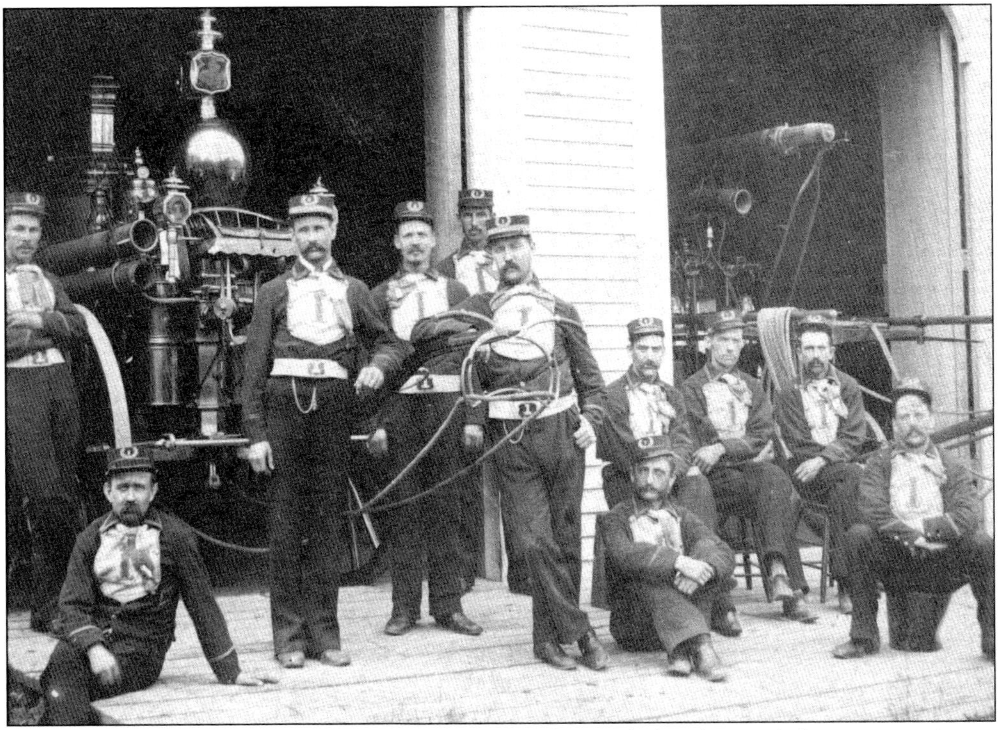

Members of the Central Fire Company pose in front of the doors of their engine house c. 1875. The firemen wear dashing uniforms, complete with cap, belt, and shieldlike shirt fronts. Steamer No. 1 and Empire No. 2 can be seen in the open doorways. Another engine house on Central Street in South Georgetown was where Washington No. 3 was housed, which was a Hunneman-built engine acquired in 1860 in partial trade for Pentucket No. 1. (Courtesy of the Central Fire Company.)

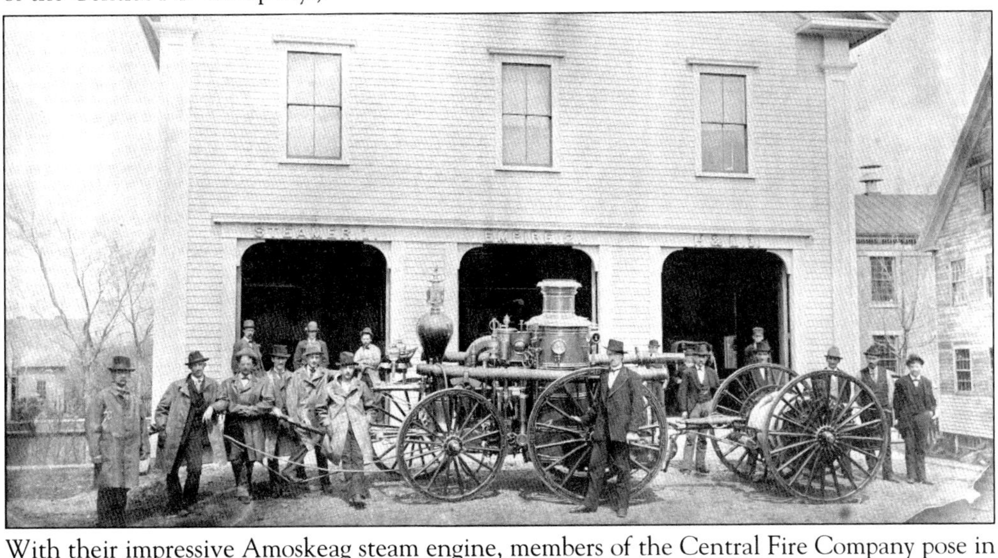

With their impressive Amoskeag steam engine, members of the Central Fire Company pose in front of their engine house on Middle Street. This house had Steamer No. 1, Empire No. 2, and Hook & Ladder No. 1 as part of the firefighting apparatus of a century ago. (Courtesy of the Central Fire Company.)

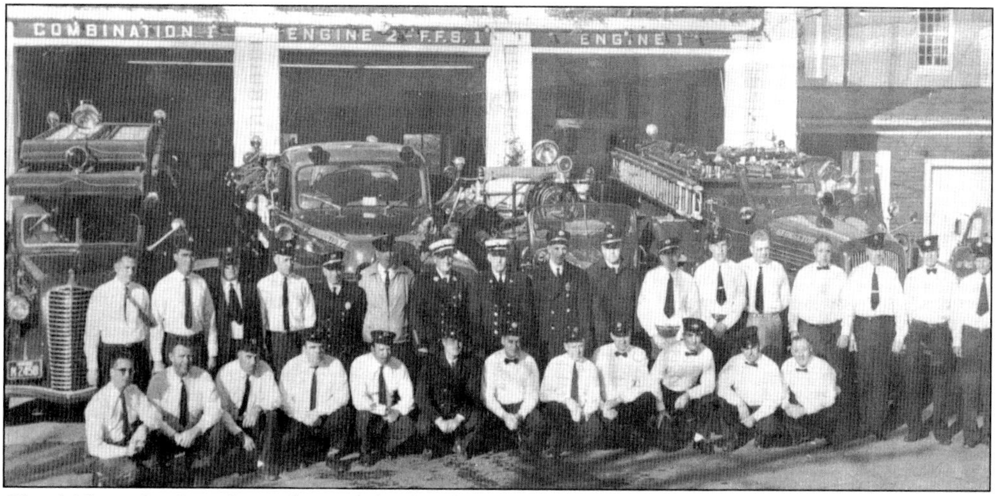

Chief Alton Cook and members of the fire department pose in front of the Central Firehouse in 1959 with their three fire engines in the doors. Established in 1923, the Central Fire Company maintains three fire trucks in its house on Middle Street. (Courtesy of the Georgetown Peabody Library.)

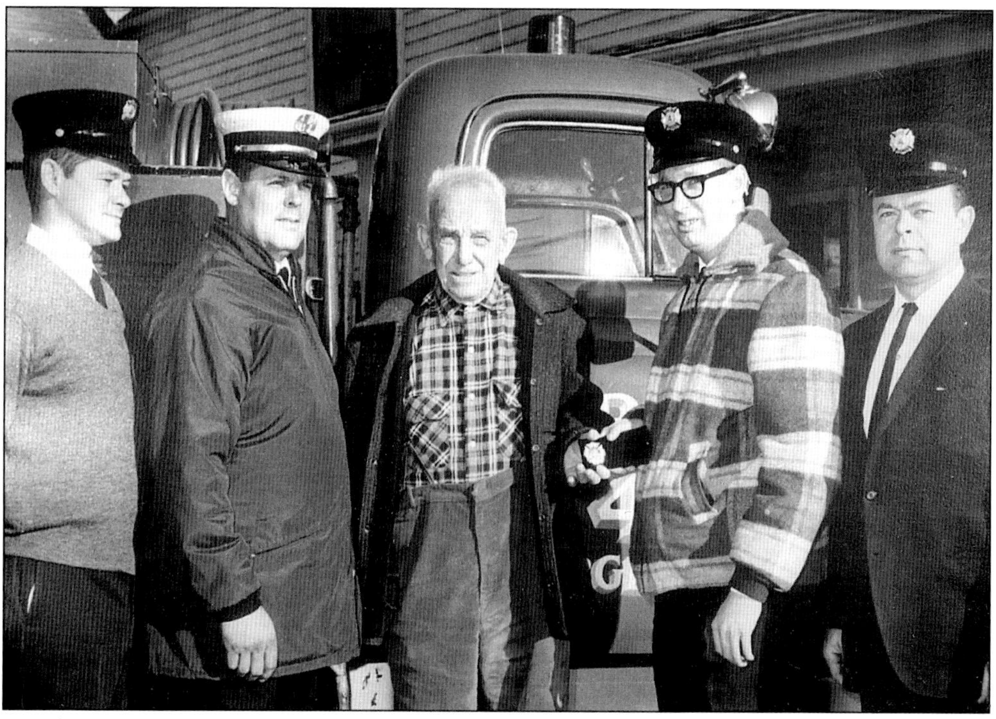

Standing outside the headquarters of Erie Fire Association No. 4 in 1967 are, from left to right, Lt. Ralph A. Mackenzie, Capt. Arthur H. Wyman, awardee Walter P. Hardy (holding his 75-year pin), president William Nutter, and treasurer Kenneth Owens. (Courtesy of Erie Fire Association No. 4.)

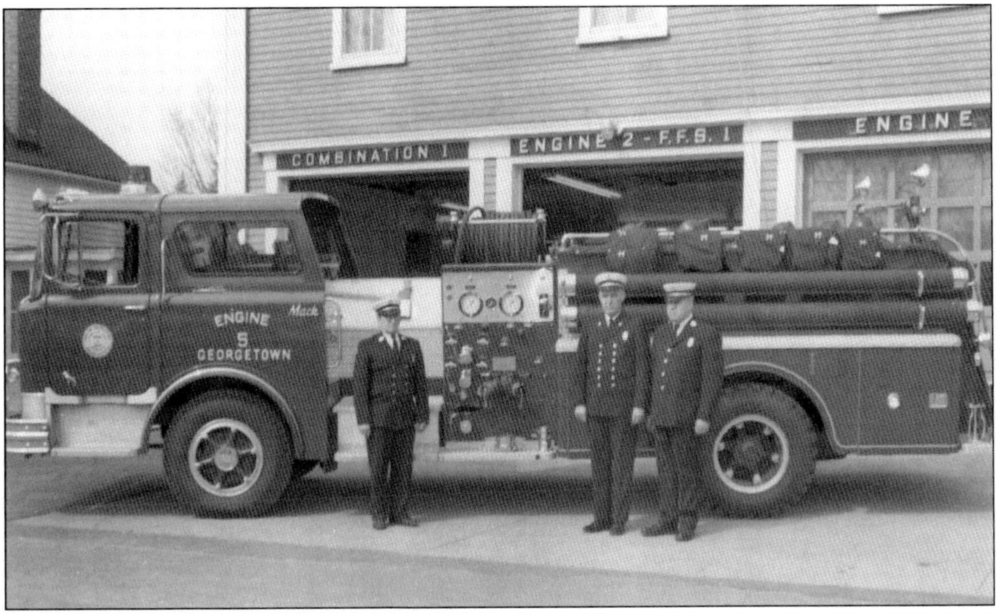

Standing in front of the Central Firehouse in 1971 are, from left to right, Chief Basil "Shrimp" Kinson, Deputy Chief William Green, and Deputy Chief Waldo Reed. Engine No. 5 is a far cry from the hand pump engines of the 19th century and provides superior firefighting capabilities for the residents of Georgetown. (Courtesy of Harold C. Roeder.)

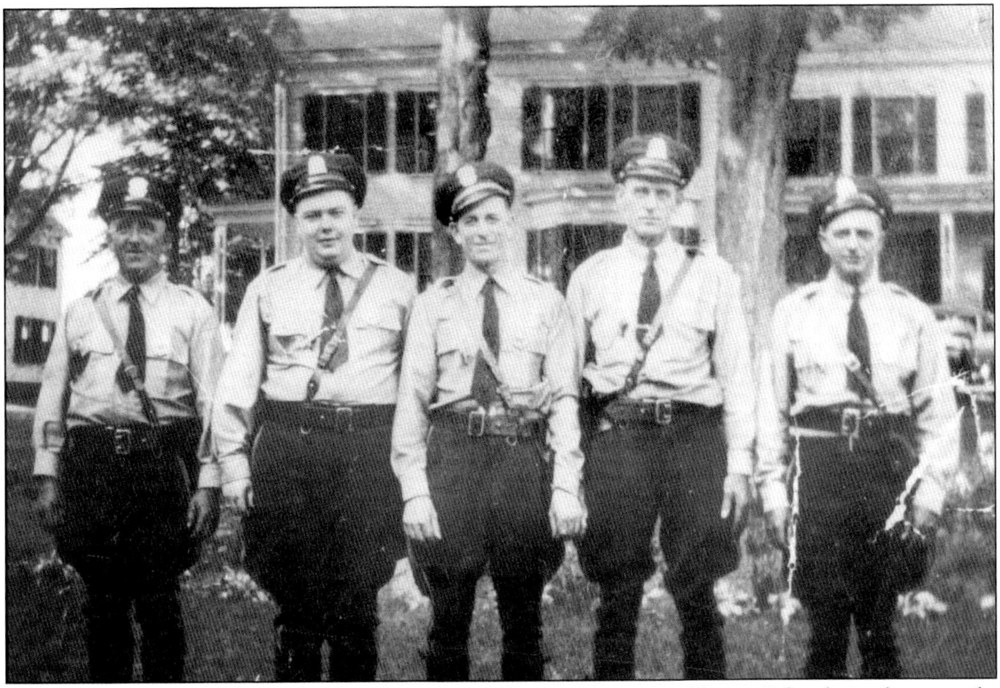

Members of the Georgetown police force in 1942 participate in a "lineup" for their photograph. From left to right are Bib Gagnon, Dick Greenleaf, Chief Louis M. Holt, Richmond "Dick" Kneeland, and Charlie Newcomb. (Courtesy of Winifred Holt Gatchell.)

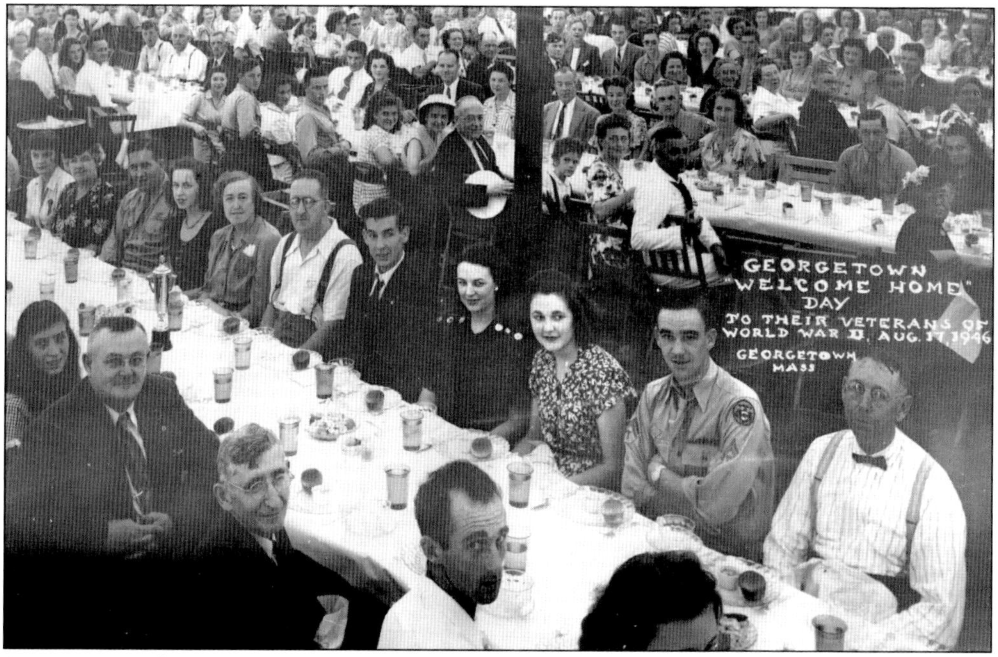

A community dinner was held under tents on Lincoln Park during Welcome Home Day, which was sponsored by the town officials of Georgetown on August 17, 1946, to welcome home and properly thank the veterans of World War II. A roast turkey dinner with all the trimmings was a way of showing the sincere thanks to the Georgetown men and women who had served in the armed forces during the war. (Courtesy of the Georgetown Historical Society.)

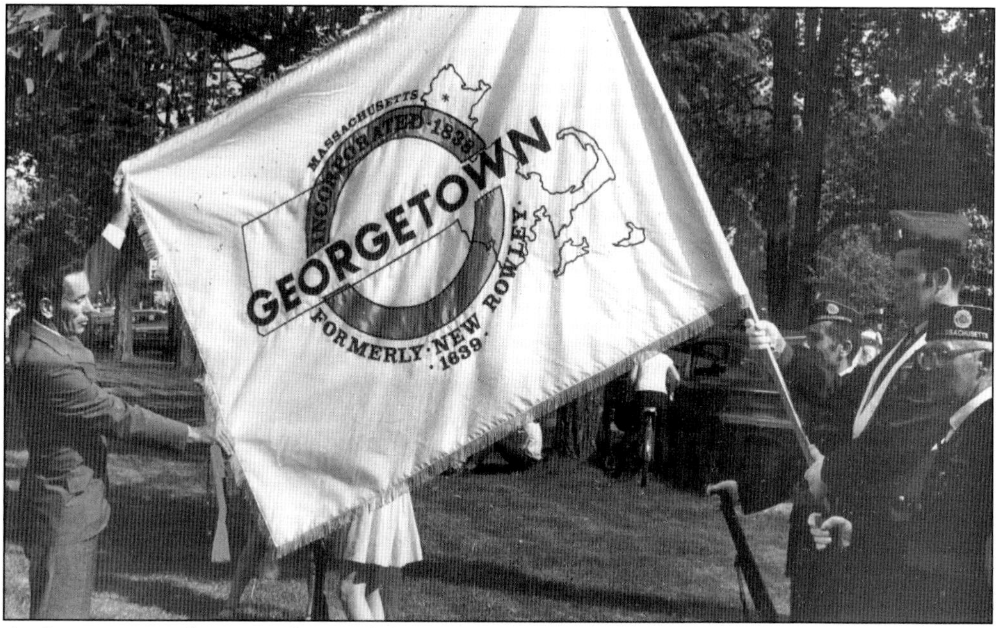

A Georgetown flag was designed by local resident Edward DesJardins and unfurled to public acclaim on Memorial Day 1970. In this photograph, Bill Handren (left) and Herbert Fuller (right) of the Rene J. Gagnon Post 211, American Legion, proudly display the new flag on Harry Murch Park. (Courtesy of the Georgetown Historical Commission.)

Two

Places of Worship

Religion can be described as the worship of a higher being, but it also involves a strong code of ethics in its systematic approach by those who seek to take part in its glories. In the last three centuries, Georgetown has gone from one meetinghouse to a wide spectrum of religious beliefs.

The first place of worship in Georgetown was established in 1731, when the West (Second) Parish of Rowley was founded in response to a petition sent to the Great and General Court by 44 residents of the western section of Rowley. Rev. James Chandler (1706–1789), a graduate of Harvard College in 1728, served as the first minister, being ordained in 1732. The new parish elected Lt. John Spofford as moderator and Jonathan Boynton as clerk. The meetinghouse and (later) the South Byfield Parish were the only places of worship in town until 1754, when several families were displeased with the services and withdrew, holding services at Hale's Corner. These people were called Separatists but eventually became known as Anabaptists. In 1785, they founded what became known as the First Baptist Church in Georgetown.

Over the next century, the Congregational and Baptist churches would be joined by the New Rowley Universalist Church, which was built on the present site of the Georgetown Memorial Town Hall. An Orthodox Congregational church, known as the Peabody Memorial Church, was built on East Main Street (now the site of the town parking lot). The Roman Catholic church (which initially worshiped in the former vestry of the Old South Church) built a church in 1907 on Central Street and, in 1964, built the present church on Andover Street. From 1916 to 1966, the Episcopalian church occupied the former School No. 4, which was known as the Old Brick Church (on West Main Street) and is now the headquarters of the Noack Organ Company. Eventually, a Church of Jesus Christ of Latter Day Saints was built in Georgetown, which showed the religious diversity of Georgetonians. The New Life Fellowship Church, on East Main Street opposite the Union Cemetery, was built as a new building for the First Baptist Church and is now an ecumenical church.

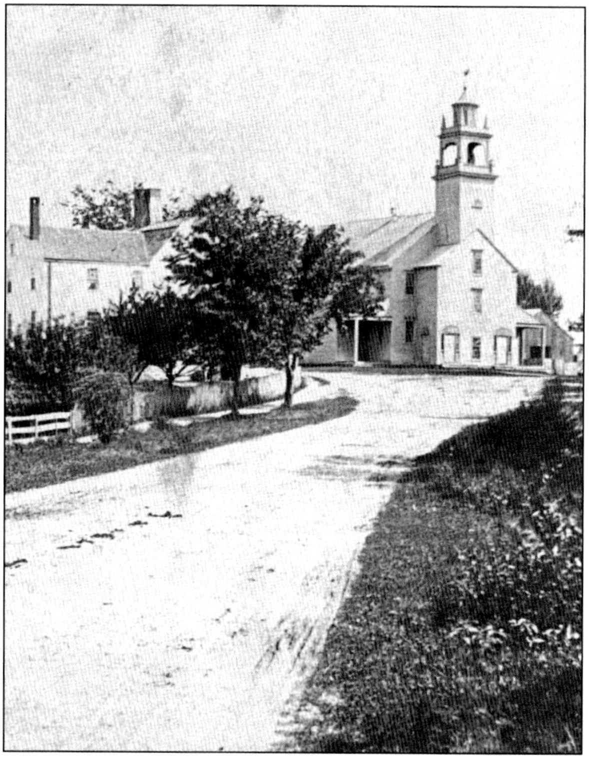

The Old South Church was raised on July 5, 1769, and stood at the Old South Green (the present corner of East Main and Elm Streets). It was an impressive New England meetinghouse, with a gilded "wether cock" (made by Daniel Thurston) on the steeple. The belfry had a bell cast in 1816 by the noted Paul Revere & Son Foundry, which was operated in Boston's North End by the former silversmith and noted patriot and his son Joseph Warren Revere. The church held its last service in the old meetinghouse in December 1874, and it was demolished a year later. The former site of the meetinghouse is now the location of the Georgetown Firemen's Memorial. (Courtesy of the Georgetown Historical Society.)

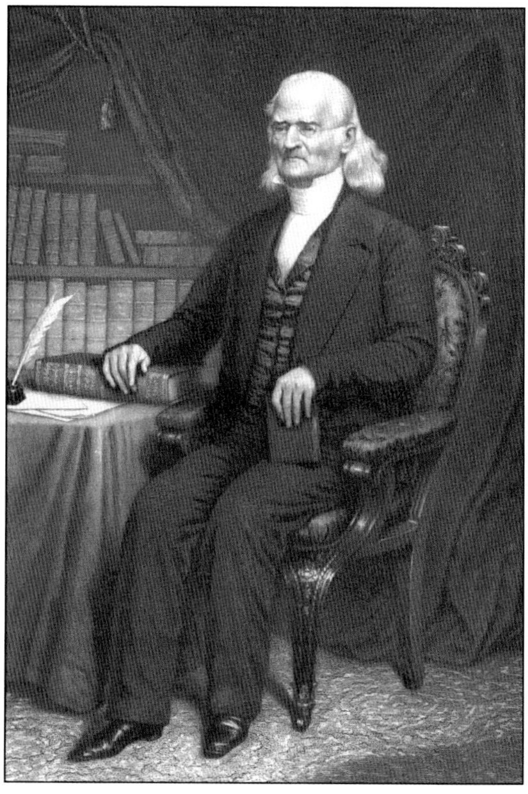

Rev. Isaac Braman (1770–1858) was ordained minister of the Old South Church in 1797. A graduate of Harvard College (Class of 1794), he was the last of 64 candidates who preached their audition-sermons at the Old South Church before he was chosen to become the settled minister. This print of the venerable minister, engraved by John Sartain from a daguerreotype, was done in 1852 and shows a man who was beloved by both his congregation and his fellow townsmen. On his tombstone in the Old Union Cemetery is carved, "Be thou faithful unto death, and I will give thee a crown of life." (Courtesy of the Georgetown Historical Society.)

Rev. Charles Beecher (1815–1900) was installed in 1857 as colleague pastor with Rev. Isaac Braman and served as the ordained minister from 1858 to 1881. A highly controversial minister whose intellectual and philosophical preaching was often in direct conflict with the beliefs of a portion of his congregation, he was nonetheless considered by most a brilliant man. His heretical views on the preexistence of souls created a schism in the congregation, some of them withdrawing in 1864 and forming an Orthodox Congregational society. With Lowell Mason, the first Musical Jubilee in the United States was held in the Old South Church, with many of the singers later participating in the Great Peace Jubilee in Boston. In 1874, the congregation abandoned the Old South Church for a new Stick-style church built across from the town hall. (Courtesy of Louise A. Richardson.)

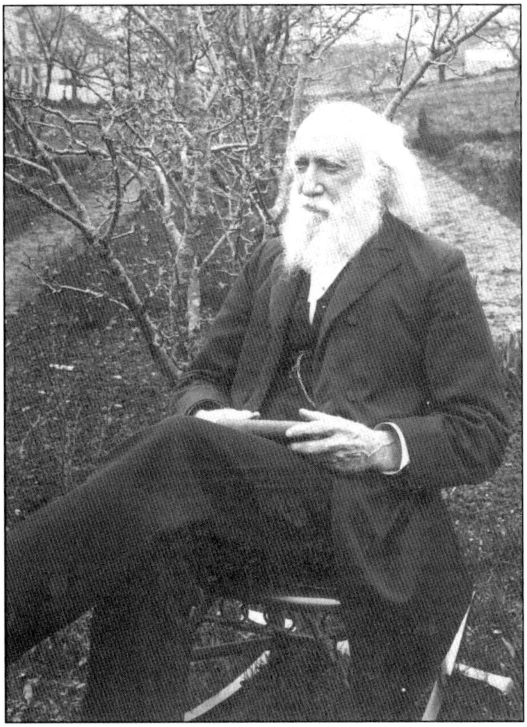

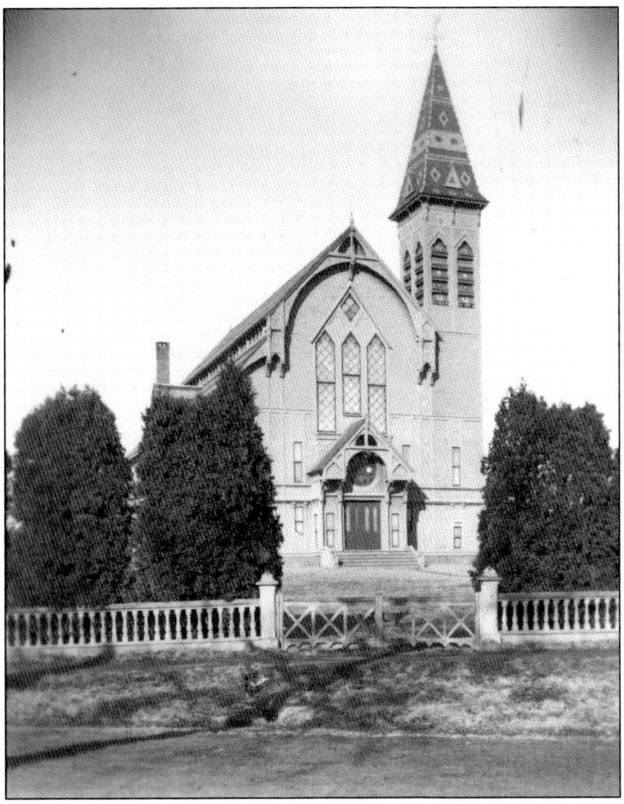

The First Congregational Church, designed by the Boston architectural firm of Peabody & Stearns, was built in 1874 at the corner of Clark and Andover Streets. An elaborate Stick-style, wood-framed church, it has a large lancet-shaped stained-glass window on the facade. The polychromatic slate roof is punctuated by a bell tower (where the Revere bell from the Old South Church was hung), which still adds great interest to the church. The church merged with the Peabody Memorial Church in 1908, and the reunited congregation worships here to this day. (From the collection of Albert E. Meader.)

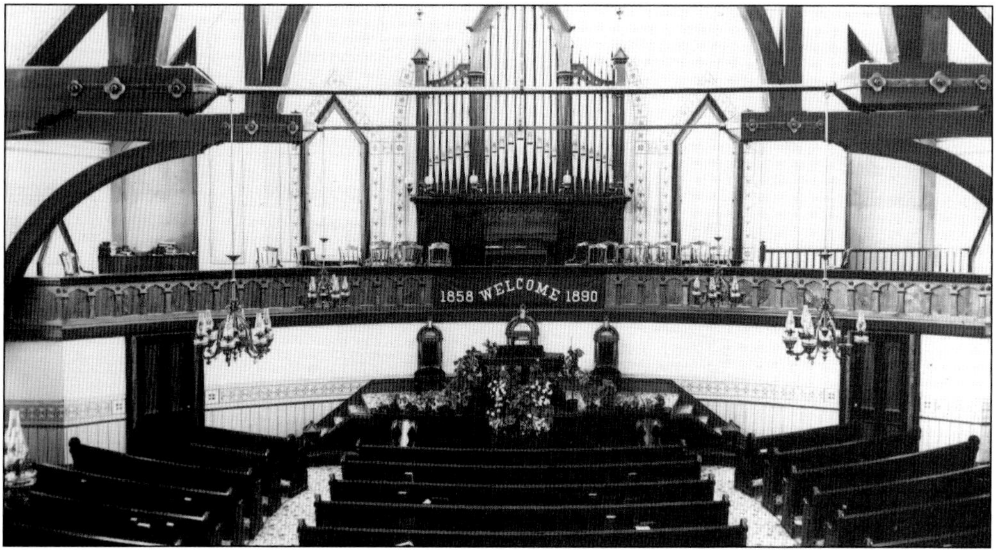

The interior of the First Congregational Church is shown in 1890 just prior to a service welcoming parishioners and friends during a return visit of Rev. Charles Beecher (minister from 1858 to 1881), who was then living in Florida and serving as a school superintendent. The three pulpit chairs were given by Fannie Holmes Cornish, who once lived in Georgetown, in memory of her parents. Note the iron tie rods connecting the wood beams and the impressive gallery above the altar. The interior was elaborately decorated with rich wood trim, a hallmark of Peabody & Stearns. (Courtesy of Homer K. Tapin.)

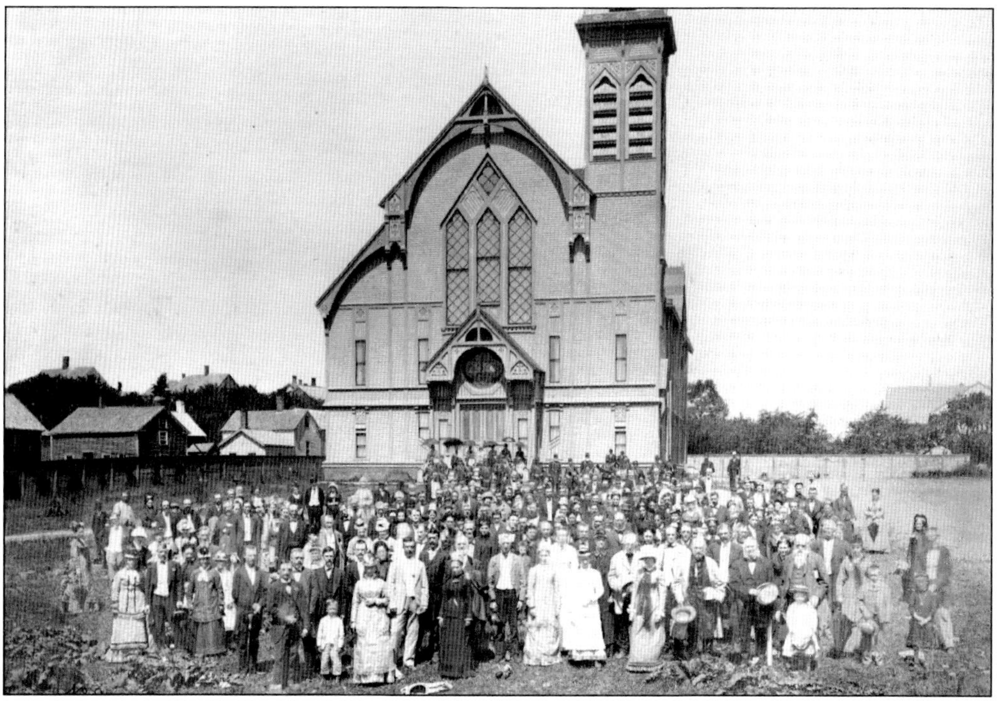

Members of the Perley family held a grand reunion of the generations in Georgetown in 1877. Here, members of the extended Perley family pose for a photograph of the generations in front of the First Congregational Church on Andover Street. (From the collection of Albert E. Meader.)

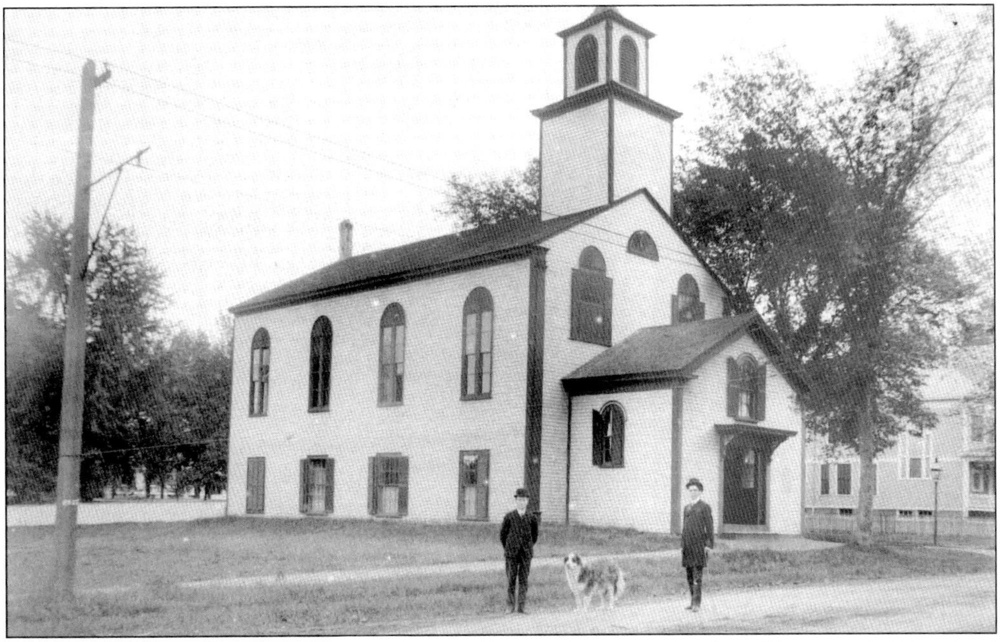

The First Baptist Church was founded in 1785 "as a Distinct Church in Union and fellowship" with the Haverhill Baptist Church, with Rev. William Ewing serving as the first minister. A new place of worship was built in 1829 at the corner of North and Parsonage Streets. It was later moved to the corner of North and Pleasant Streets, where the congregation worshiped until the old church was sold and remodeled as a private residence and photographer's studio. (Courtesy of Louise A. Richardson.)

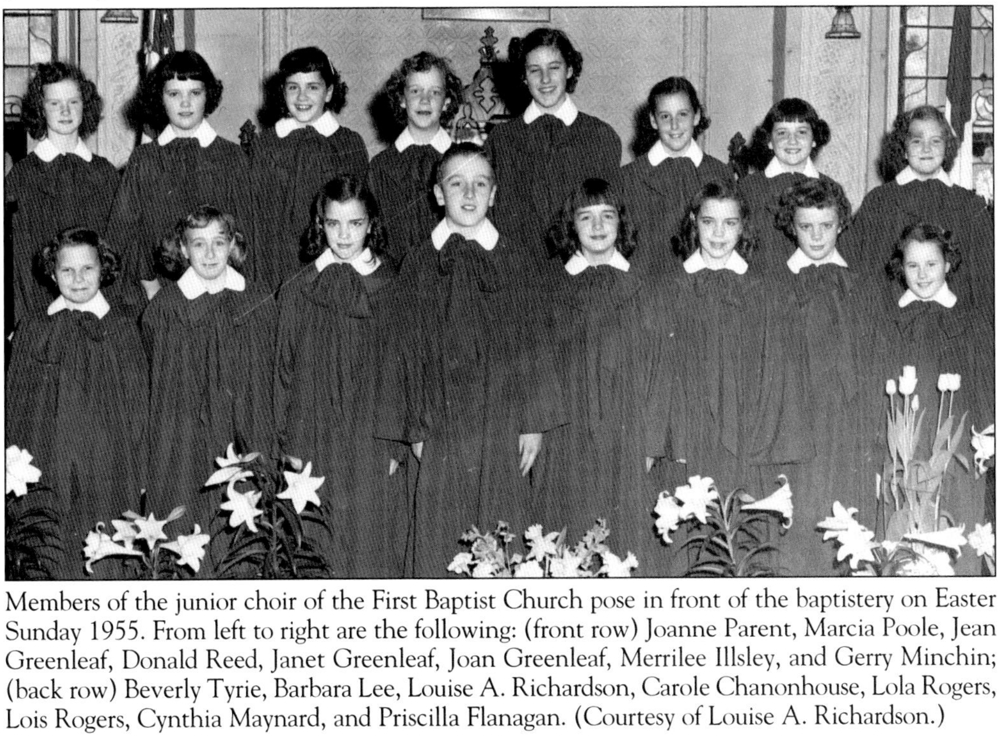

Members of the junior choir of the First Baptist Church pose in front of the baptistery on Easter Sunday 1955. From left to right are the following: (front row) Joanne Parent, Marcia Poole, Jean Greenleaf, Donald Reed, Janet Greenleaf, Joan Greenleaf, Merrilee Illsley, and Gerry Minchin; (back row) Beverly Tyrie, Barbara Lee, Louise A. Richardson, Carole Chanonhouse, Lola Rogers, Lois Rogers, Cynthia Maynard, and Priscilla Flanagan. (Courtesy of Louise A. Richardson.)

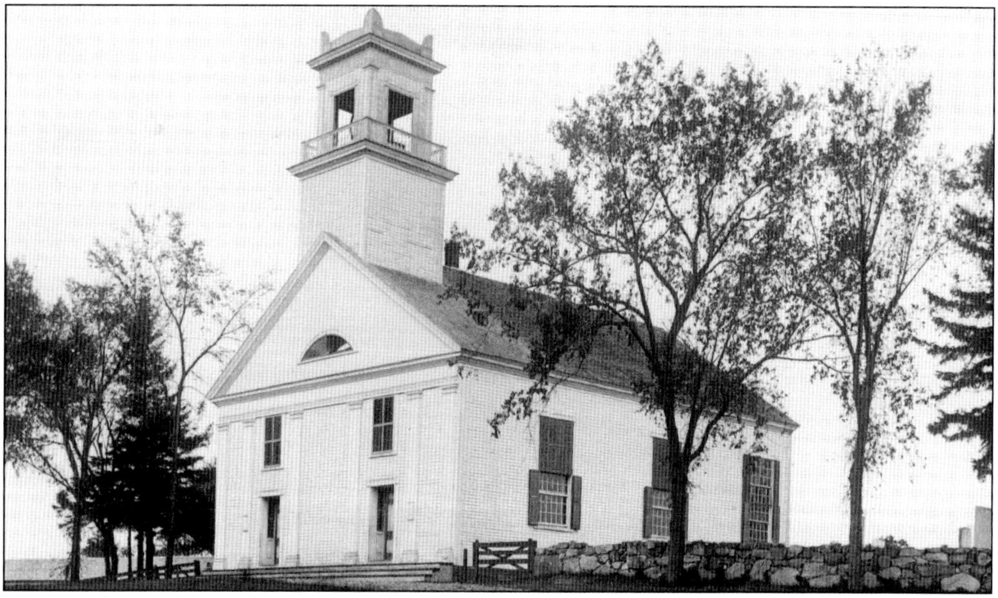

The South Byfield Parish was organized in 1702 and called Byfield in honor of the Honorable Nathaniel Byfield of Boston, who presented the parish a bell. Rev. Moses Hale of Newbury served as the first pastor from 1706 to 1744. In 1710, it was incorporated as "the Parish or Precinct upon Newbury Falls, commonly called Byfield." The Greek Revival–style church was built in 1833 after a fire had destroyed the original church two years earlier. The meetinghouse had two entrances surmounted by windows, with Doric pilasters supporting a pediment with a louvered demilune window. It also had a simple belfry with corner amphimions. On the side of the meetinghouse is the old cemetery where many of Georgetown's early ancestors were buried. (From the collection of Albert E. Meader.)

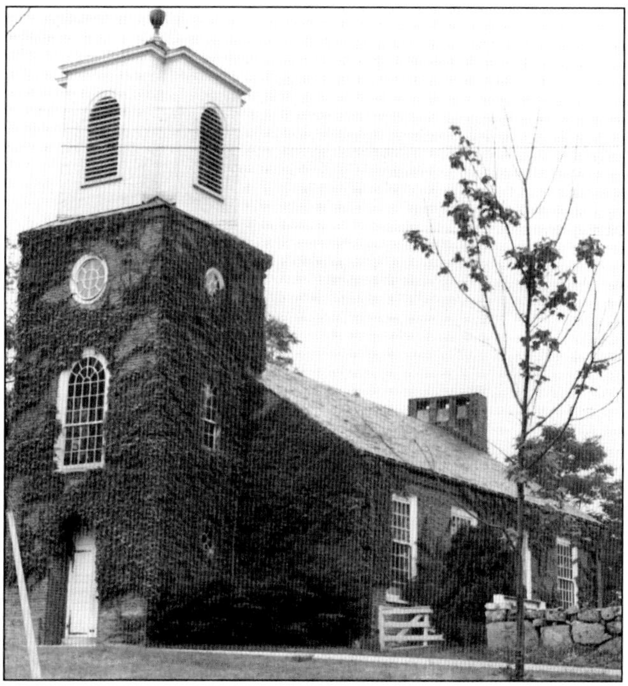

This structure of the South Byfield Parish was built in 1933. Its belfry is classic in its simplicity. The church was built in the Georgian Revival style with an impressive arched and mullioned window in the tower, which was surmounted by an ocular window. The side windows were simple mullioned windows, and the belfry was surmounted by an urn finial. The building is now a private residence. (From the collection of Albert E. Meader.)

The Peabody Memorial Church was designed by architects Gridley J. Fox Bryant and Arthur Gilman of Boston. A high-style brick Italianate church, it was built between 1866 and 1867 by Charles Carleton of Haverhill. Its pinnacled tower and four-sided clock, made by the Howard Clock Company of Roxbury, was a prominent feature of Georgetown. According to the express wish of George Peabody, the contractor was charged to "build the church so thoroughly and substantially, that no repair should be required for a hundred years." However, after the congregation reunited with the Congregational church, the former church was sold in 1915 to the town and was known as Peabody Memorial Hall, being used for town meetings until it was destroyed by fire in 1920. (Courtesy of the Georgetown Historical Society.)

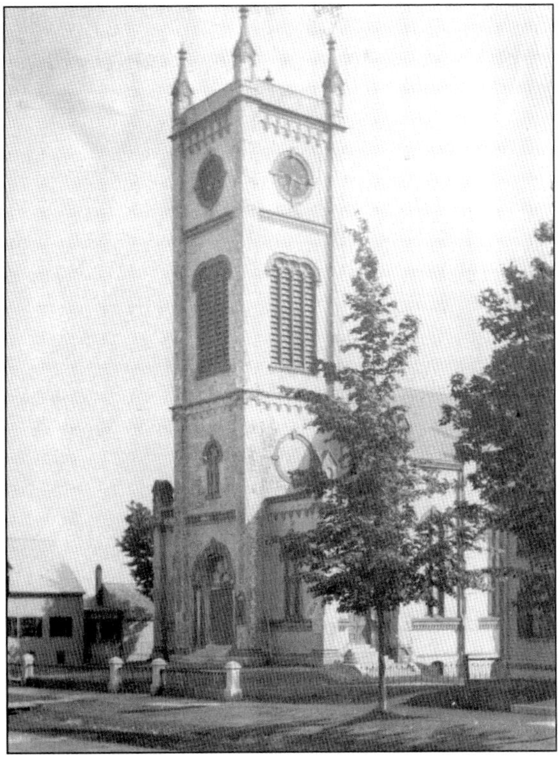

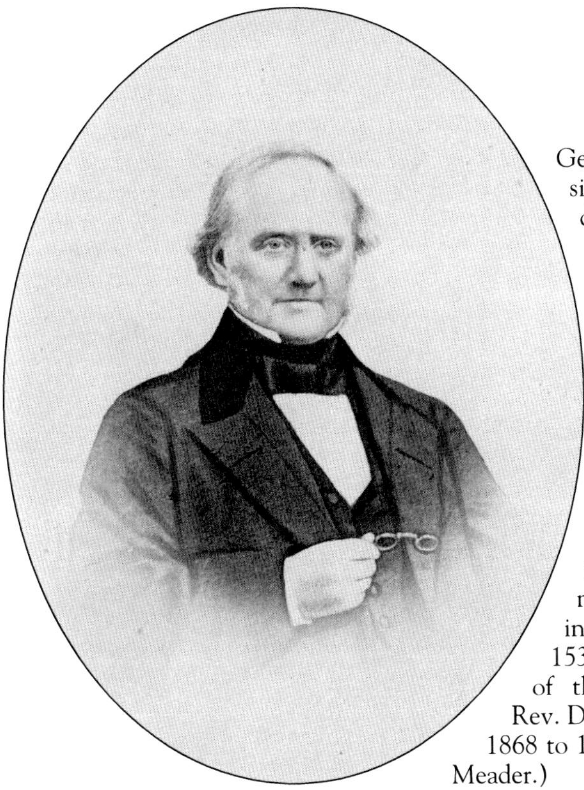

George Peabody (1795–1869) and his sister Judith Peabody Russell Daniels donated the funds to build the Peabody Memorial Church in memory of their mother, Judith Dodge Peabody (1770–1830). George Peabody was a successful London banker who had been presented with the Freedom of the City of London and honored by a statue in London that was unveiled by Edward, Prince of Wales, in recognition of his overwhelming generosity in the founding of the Peabody Trust. In donating the funds for the church, Peabody sought to memorialize his mother, who was born in Georgetown in a house now located at 153 West Main Street. The first minister of the Peabody Memorial Church was Rev. David Dana Marsh, who served from 1868 to 1888. (From the collection of Albert E. Meader.)

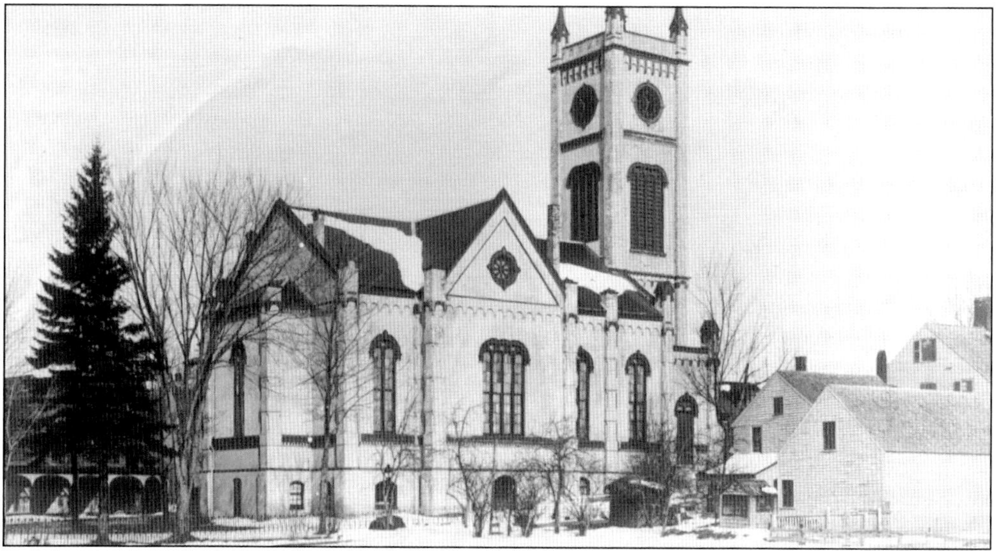

In this c. 1875 view of Peabody Memorial Church from the rear, the impressiveness of the brick structure is apparent in the use of red brick and massive stained-glass windows. The bell was sent by George Peabody from London and was inscribed with his and his sister's name. On the far left are the horse sheds, which were built so that horses would be protected from inclement weather during services. (Courtesy of the Georgetown Historical Society.)

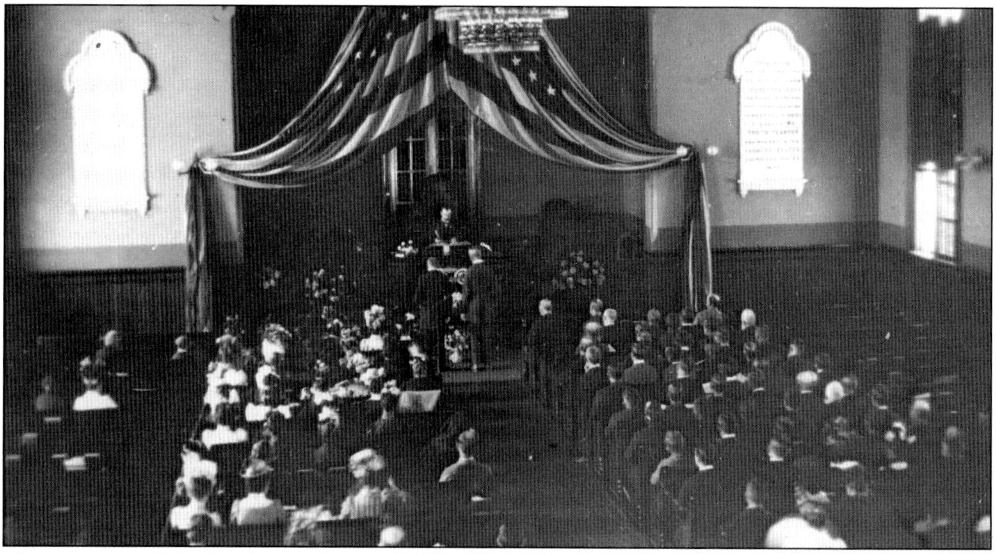

The interior of the Peabody Memorial Church was painted a French gray with a blue ceiling and had two memorial tablets on either side of the pulpit. The marble tablet on the left was to the memory of Rev. Isaac Braman (1770–1858), who was ordained pastor of the Old South Church in 1797. The marble tablet on the right was to the memory of Judith Dodge Peabody (1770–1830), in whose memory the church was erected in 1866–1867. Members of the Peabody family donated the altar furniture, made of chestnut like the church trim. The communion service was donated by Julia Peabody Chandler, and the chandeliers were donated by Jeremiah D. Peabody. The clock, communion table, and hymnbooks were presented by the nephews of George Peabody. The magnificent organ was presented by George Jewett Tenney and his son Richard Tenney. (From the collection of Albert E. Meader.)

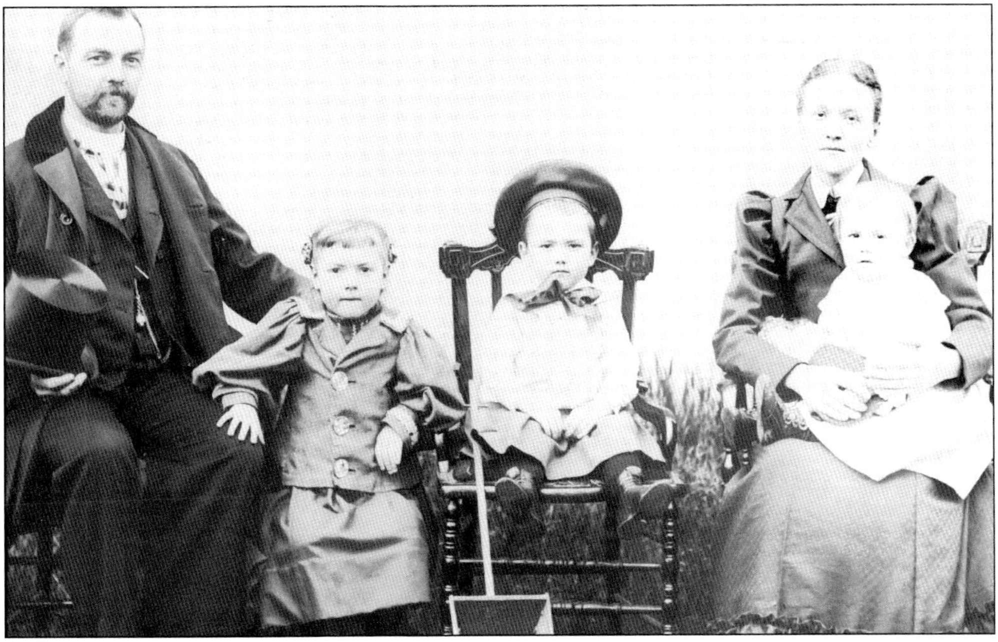

Rev. Charles Julian Tuthill served as minister of the Peabody Memorial Church from 1894 to 1901. He lived with his family at 25 East Main Street. From left to right are Reverend Tuthill, Margaret Tuthill, Samuel Tuthill, and Mrs. Tuthill, who holds their baby. (Courtesy of the Georgetown Historical Society.)

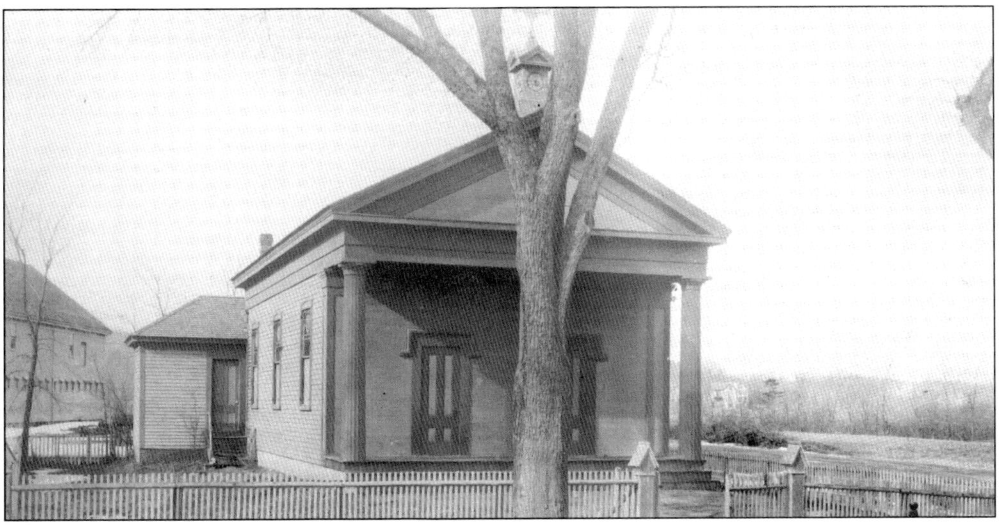

Rev. Henry Lennon of Newburyport held the first Roman Catholic mass in Georgetown at the home of James McLain at 27 Andover Street (the Carleton Home since 1902). The original vestry of the Old South Church was built in 1852 and was used by the members of the Orthodox Memorial Society (later the Peabody Memorial Church) from 1864 to 1868. It was sold to the Roman Catholics in Georgetown in 1870. The former vestry was dedicated by Archbishop John J. Williams, and masses were held here for the next 37 years. The first pastor in Georgetown was Rev. Richard Cummins, who was succeeded in 1871 by Rev. John Cummins, his uncle. Devoid of its columns, the deconsecrated church stood until recently on East Main and Elm Streets as a storage warehouse. (Courtesy of the Georgetown Historical Society.)

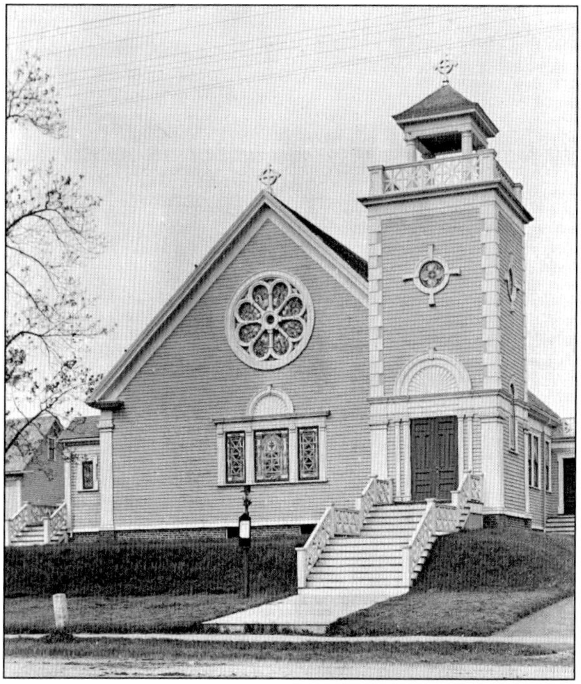

Old St. Mary's Roman Catholic Church was a wood-framed Colonial Revival church built in 1907 on Central Street (now the site of a shopping center across from the Georgetown post office). It was dedicated by Rt. Rev. John Brady, auxiliary bishop of Boston. A simple asymmetrical church, it was embellished with a bell tower that had corner quoining. It also featured a modified Palladian window with stained glass on the facade and a magnificent rose window. This church was extensively damaged by fire in 1962. It was decided at that time to build a new church rather than rebuild the old one, which was demolished in 1965. (Courtesy of the Georgetown Historical Society.)

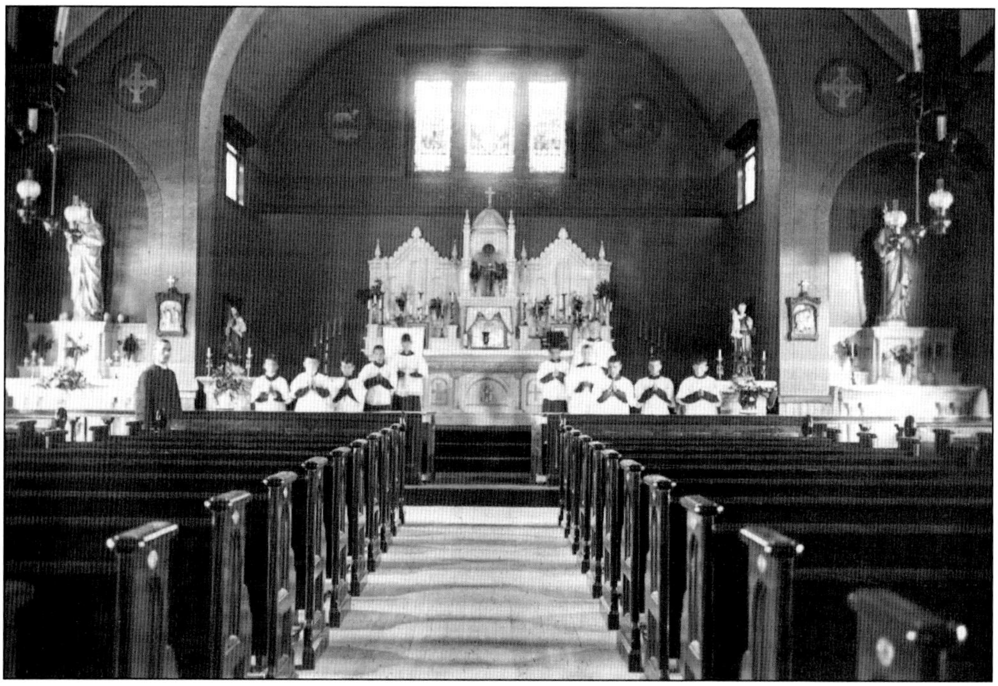

The altar of St. Mary's Roman Catholic Church was of carved white marble. Fr. Michael P. Mahon, who served as pastor from 1909 to 1914, stands on the far left with cherubic altar boys in front of the altar. Mahon was a noted scholar, speaking Gaelic, Greek, Latin, and French. He was a well-known writer for the *Pilot,* the leading newspaper in the Boston Catholic community. The statues of Jesus Christ (left) and St. Anthony (right) were purchased in France. (From the collection of Albert E. Meader.)

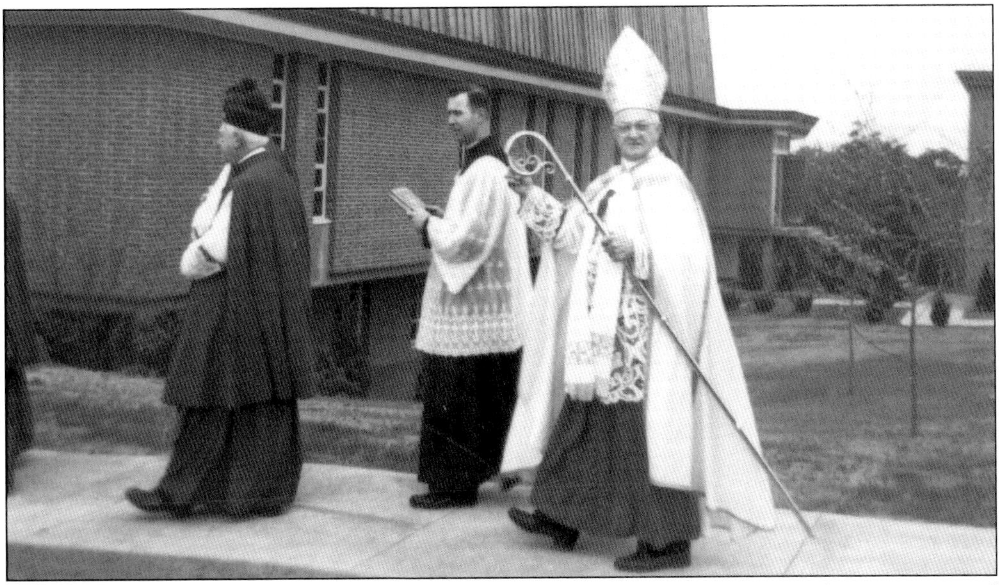

The present St. Mary's Roman Catholic Church was built in 1963 on Andover Street and dedicated on June 7, 1964, as a modern edifice reflecting the changes wrought by Vatican II. Set on the edge of a large macadam parking lot, the one-story brick church with a pressed-copper, cantilevered roof serves a more broad-based Roman Catholic community than the early masses in the Civil War era. Here, Rt. Rev. Jeremiah F. Minihan, auxiliary bishop of Boston, leads the procession into the new church during the dedication ceremonies. (From the collection of Albert E. Meader.)

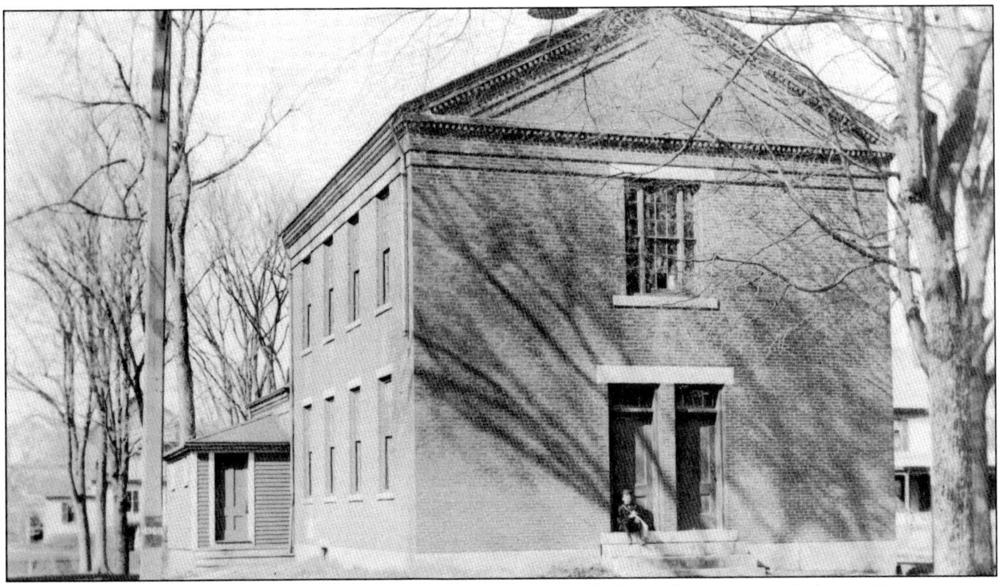

The Old Brick Schoolhouse (No. 4), at the corner of West Main and School Streets, was used for town offices and high school classes after 1906. All Saints Episcopal Church rented the second floor in 1916 for services and eventually purchased the school from the town in 1917, worshiping here until 1966, when it was deconsecrated. Rev. Glenn Tilley Morse, a noted antiquarian, served this parish. The Noack Organ Company purchased the former school-church building in 1970. (From the collection of Albert E. Meader.)

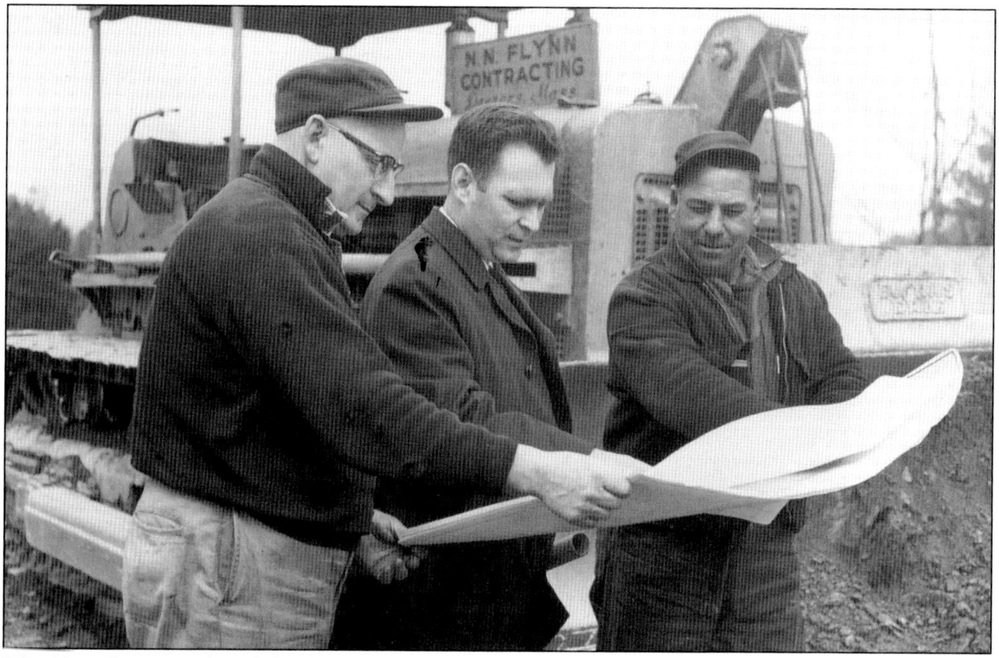

The First Baptist Church built a modern church in 1966 at 186 East Main Street, on a knoll overlooking the historic Union Cemetery. Pictured at the building site are, from left to right, H. Clark Budd, building chairman; Rev. Bernard L. Hughes, pastor of the First Baptist Church; and William Maynard, the bulldozer operator for the N.N. Flynn Contracting Company. Today, the church is known as the New Life Community Church. (Courtesy of the Georgetown Historical Commission.)

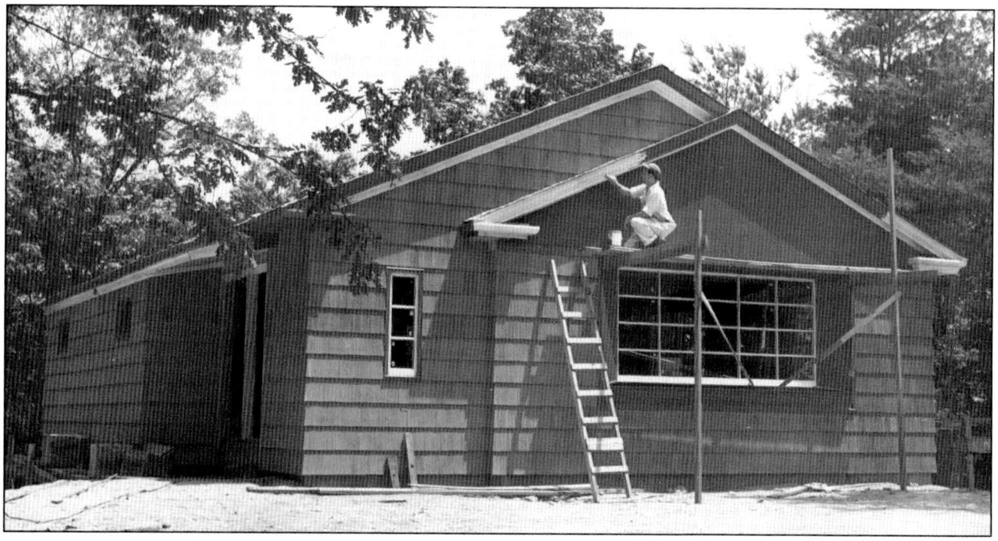

The Church of Jesus Christ of Latter Day Saints first worshiped in Georgetown in the Odd Fellows Hall and erected a place of worship in 1954 at the corner of Andover Street and Canteberry Drive. The congregation built a small church on Jewett Street in 1968. It was designed by a member of the church, Ellsworth Tidd of the Lawrence architectural firm of Ashton, Huntress & Pratt. In this photograph, Tidd is applying a primer coat of paint to the pedimented gable of the first church. (Courtesy of the Georgetown Historical Commission.)

Three

SCHOOLS

The first known school in Georgetown was built in 1737. In 1795, a red schoolhouse was built on Andover Street (the present site of the Civil War Soldiers' Monument) and served the needs of the parish until the incorporation of Georgetown in 1838. The first Georgetown School Committee was elected in 1839 and consisted of Rev. Isaac Braman, pastor of the Old South Church; Rev. John Burden, pastor of the First Baptist Church; and Rev. James Peabody of Byfield Parish Church. One representative from each of the seven school districts included Col. Joseph Kimball (No. 1), Cornelius Baker (No. 2), Edward Poor (No. 3), Jeremiah Russell, Esq. (No. 4), Charles Hills (No. 5), Gorham P. Tenney (No. 6), and Dea. Green Wildes (No. 7). It was the duty of the school committee to hire and compensate the teachers and to provide fuel and school supplies and routine maintenance of the one-room schoolhouses. The first high school was opened in 1856 on the first floor of the town house, with William Reed as teacher. Here it remained until fire destroyed the building in 1898.

This routine was to hold forth until it was changed to three trustees. In 1899, the Perley Free School was built and named after John Perley, who had left a fund to the town to support a high school. Designed by Clarence Hoyt as a Classical Revival brick-and-granite schoolhouse, it was built on North Street, near the square and library. It served generations of schoolchildren until it was destroyed by fire in 1935, after which it was rebuilt and renamed the Perley High School. The high school became known as the Georgetown High School in 1961, when it relocated to Atwood's Hill in the new school designed by Ellsworth Tidd of the Lawrence architectural firm of Ashton, Huntress & Pratt. Under the direction of James H. Boynton (who served as principal of the Perley High School), great achievements in education were accomplished. This gentleman, a 10th-generation descendant of the first schoolteacher in Rowley, continued the vision of his ancestor in the 17th century into the 20th century. Today, in addition to the Georgetown High School, the students attend the Perley Elementary School (kindergarten through grade two) and the Penn Brook School (grades three through six).

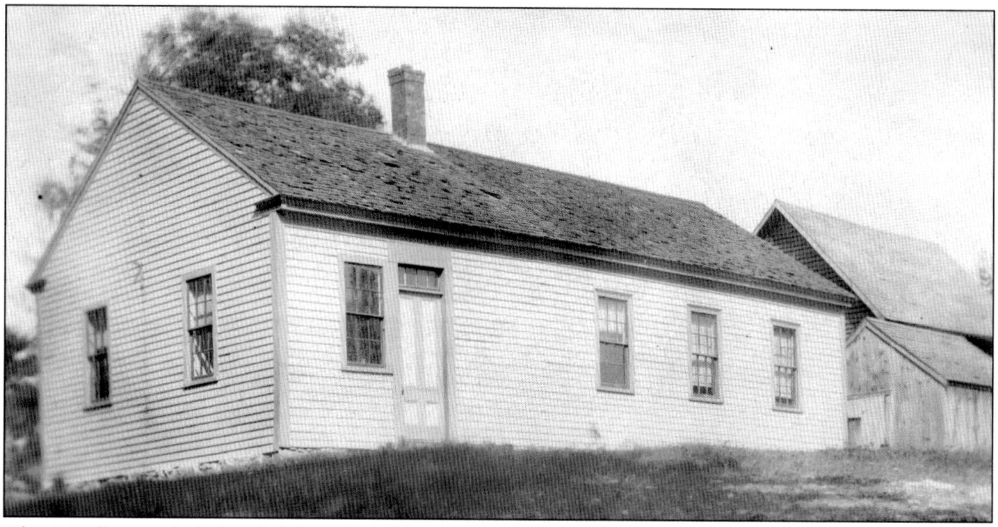

The Marlborough School (No. 1) was located near 188 East Main Street. Marlborough Village (formerly known as Elders Plain in honor of Elder Humphrey Rayner) was renamed in honor of the English duke of Marlborough, whose family was acquainted with Rev. John Rayner, who was educated at Cambridge University. Sold by the town in 1905, the school was later divided, with a portion being used by the Camenker family as a henhouse and the other portion being moved to Groveland and remodeled as the home of the Dechesne family. (Courtesy of the Georgetown Historical Society.)

Spirit of departed schoolmates who on earth we loved so well
Are you all in bliss united, do you still in friendship dwell?

—Anonymous

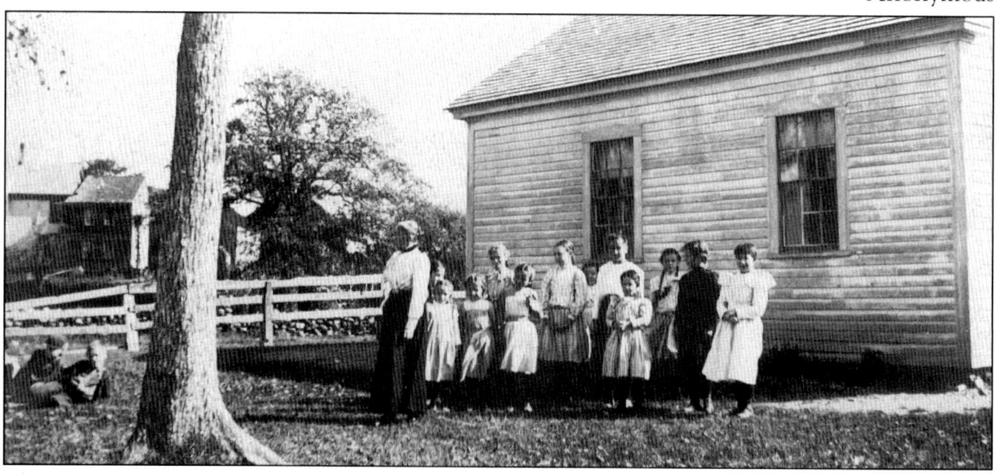

The Andover Hill School (No. 3) was built in 1828 on Andover Street. A simple gable-end Greek Revival building, it had no embellishment, as was the case with all of the early schoolhouses. The teacher in this *c.* 1885 photograph is Sarah Lowe (1832–1905). Lowe taught in the Georgetown school for 41 years. Upon her death, her headstone in Harmony Cemetery was erected through the generosity of her friends and former students. The Hill School later became a storage shed for Samuel Batchelder (and, later, the Perley family) until it was moved by the Georgetown Historical Commission in 1984 to a site on East Main Street adjacent to the Brocklebank Museum. (From the collection of Ida Louise Weston Morse.)

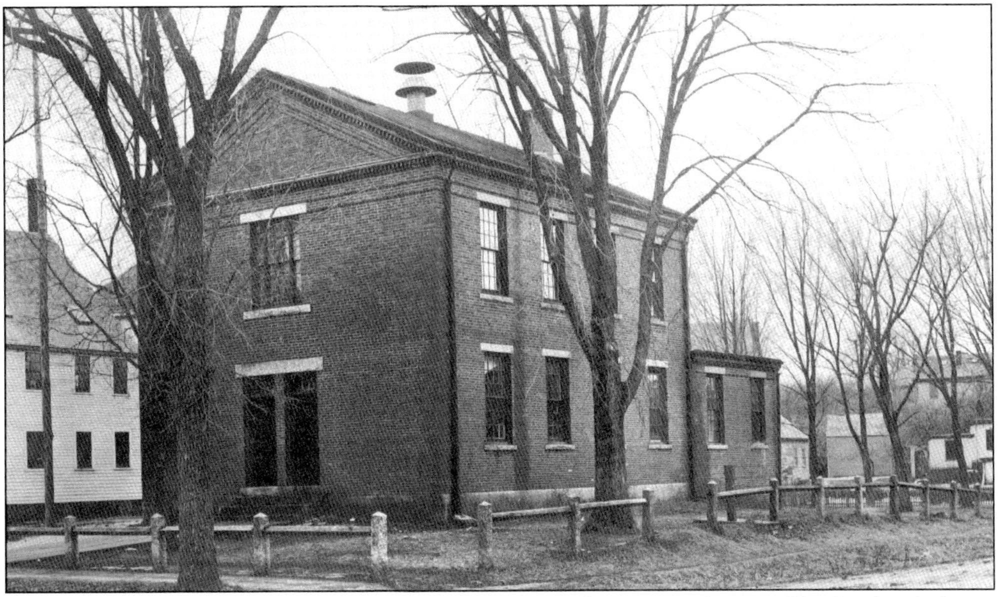

The Old Brick Schoolhouse (No. 4) was built in 1854 for intermediate and high school classes near the corner of School and West Main Streets. This school was to be used as the local recruitment office during World War I. The congregation of All Saints Episcopal Church worshiped here from 1916 to 1966. Today, the former schoolhouse and church is the Noack Organ Company, a well-known organ manufactory. Seen on the left is the Noyes Shoe Shop, now Scala's Antique Shop. (Courtesy of the Georgetown Historical Society.)

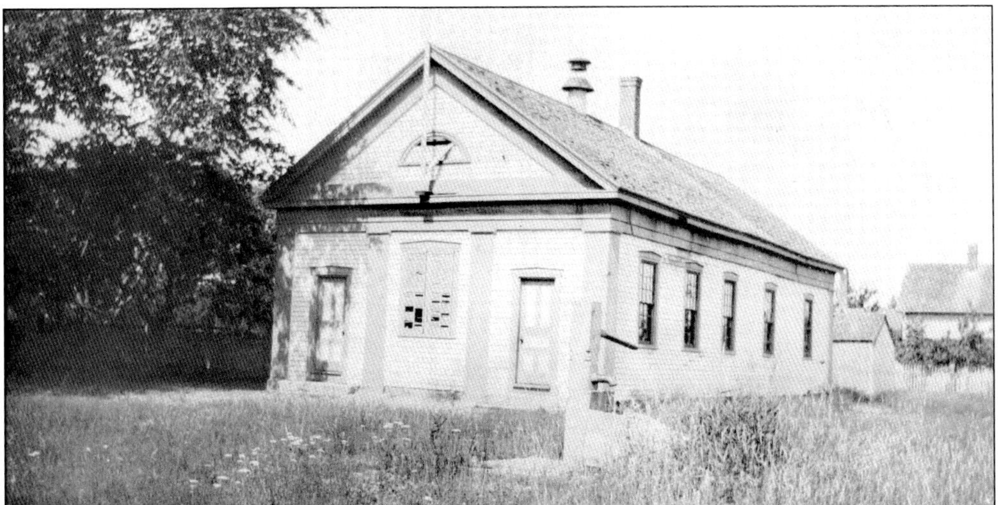

The Old North School (No. 5) is at the corner of Boardman and North Streets and was built in 1851. For many years, Sara E. Horner (1828–1906) taught at this schoolhouse with 80 students, with an average attendance of 54 in 1848. This school still stands though extensively remodeled as a two-story apartment house. (Courtesy of the Georgetown Historical Society.)

Tell me! Do you still remember scenes of childhood and of youth
In the Old Red Centre Schoolhouse where we all were taught the truth?

—Anonymous

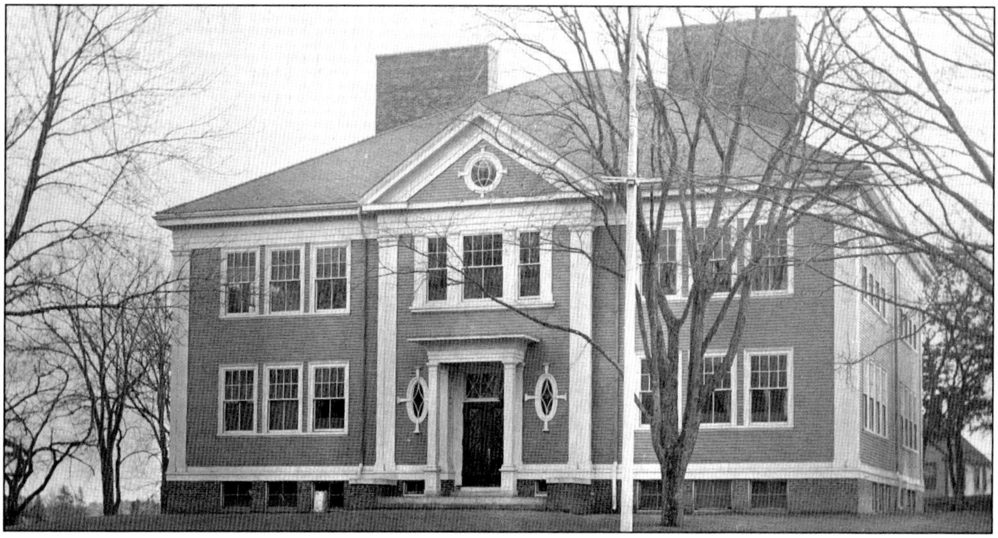

The Georgian Revival Central School, designed by Cooper & Bailey, was built in 1905 at the corner of Library and Central Streets. With monumental Doric pilasters supporting a pedimented gable, the facade is embellished with an oculus in the pediment and symmetrical elliptical oculi on either side of the entrance, which is framed with bold Tuscan pilasters. Frank Irving Cooper and Elmer Smith Bailey were in partnership from 1899 to 1914, specializing in school architecture. In 1905, all one-room schoolhouses in Georgetown were closed and sold, after which students attended the Central School. Today, the Central School is used as the town hall. (Courtesy of the Georgetown Historical Society.)

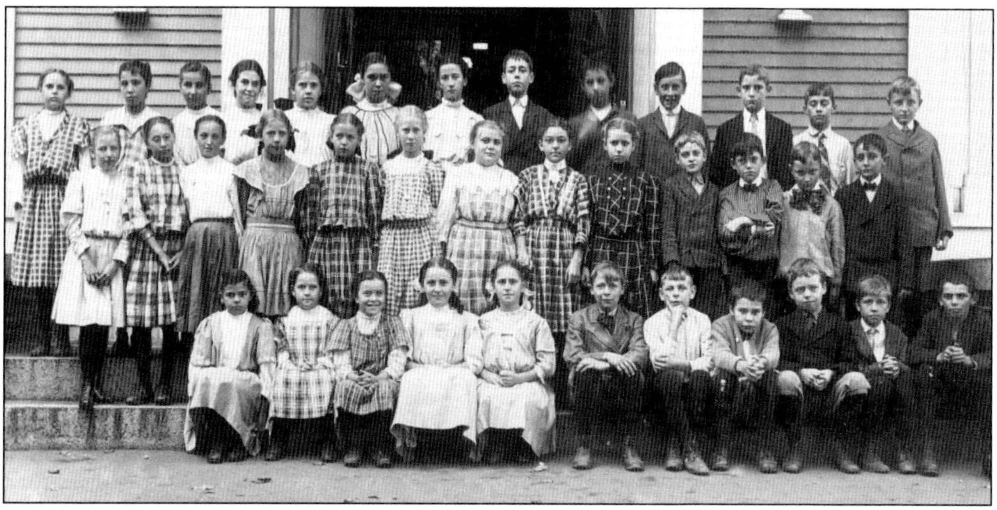

Sixth-grade students at the Central School pose in 1908. From left to right are the following: (front row) Alice Brown, Lauretta Adams, Delia Flagg, Mary Hamelin, Harriet Wilkins, Oscar Dole, Herbert Jackson, Karl Hamelin, Louis de Rochemont, Robert Rogers, and David Ross; (middle row) Gladys Stockman, Beatrice Steeves, Helen Brocklebank, Emily Poor, Alice Davis, Helen Hardy, Alice Hoyt, Alice Spaulding, Helen Pillsbury, Arthur Holt, Louis Carney, Harold Pedder, and Stanley De Quoy; (back row) Blanche Spaulding, Florence Hould, Vera Murch, Dorothy Brownell, Rhue Marden, Ethel Woodman, Mary Barbour, John Palmer, William Matthews, George Mooney, William Woodman, James Frost, and James Pedder. (Courtesy of the Georgetown Historical Society.)

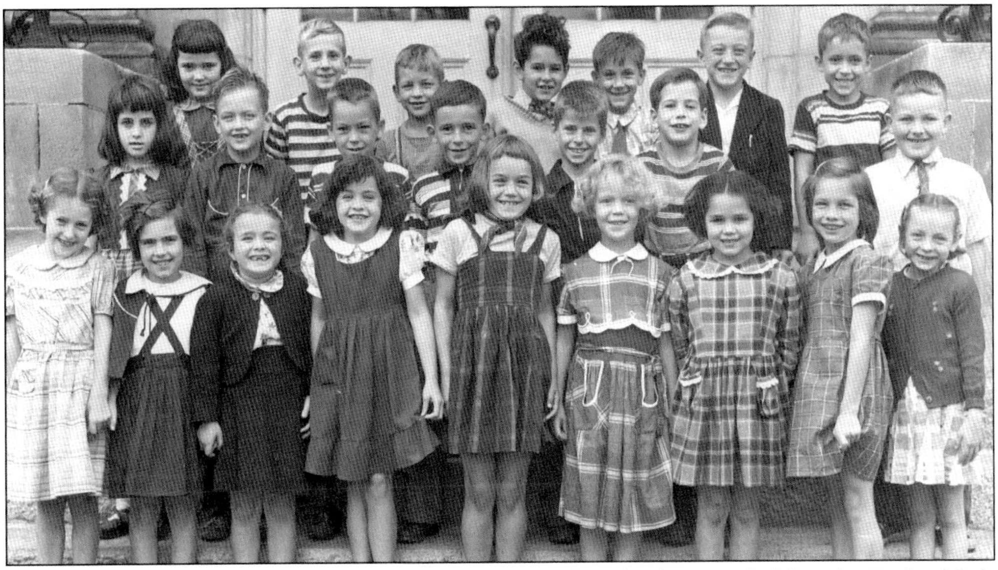

Because of overcrowding, Mrs. Peardon's 1952 second-grade class was held at the Perley High School rather than at the Central School. From left to right are the following: (front row) Arlene Hochmuth, Priscilla Roode, Helen Hollis, Louise A. Richardson, Miriam Fernald, Carole Chanonhouse, Susan Parker, Karen Strogney, and Ruth Brocklebank; (middle row) Sarah Boyland, Glen Dodge, Richard Hooper, Verne Hardenbrook, Wayne Coolen, William Fuller, and David Beaudoin; (back row) Barbara Lee, Gerald Finnigan, Dennis Simcoe, Timothy Pepin, David Flynn, Donald Reed, and James Tidd. (Courtesy of Louise A. Richardson.)

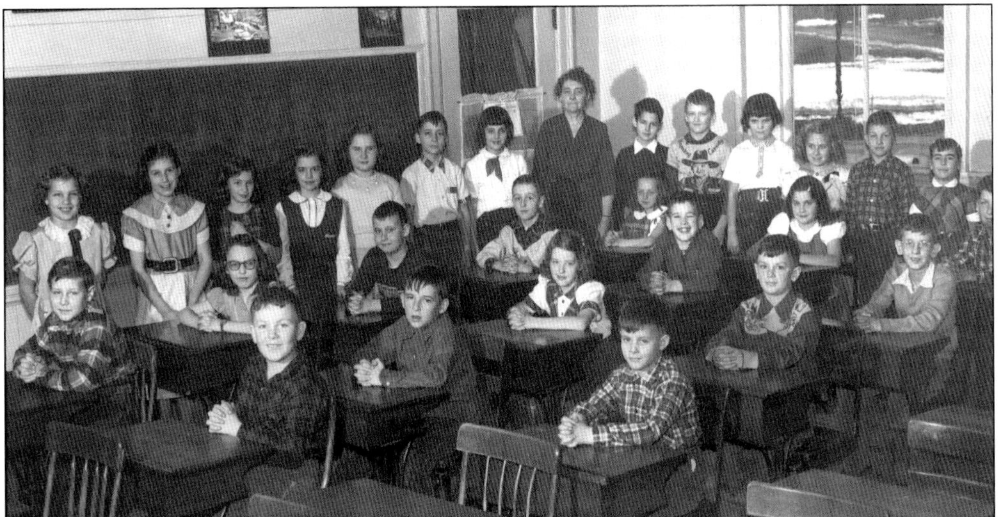

Miss Hardy's fourth-grade class at the Central School is shown here in 1954. Standing, from left to right, are Karen Strogney, Lois Rogers, Elaine Handren, Jean Greenleaf, Ronna Falabella, James Tidd, Sarah Boyland, Miss Hardy, Timothy Pepin, Glen Dodge, Barbara Lee, Susan Laramee, Dennis Simcoe, and Priscilla Roode. Sitting, from front to back, are the following: (left row) Peter Alder, Sharon Hills, Paul Terreaux, Donald Reed, and Ruth Brocklebank; (middle row) David Beaudoin, Verne Hardenbrook, Arlene Hochmuth, William Fuller, and Louise A. Richardson; (right row) Donald Jones, Christopher Goodwin, Gerald Finnigan, and Ronald Coolen. (Courtesy of Louise A. Richardson.)

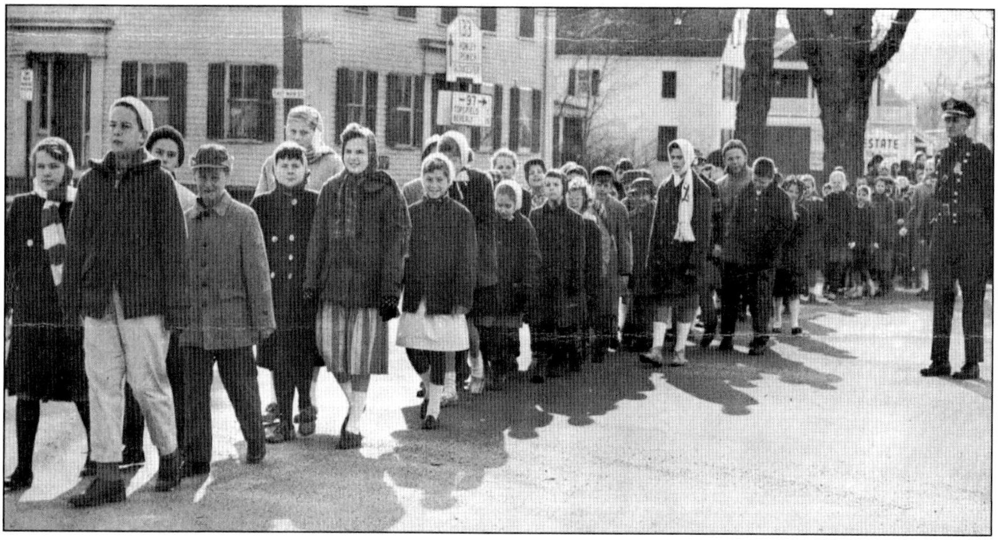

In 1958, students from the Central School are seen walking to the cafeteria of the Perley High School for lunch. On the right, Georgetown police chief Richmond "Dick" Kneeland can be seen monitoring the more than 200 students who made this trip daily. In the background is the Odd Fellows Hall, a Greek Revival house built c. 1840 by Theodore Elliott and now used by the King Davis Agency. (Courtesy of the Georgetown Peabody Library.)

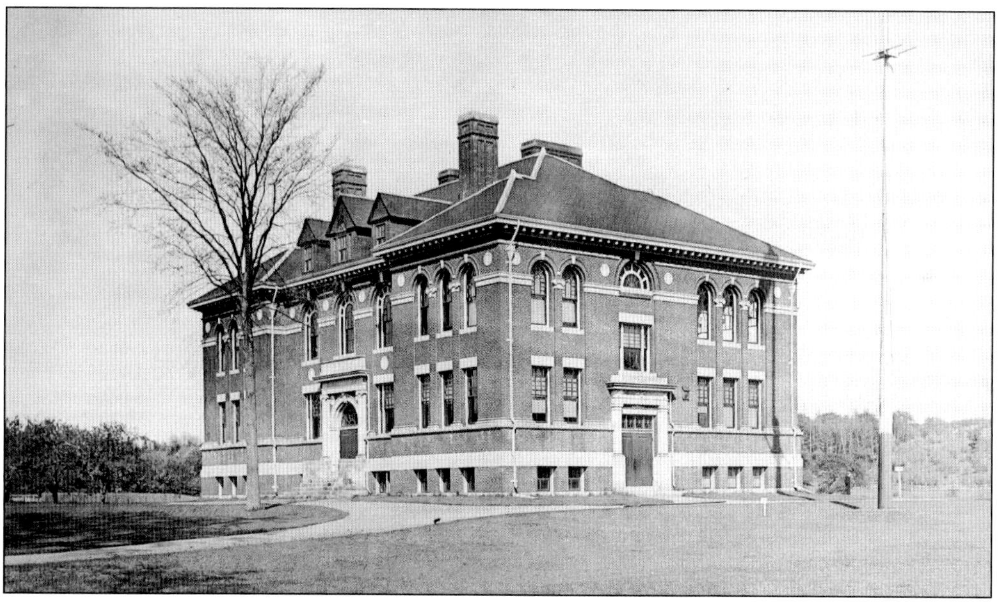

The Perley Free School, designed by Boston architect Clarence P. Hoyt, was built as a high school in 1899 on North Street and was named for philanthropist John Perley (1782–1860). The interior was destroyed by fire in subzero weather in 1935 and was rebuilt by the Sturgis Association of Boston. It now serves as a school for kindergarten to second grade. (Courtesy of the Georgetown Historical Society.)

John Perley was a native of Rowley. The son of John and Lydia Perley, he was a successful merchant in Danvers until 1830, when he moved to New York. Upon his death, he was buried in the center lot at Harmony Cemetery with a grand, Gothic Revival, white Italian marble monument that was an exact replica of one erected in England to the memory of Sir Walter Scott. He bequeathed his estate to benefit not only his relatives but also the First Congregational Church in Georgetown, the Linebrook Church, the needy of Georgetown, and the remainder "to accumulate until the Trustees [of the Perley Estate] deemed the amount sufficient to build and equip the school and have a fund to carry it on with." (From the collection of Albert E. Meader.)

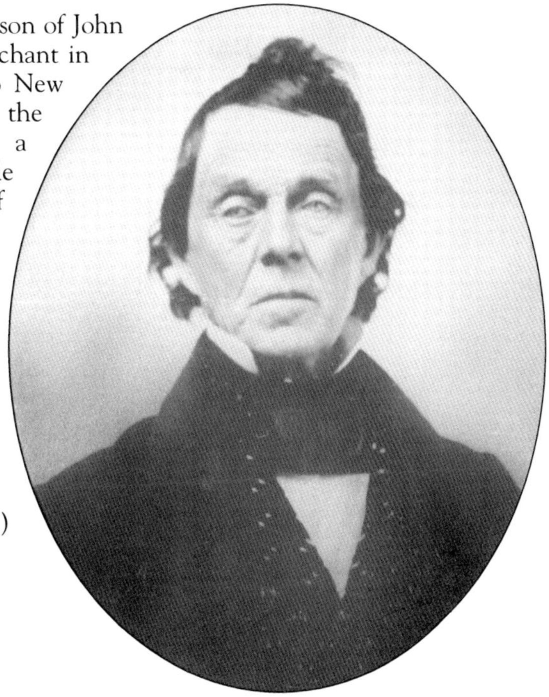

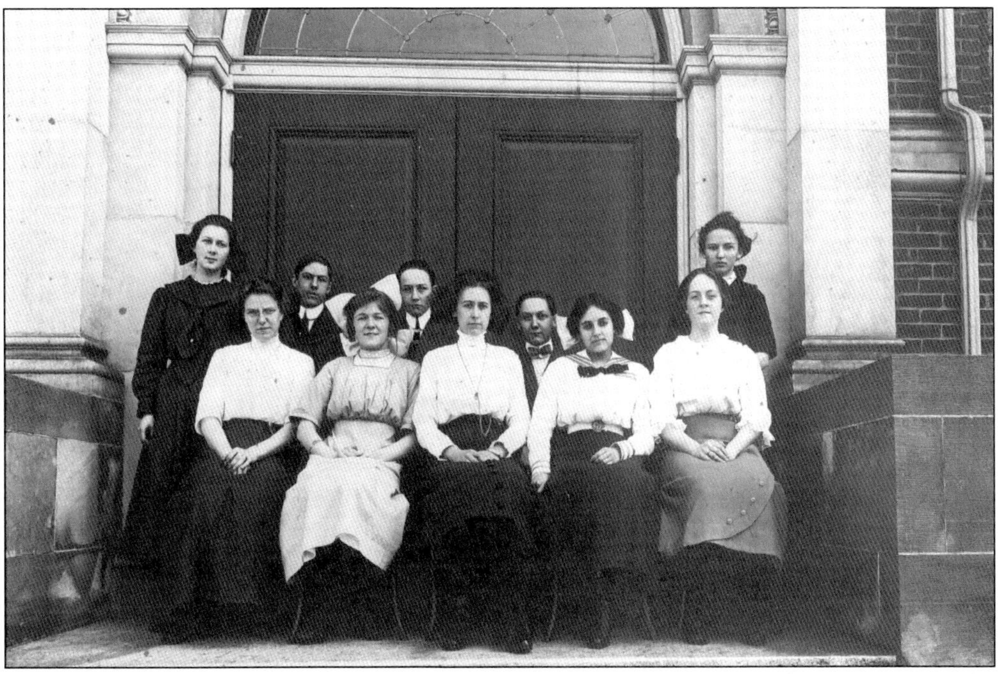

Members of the 1904 graduation class of the Perley Free School pose on the front steps of the school. From left to right are the following: (front row) Eva Harriman, Alberta M. Hatfield, teacher Marie A. Watson, Eule Waterhouse, and M. Gertrude Thwing; (back row) Charlotte C. Haskell, Oliver W. Larkin (later a Pulitzer Prize winner for the 1949 book *Art and Life in America*), Robert B. Adams, Charlotte M. Falconer, and Satira T. Stetson. (Courtesy of the Georgetown Historical Society.)

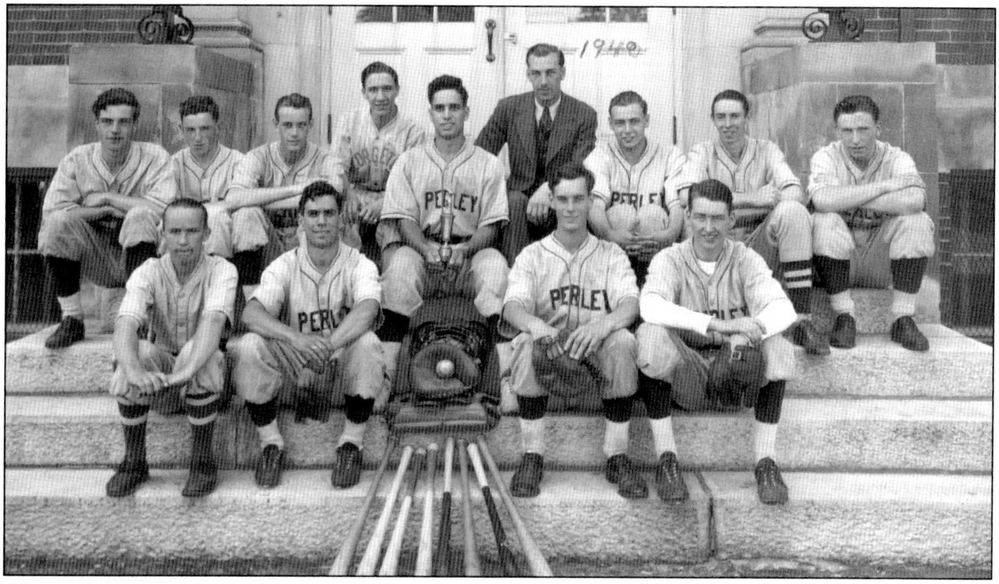

The 1940 baseball team of the Perley High School poses on the front steps of the school with an artistic arrangement of equipment in front. From left to right are the following: (front row) Malcolm Morse, John Mello, Irving Robinson, and Irving Bean; (back row) William Gatchell, Ralph Stetson, Robert Bent, Harold Roberts, captain Cliff Mello (holding the championship award), coach James H. Boynton (who later became the high school principal), Kenneth Poole, Roland Spofford, and Robert Jones. (Courtesy of James H. Boynton.)

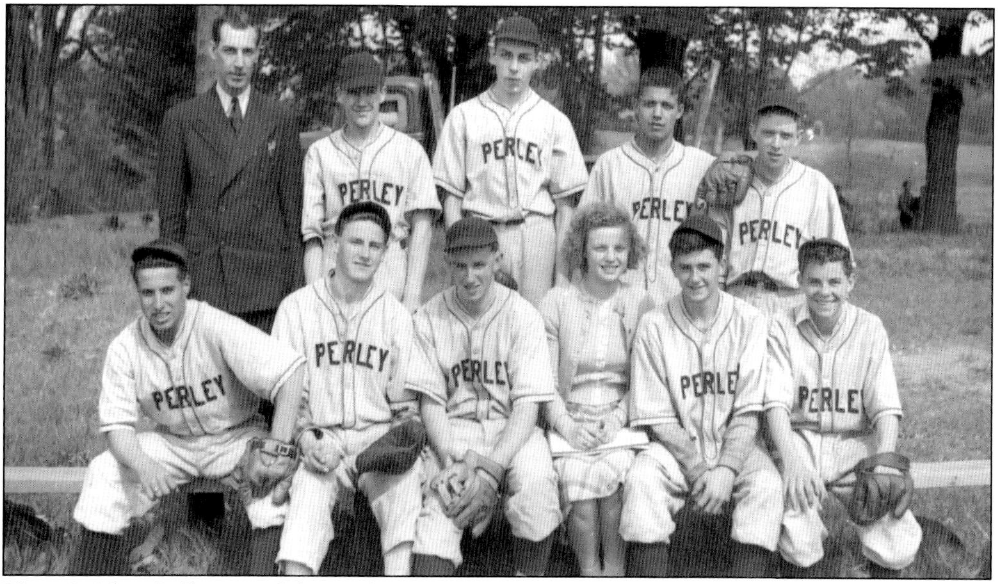

The 1942 baseball team of the Perley High School includes, from left to right, the following: (front row) Philip Biron, John Wilkins, Ralph Stetson, scorekeeper Ruth Longley, George Tolman, and Herbert Kent; (back row) coach James H. Boynton, Merton Roberts, Raymond "Bud" Chase, Leo Soucy, and Dennis Spaulding. The most famous baseball player from Georgetown was Fred Tenney (1871–1952), who played for the Boston Beaneaters, which won league pennants in 1897 and 1898. Tenney later played for the New York Giants and was noted for his running speed. (Courtesy of James H. Boynton.)

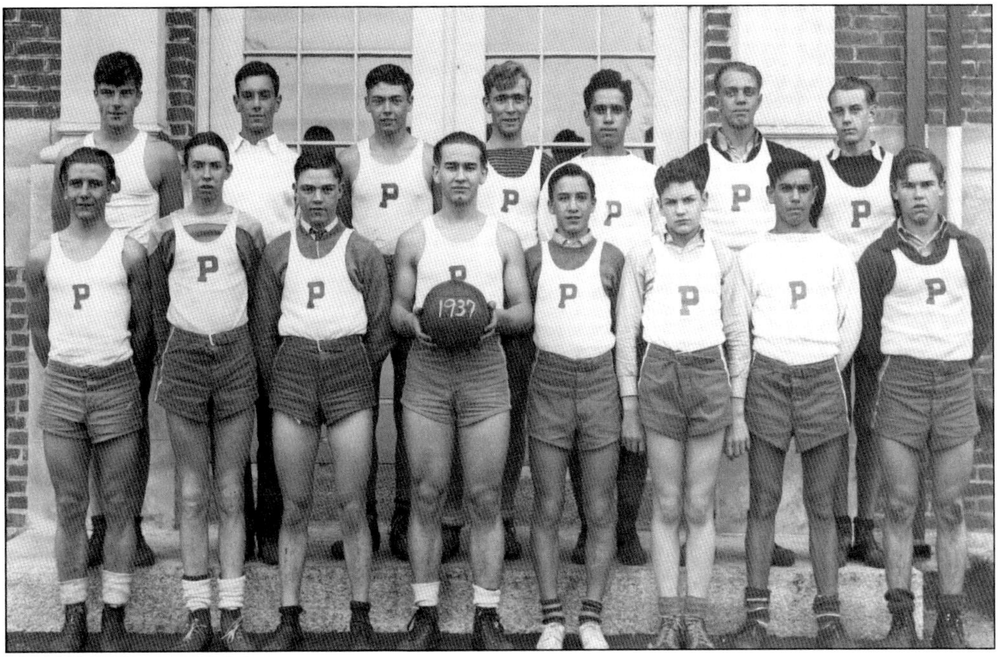

The 1937 soccer team of the Perley Free High School poses outside the school. From left to right are the following: (front row) Richard Rogers, Roland Spofford, Charles Flanders, captain Frank Roberts, Harold Roberts, Edward Williams, John Mello, and Ernest George; (back row) William Gatchell, Irving Robinson, Kenneth Poole, James Shute, Clifford Mello, John Lancaster, and Robert Bent. This was the second year that soccer was coached at the Perley High School, having been introduced by James H. Boynton. (Courtesy of James H. Boynton.)

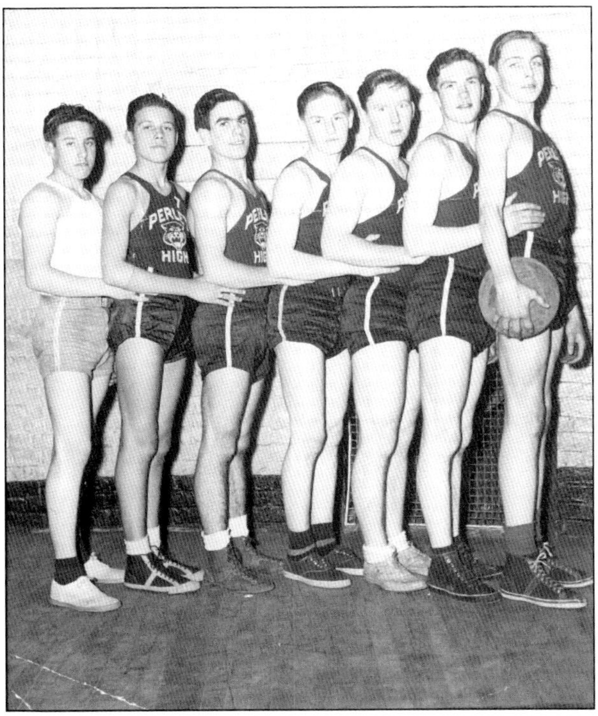

The lineup of the Perley High School basketball team in 1941 includes, from left to right, Phil Biron, Leo Soucy, John Mello, John Wilkins, Bob Jones, Bill Gatchell, and Raymond "Bud" Chase. Note the wide array of footwear of the ballplayers. (Courtesy of James H. Boynton.)

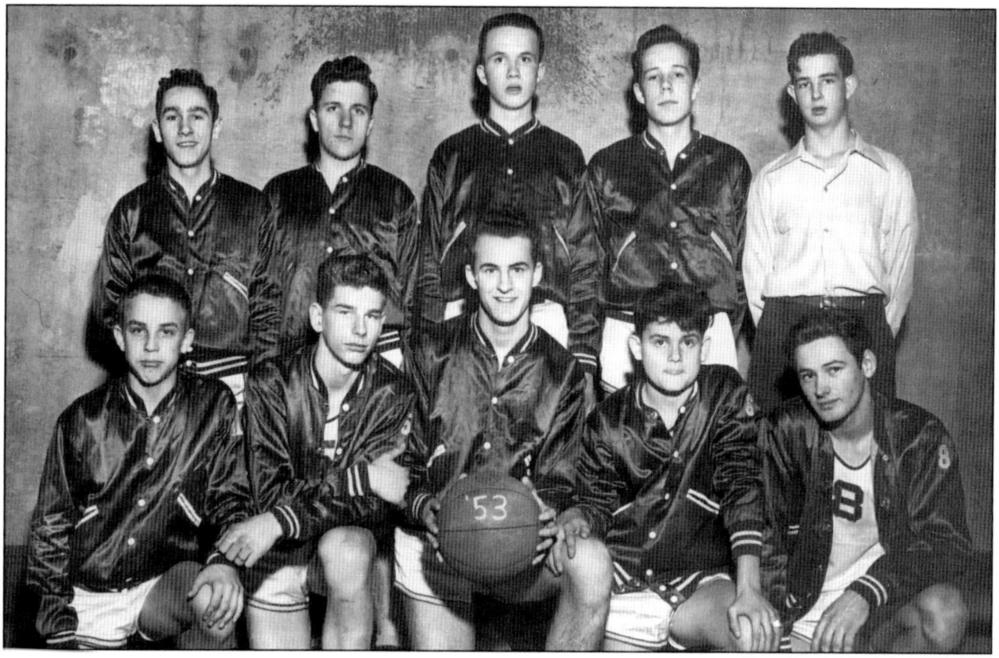

The 1953 varsity basketball team at the Perley High School includes, from left to right, the following: (front row) Calvin Pingree, Donald Cragg, Arthur Marceau, William Prescott, and Roy Thompson; (back row) Robert Reed, Robert Frost, Glen Smerage, George James, and Richard Phillips. A new gymnasium was built in 1949 by Alfred E. Tidd & Son from designs provided by his son Ellsworth Tidd of the Lawrence architectural firm Ashton, Huntress & Pratt. The flier for the gymnasium's dedication said that with "indefatigable activity, and with the complete cooperation of the School Committee [Alfred E. Tidd] has made this Perley Gymnasium a reality. No other single person has made a greater contribution." (Courtesy of James H. Boynton.)

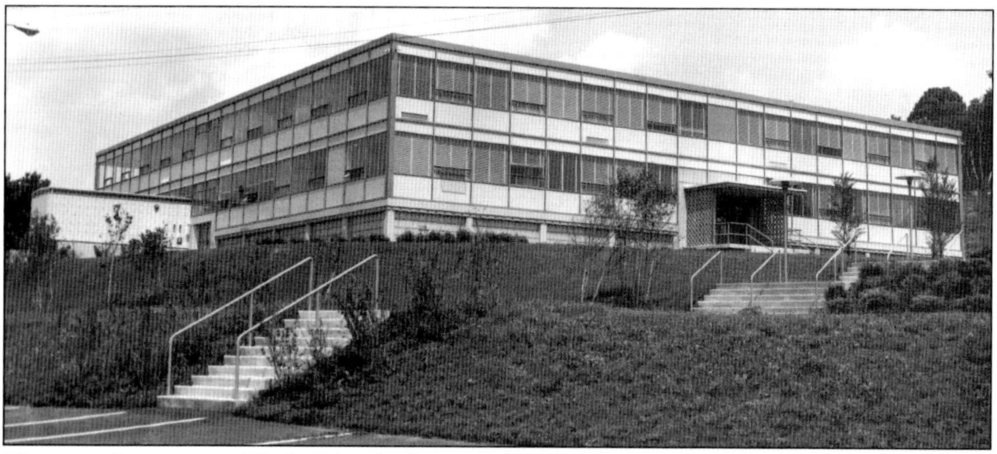

The new Georgetown High School, designed by Ellsworth Tidd, was built in 1962 by the Georgetown contracting firm of Alfred E. Tidd & Son. Built on Atwood's Hill (overlooking the center of town and within convenient walking distance of the library), this modern school was a great dichotomy from the early-19th-century one-room schoolhouses in town. The high school colors are blue and white, and the school motto is "He Conquers Who Endures." (Courtesy of the Georgetown Historical Commission.)

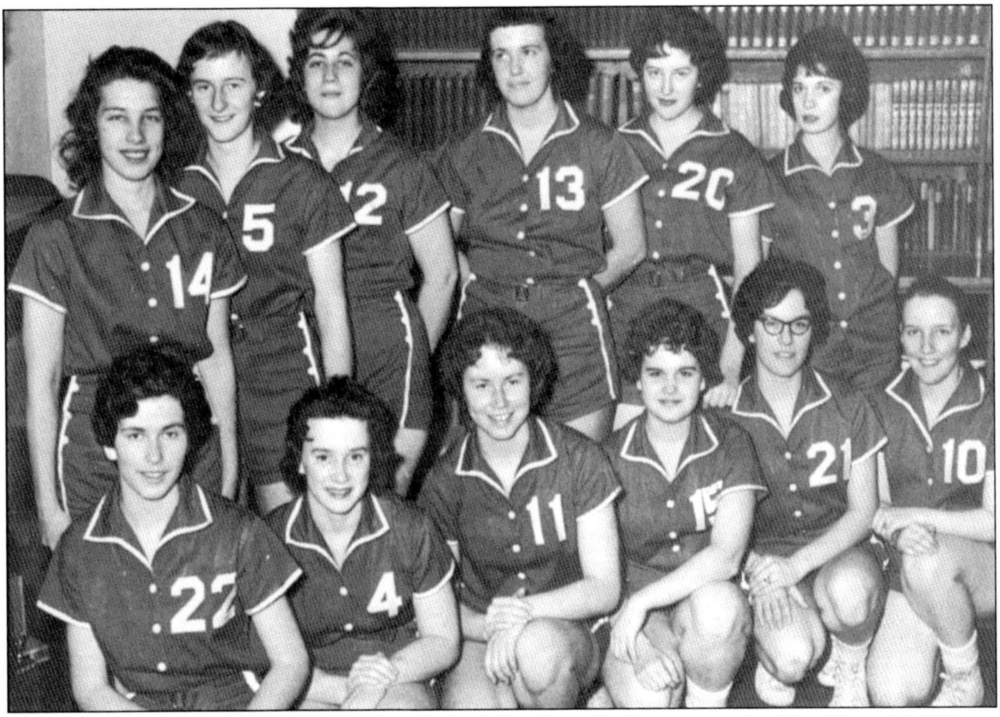

The girls' varsity basketball at Perley High School in 1961 was coached by Carol N. Visser. From left to right are the following: (front row) Diane Thibeault, Candace Mae Cookson, co-captain Joy Marshall, co-captain Florence Abend, Marguerite Lacey, and Phyllis Ricker; (back row) Karen Strogney, Cynthia Powell, Kathy Burke, Joan Kinney, Arlene Hochmuth, and Sue Whelpley. The team won nine games and only lost three during the season. (Courtesy of Louise A. Richardson.)

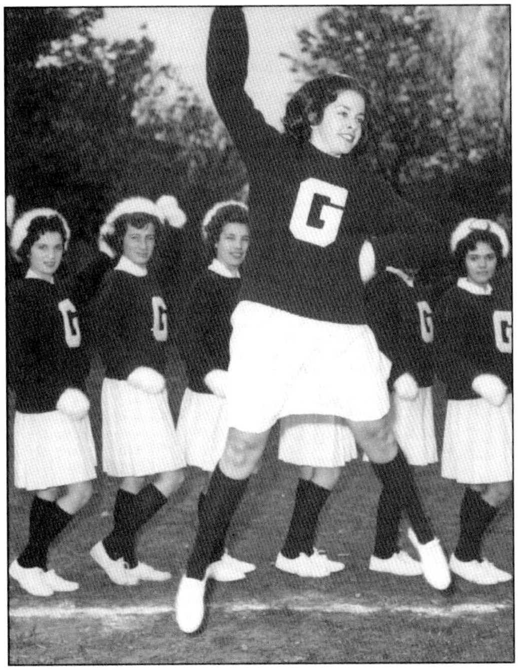

Louise A. Richardson, captain of the senior football cheerleaders, leads a rousing cheer during a Georgetown football game in 1961. In the rear, from left to right, are cheerleaders Suzanne Whelpley, Jennifer Young, Karen Strogney, Pat McAndrew (obscured), Barbara Schmidt (obscured), and Barbara Lee. The cheerleaders' uniforms were blue football sweaters and white pleated skirts with fetching angora mittens and caps. (Courtesy of Nicole C. Franciscovich.)

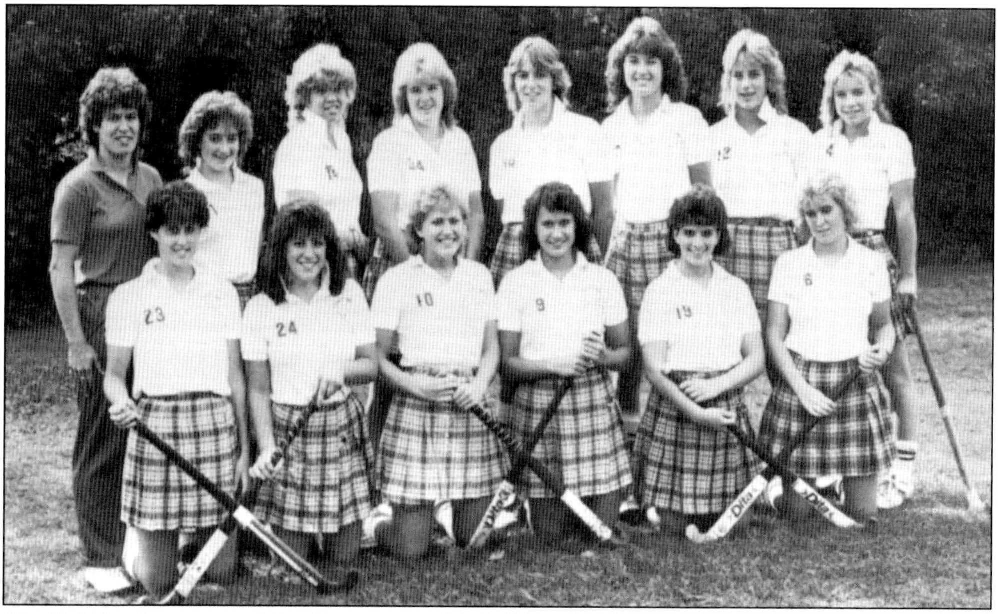

The field hockey team of the Georgetown High School is shown in 1986. From left to right are the following: (front row) Stacey Sears, Sarah Lee McQuillan, Elissa Haller, Karen Spiliotis, Heidi Burdett, and Suzanne Huber; (back row) coach Rose Anne Giannelli, Colleen Reddy, Traci Strogney, Debbie Kehoe, Galadriel Gilman, Virginia Games, Cynthia Stewart, and Brenda Holt. (Courtesy of Nicole C. Franciscovich.)

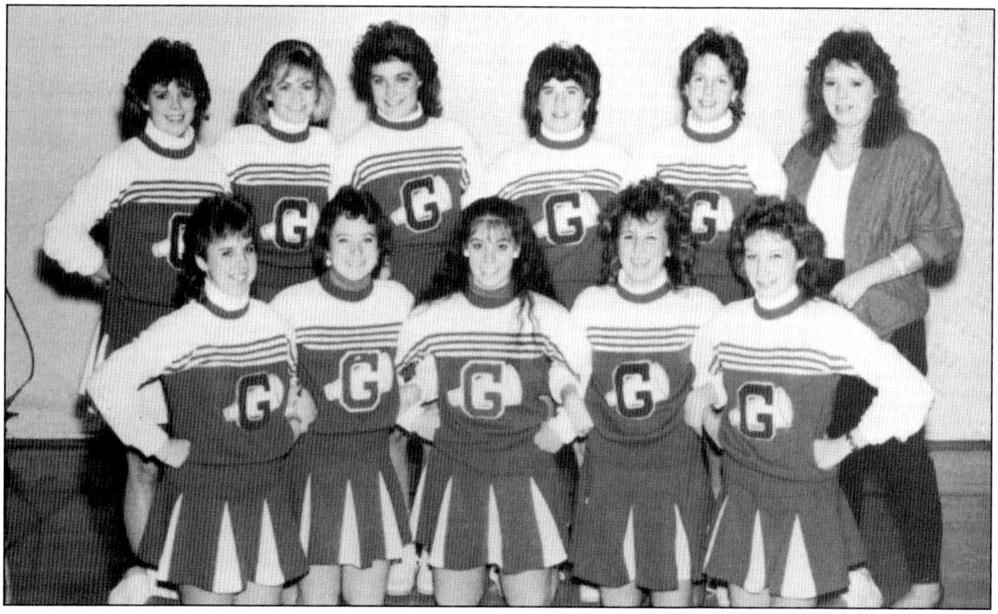

The basketball cheerleaders at Georgetown High School pose in 1986. From left to right are the following: (front row) Amy Pingree, Laurie White, captain Renee Gasbarro, Deanna Walters, and Holly Kirkey; (back row) Kristen Robinson, Nicole Franciscovich, Laurel Apprich, Stephanie Lind, Kimberly Morrisson, and advisor Missy Tripp. (Courtesy of Michael P. Franciscovich.)

Four

The Georgetown Peabody Library

The Georgetown Peabody Library was established through the generosity of the great philanthropist George W. Peabody (1795–1869), whose mother was born in Georgetown. A successful and benevolent merchant, Peabody had been born in South Danvers (later named Peabody in his honor) and was an immensely successful banker in London. In 1837, Peabody established Peabody & Company, merchants and money brokers, Wamford Court, London. He brokered bonds for the United States, often donating his broker's fee to charity and thereby receiving great acclaim as a truly beneficent person. During his lifetime, he donated millions of dollars to charity. He also provided the funds necessary to build and equip town libraries not just in Georgetown but in Thetford, Vermont, and in Danvers, Peabody, and Newburyport.

George Peabody often visited his sister Judith Peabody Russell Daniels, who lived at 25 East Main Street, staying with her when he visited Massachusetts. In 1866, at the laying of the cornerstone of the Peabody Memorial Church (for which he donated the necessary funds to build), he announced to those assembled that he was also donating the funds to establish a public library in Georgetown. Built on Library Street directly behind the Peabody Memorial Church, the wood-framed Italianate library was designed by the Boston architectural firm of Bryant & Gilman and was opened in 1868. In 1871, Peabody's sister donated the funds to build a lecture and concert hall, which greatly enlarged the already crowded library. Peabody also donated an endowment fund and 2,400 books from London, which he said were printed "better and more cheaply" than in the United States. This library served the needs of the public until the late 19th century, when the trustees sought to erect a larger library.

The present library was built on Lincoln Park, the land having been donated to the town for the library by Milton J. Tenney and his sister Lucy Tenney Brown, the children of George J. Tenney. The library was designed by the Boston architectural firm of Cooper & Bailey and built by contractor Edwin H. George. It was opened to the public on September 1, 1909. The following have served as librarian: Orlando B. Tenney (1869–1870), Richard Tenney (1871–1880), Henry Nelson (1880–1887), Mrs. S.A. Holt (1888–1898), Sarah T. Noyes (1899–1909), Lois P. Noyes (1909–1929), Pearl A. Poole (1929–1971), Jean B. Hamelin (1971–1983 and 1984–1986), and Richard St. Pierre (1983–1984). Those serving as library director include Betsy McNamara (1986–2000, made director in 1996), Diane Giarusso (2000), and Nanci Milone Hill (2000–2001).

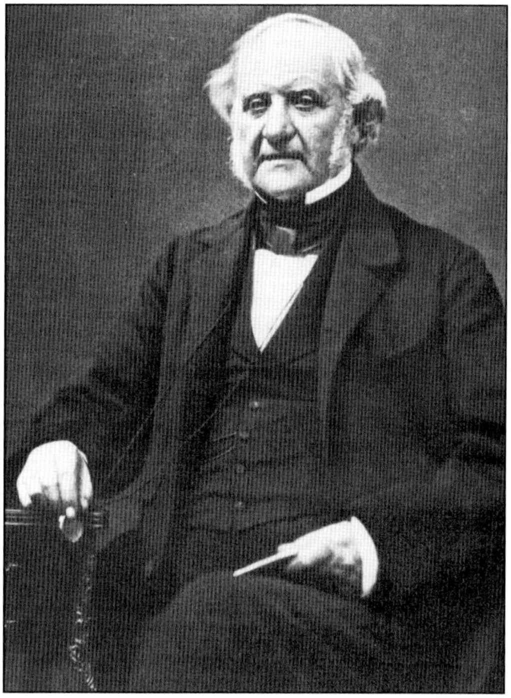

George W. Peabody was honored by the town with this resolution: "That with the liveliest emotions of pleasure we receive from George Peabody his letter of gift bestowing upon us a valuable library and Library building with the means to aid in their improvement and perpetuity, and that we accept the proffered gifts on the conditions conferred, and for ourselves and our posterity return our most heartfelt thanks to the generous donor, who, while persistently refusing rank from royalty, by his vast and numerous donations, has become among men, by letters patent from the whole civilized world, worthy of the title of Prince of Givers." Peabody, who was once quoted as saying that "education [is] a debt due from present to future generations," ensured that his munificence in extolling the virtues of learning continued long past his death. (Courtesy of the Georgetown Peabody Library.)

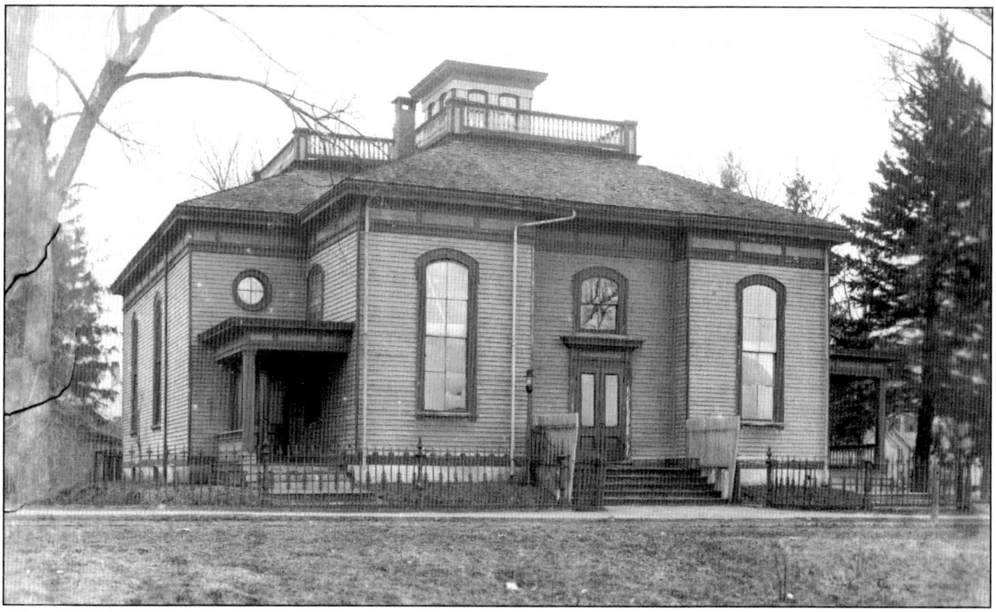

The first library in Georgetown was built on Library Street, directly behind the Peabody Memorial Church (today the town parking lot). Designed by Gridley J. Fox Bryant and Arthur Gilman, the library was completed in 1867 but was not opened until July 3, 1868. The first librarian was Orlando B. Tenney. Judith Peabody Russell Daniels, the sister of George Peabody, donated the funds in 1871 to build a lecture and concert hall. After the new library at Lincoln Park was opened in 1909, this building was used for various purposes, including town meetings and silent movies accompanied by a pianist, until it was demolished by Howard Pillsbury in 1934. (From the collection of Albert E. Meader.)

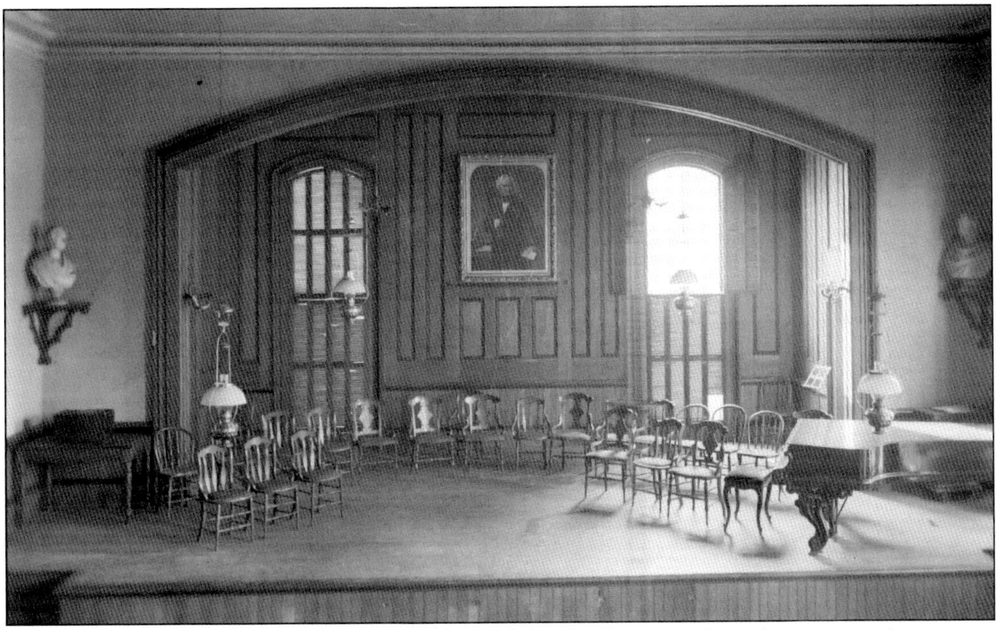

Library Hall had a lecture and concert hall added that had a stage where lectures, performances, and musical recitals were held. The addition was designed by Bryant & Gilman and was built in 1872. The large, impressive portrait of George Peabody can be seen dominating the space between the windows. (From the collection of Albert E. Meader.)

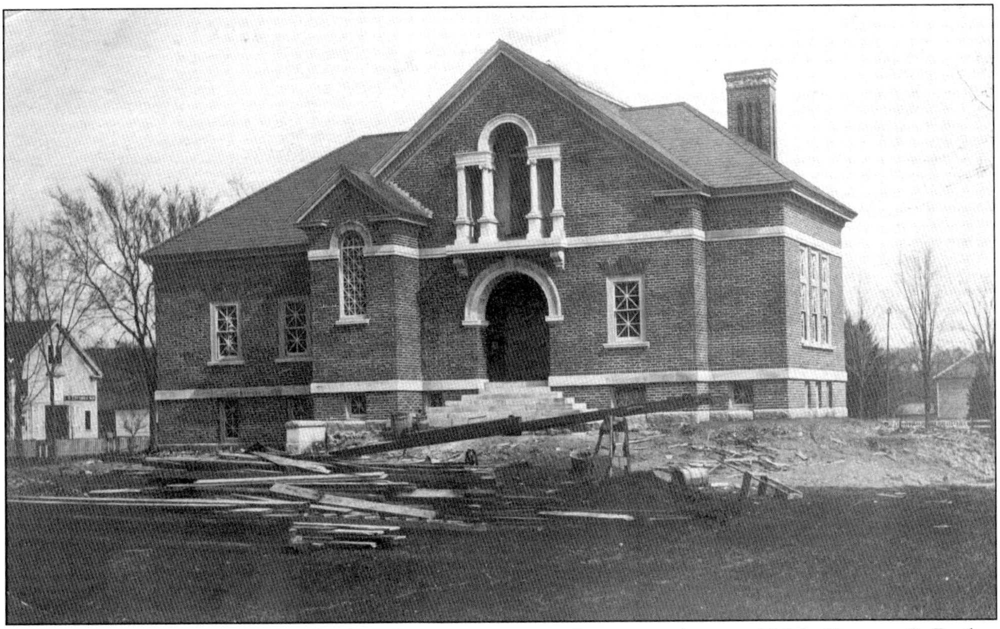

The present Georgetown Peabody Library nears completion in August 1905. Cooper & Bailey designed the brick-and-limestone facade as an asymmetrical Classical Revival building with a massive Palladian porch above an archway, which had the entrance set back a few feet. With the use of windows with peristyle mullions, the library was an elegant building on Lincoln Park, facing Park Street. (Courtesy of the Georgetown Historical Society.)

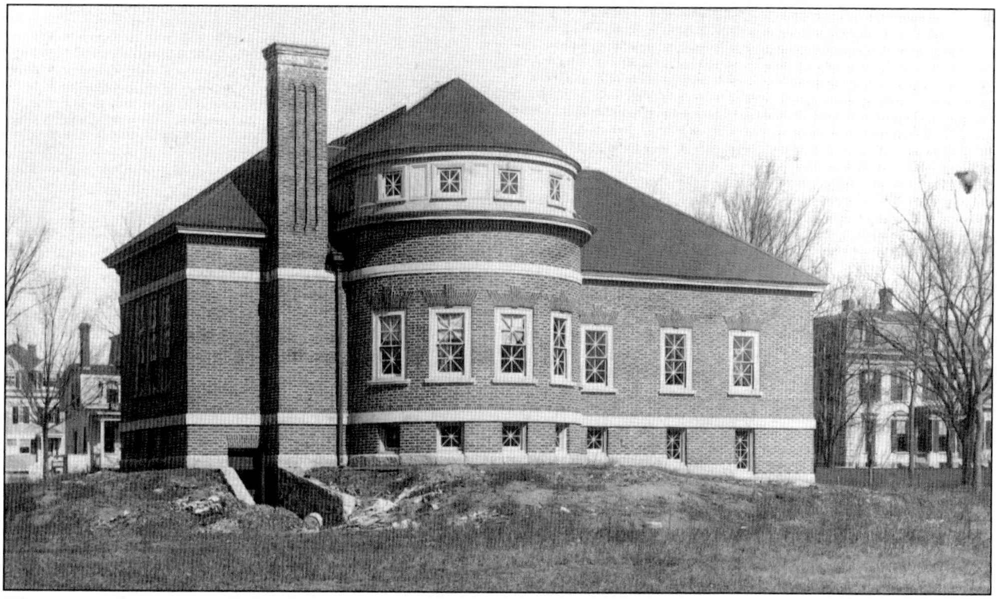

The rear elevation of the library has a swell-bay facade with a conical roof surmounting a squat tower with square, mullioned windows. With the limestone stringcourses and traditional brick, even the rear of the library creates an impressive view from the street. On the far right is the Osgood House (at 10 Pleasant Street), facing Lincoln Park. (Courtesy of the Georgetown Historical Society.)

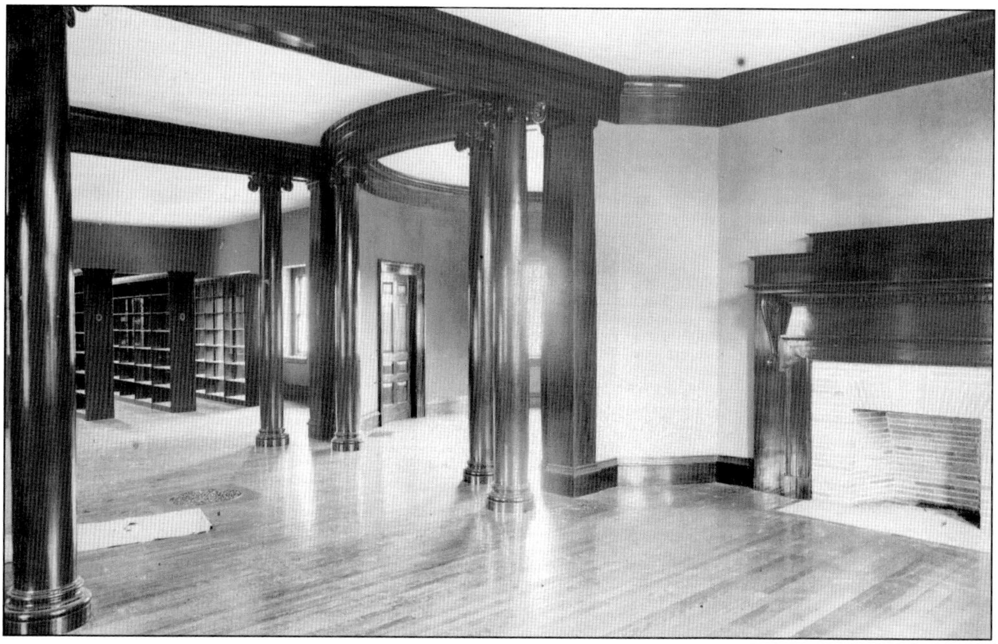

The interior of the library is pictured in August 1909 without any furnishings or books. Cooper & Bailey used Ionic columns to separate the reading room and book stacks as well as the circular room in the rear. The massive fireplace had a mantle in the same rich wood of the columns and woodwork. The bookshelves were designed by the Art Metal Construction Company of Ohio. (Courtesy of the Georgetown Historical Society.)

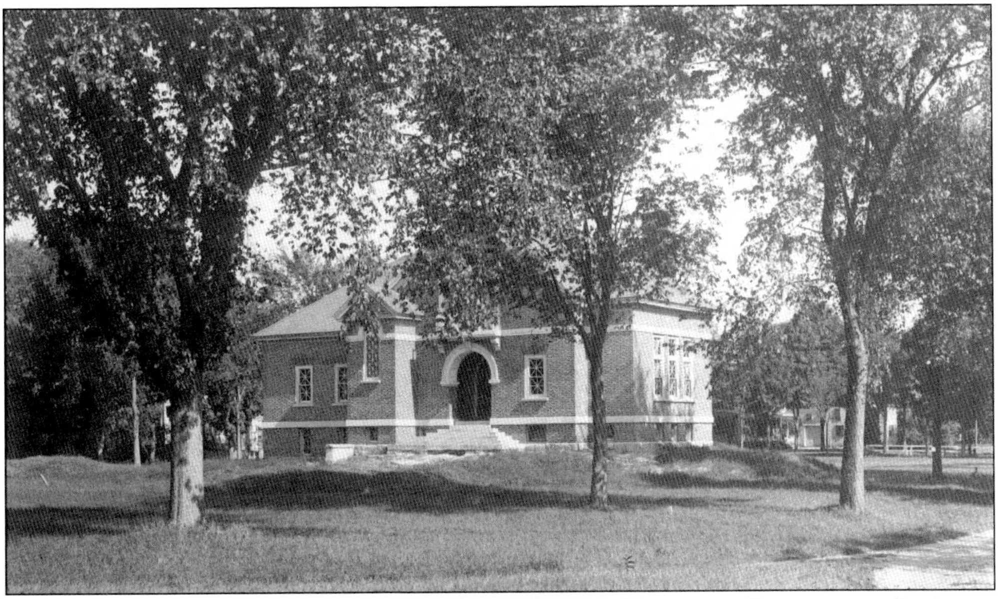

The grounds surrounding the library were designed in 1905 by native Georgetonian landscape architect Willard Weston Gay. A graduate in 1891 of Amherst College, Gay laid out the grounds on Lincoln Park to incorporate the mature shade trees with curvilinear walks and subtle plantings that enhanced the library. Gay's landscape plan enhanced the classical design executed by Cooper & Bailey. The Rene J. Gagnon Post 211, American Legion, erected a flagpole in front of the library in 1956. (Courtesy of the Georgetown Historical Society.)

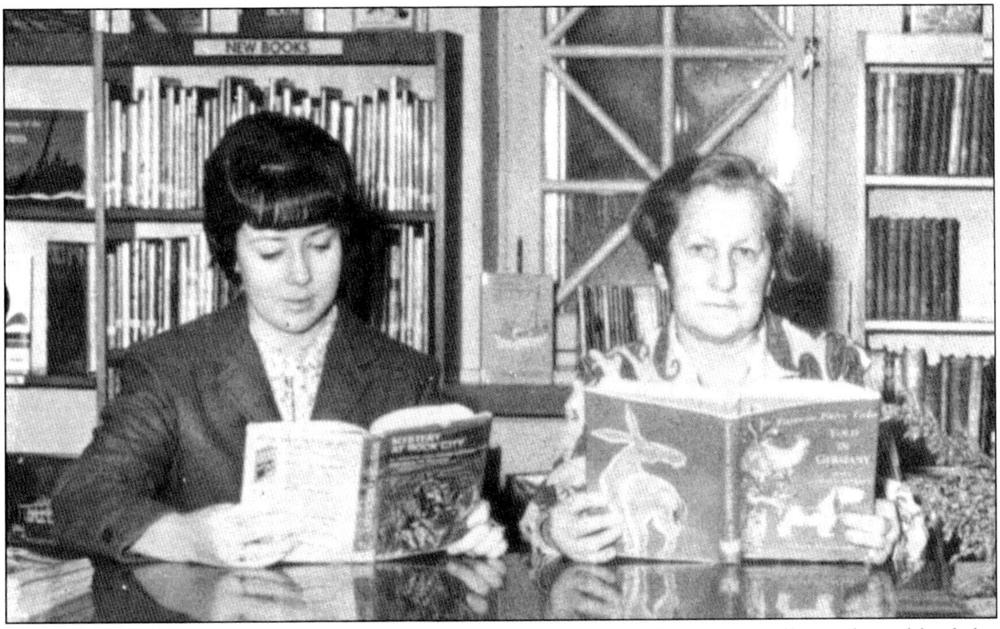

On January 24, 1964, the children's room (designed by local resident Ellsworth Tidd of the architectural firm of Ashton, Huntress & Pratt) was officially opened in the basement of the Georgetown Peabody Library. In this photograph, librarian Pearl A. Poole (right) and her student-assistant Candice Marshall sit at the children's room desk, awaiting their young patrons. (Courtesy of the Georgetown Peabody Library.)

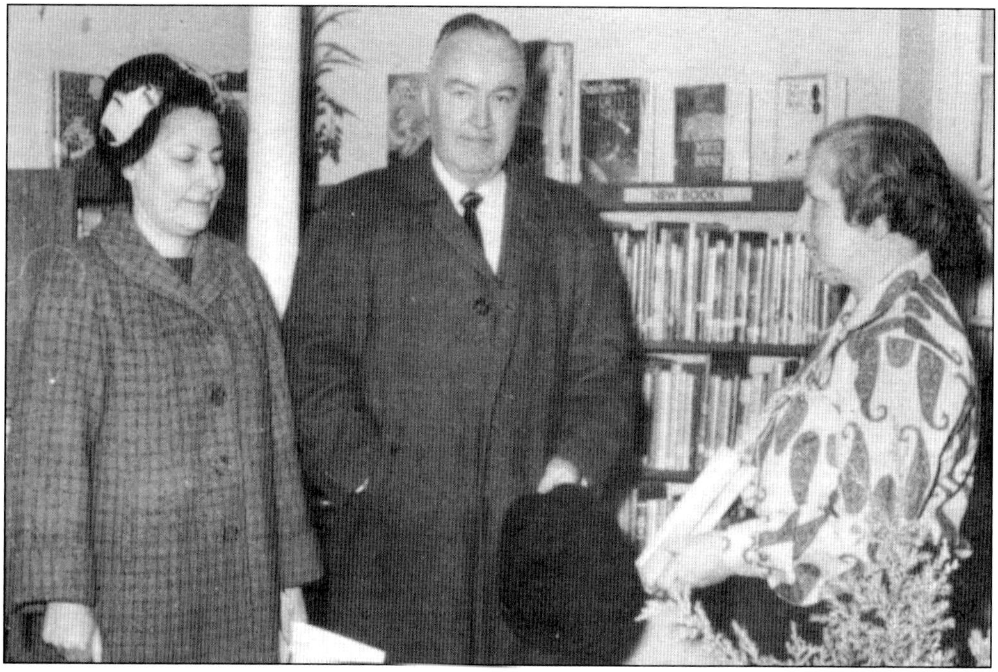

Librarian Pearl A. Poole greets Mrs. Richard J. Sullivan (head librarian of the State Regional Library Center in North Reading) and her husband, Richard J. Sullivan (head of the state board of library commissioners), to the opening in 1964 of the children's room of the Georgetown Peabody Library. (Courtesy of the Georgetown Peabody Library.)

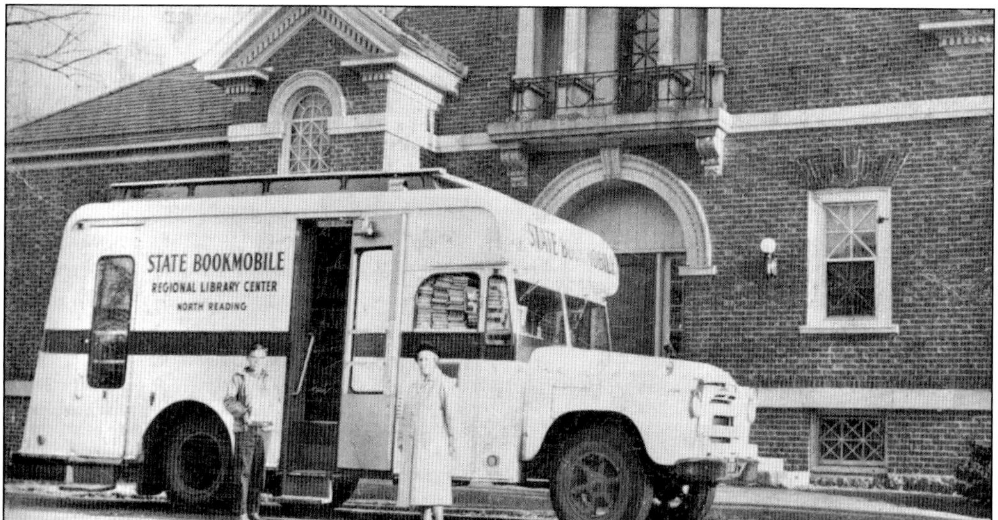

The State Bookmobile of the Regional Library Center in North Reading stops in front of the Georgetown Peabody Library in 1963, with Richard Proulx to the left of the door and librarian Pearl A. Poole to the right. The 1963 town report said that "once a month the State supported Bookmobile comes to Georgetown from its regional headquarters in North Reading, bringing a selection of some 1,500 books. From these books the librarian chooses at least 200 volumes of interest to local readers to supplement the library collection and thereby always having a good selection of new books for the library borrowers." (Courtesy of the Georgetown Peabody Library.)

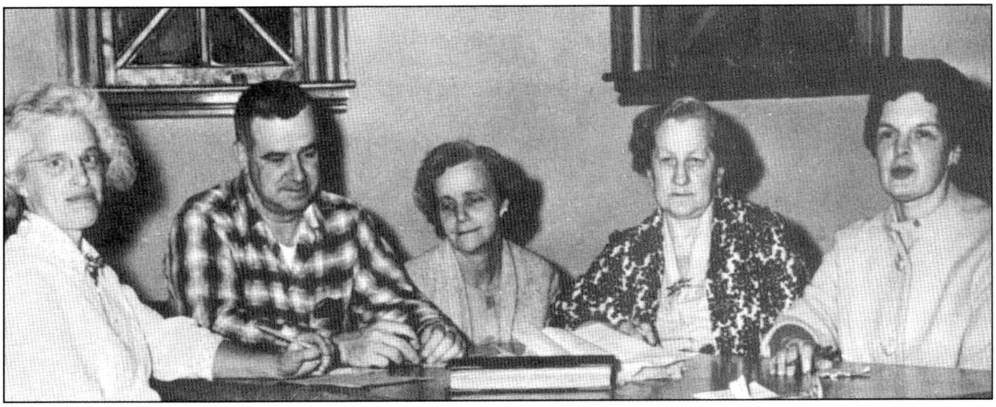

The trustees of the Georgetown Peabody Library in 1964–1965 include, from left to right, Carol Graf, secretary; Homer K. Tapin, chairman; Natalie P. Tidd; Pearl A. Poole, librarian; and Marcia Jane Field. (Courtesy of Homer K. Tapin.)

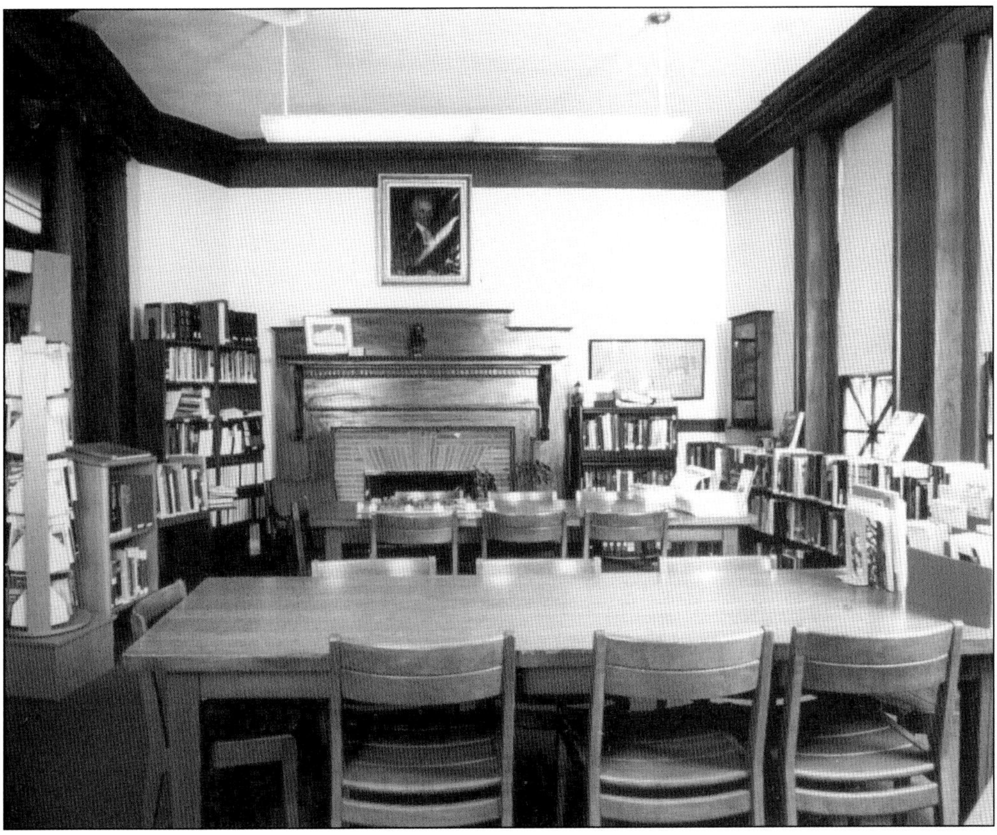

The reading room at the library is an attractive space with rich woodwork and a large fireplace and mantle at one end. The handsome portrait above the fireplace is of Rev. Isaac Braman, minister of the Old South Church from 1797 to 1858. Opposite this wall is a gilt-framed portrait by A. Bertram Schell of benefactor George Peabody, showing him with an envelope addressed to the town of Georgetown in his hand. (Courtesy of the Georgetown Peabody Library.)

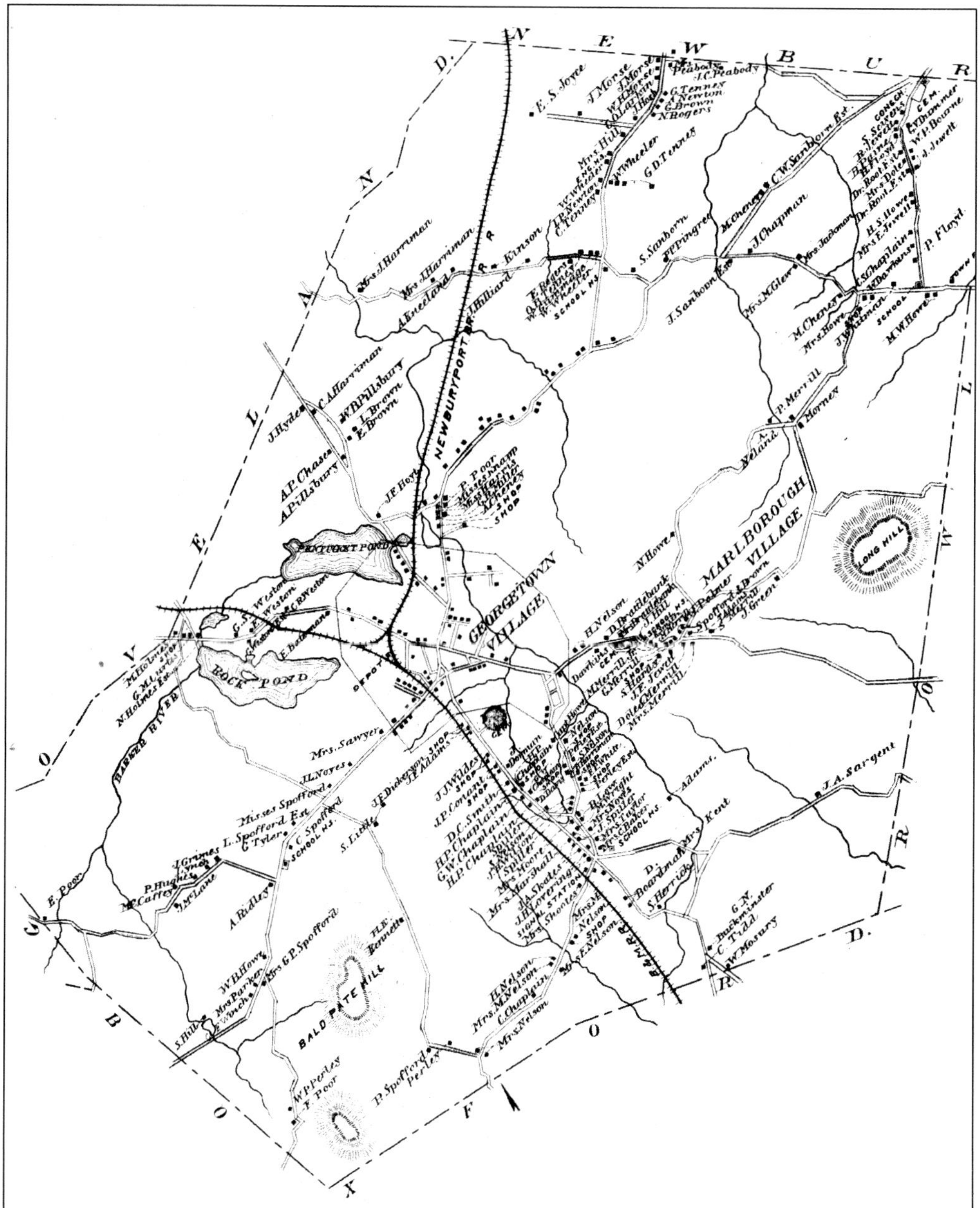

The 1884 map of Georgetown shows a far more built-up town over four decades after it had been incorporated. In the center is the route of the Boston & Maine Railroad, with a signal station in South Georgetown (Baldpate Depot) and the Georgetown Depot, at Moulton Street and Railroad Avenue. On the right is the route of the Newburyport Branch Railroad, which headed northeast through Newbury to Newburyport. Most of the houses, churches, schools, and shops are identified. The street plan would remain largely intact for the next few decades. (Courtesy of the Georgetown Peabody Library.)

Five

Modes of Transportation

The first real aspect of modern travel came to Georgetown in 1850, when the Boston & Maine Railroad opened the Georgetown & Danvers Railroad and a passenger depot at Railroad Avenue. This wood, shedlike building would serve as the depot for passengers travelling to Boston or points north and would be replaced in 1872 by an interesting Victorian depot, complete with gingerbread trim along the cornice of the hip roof. By the late 19th century, the Boston & Maine Railroad was an important means of transportation, with a depot in Georgetown Square and a signal station at South Georgetown known as Baldpate Station, where passengers destined for the Baldpate Inn would stop for the famous Tally-Ho. In the 1880s, the original railroad line was augmented with the Newburyport Branch, which ran northeast from the square.

The Haverhill, Georgetown & Danvers Railway and the Georgetown, Rowley & Ipswich Street Railway began the service of streetcars through Georgetown on June 2, 1896, with Joseph Standish as conductor and Benjamin F. Bartlett the controller of the first car. As the streetcar approached Georgetown from Groveland, nine little girls dressed in red, white, and blue sang the national anthem to the delight of the guests on the car. With more than five miles of tracks and a wood trestle (Weston's Trestle), the street railway offered local transportation in and around Georgetown. The Georgetown Carhouse, where the streetcars were held overnight, was a large building on West Main Street, adjacent to the Weston-Larkin family property. Another carbarn, with the superintendent's office, was located in Byfield.

The street railway would continue until 1919, when the line between Dummer Academy Junction and Georgetown of the Georgetown, Rowley & Ipswich Street Railway was abandoned. The Haverhill, Georgetown & Danvers line between Haverhill and Georgetown continued until 1930, when buses took over the route. Although the streetcars were no longer serving the residents of Georgetown, they remain in the public's memory as the Trestle Way Apartments. The apartments were named after Weston's Trestle, which was built in 1896 to allow the streetcars to pass over the Boston & Maine tracks.

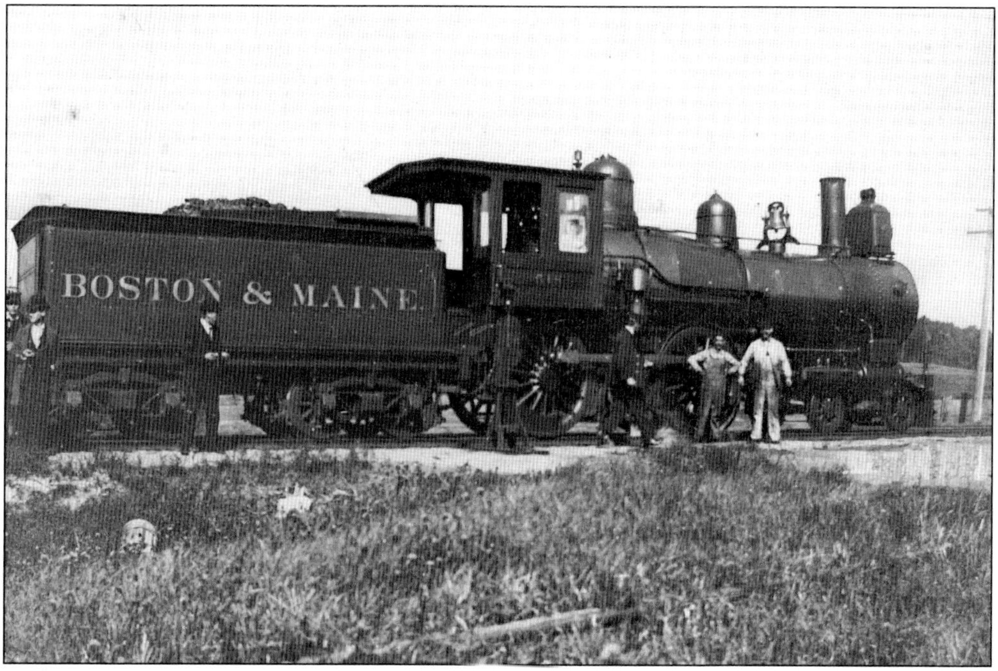

In this c. 1890 photograph, the train conductor and coal shoveler of a Boston & Maine train pose alongside the engine at the Georgetown Depot. On the front of the engine is a bell that the conductor would ring via a rope to alert people near the tracks that the train was approaching. On the left, passengers await the departure of the train. (From the collection of Albert E. Meader.)

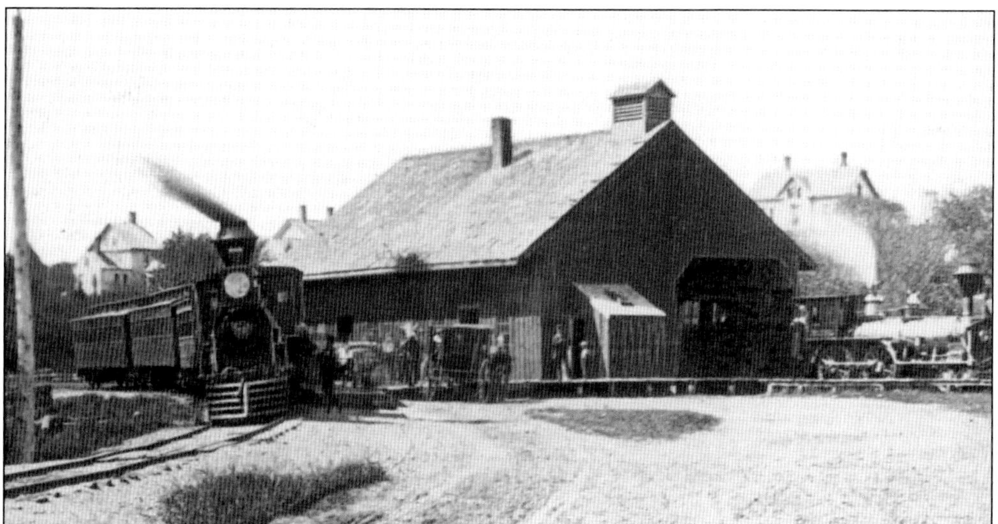

The original depot at Georgetown Square was built in 1850 at the junction of Moulton Street and Railroad Avenue as a shedlike building set between the north and south railroad tracks of the Boston & Maine Railroad. Known as the "Newburyport & Boston Merchants' Limited," the train allowed businessmen to commute to Boston for business. On the left, a train heads south toward Baldpate Depot in South Georgetown and thence to Boston. This depot was replaced with a new one in 1872. (From the collection of Albert E. Meader.)

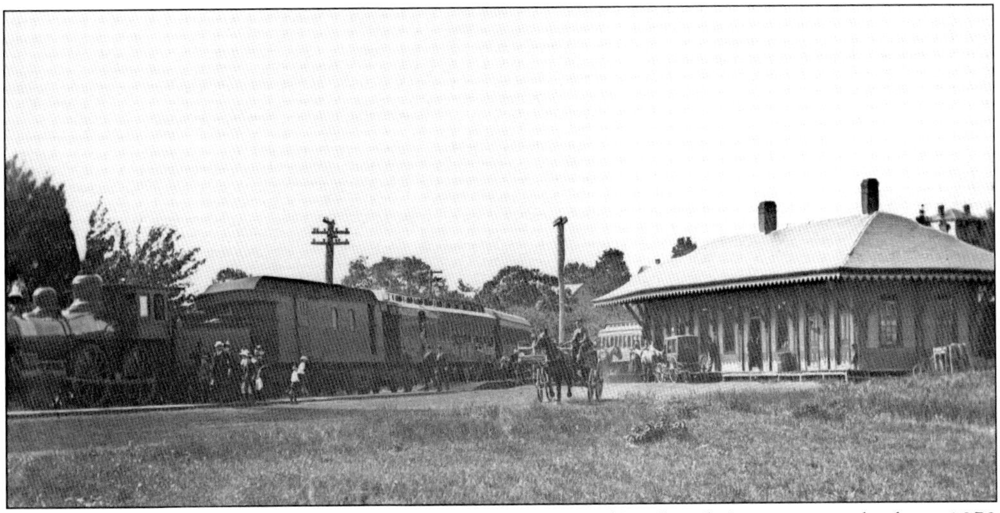

The second depot in Georgetown, at Moulton Street and Railroad Avenue, was built in 1872 as a long, wood building with an overhanging hip roof with gingerbread trim along the eaves. On the left, passengers disembark the train. A horse-drawn carriage can be seen in the center, probably to pick up luggage being unloaded from the train. The depot was demolished in 1942, as passenger use of the line was severely affected by the ascendancy of the automobile. (Courtesy of Homer K. Tapin.)

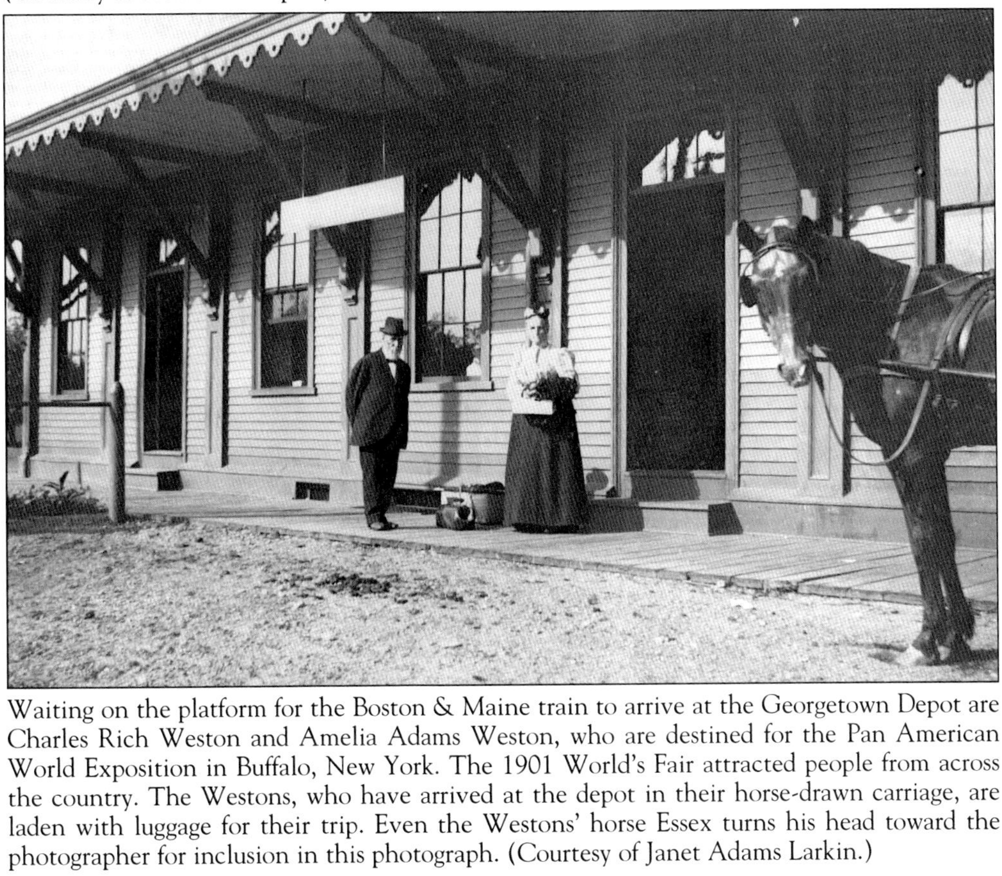

Waiting on the platform for the Boston & Maine train to arrive at the Georgetown Depot are Charles Rich Weston and Amelia Adams Weston, who are destined for the Pan American World Exposition in Buffalo, New York. The 1901 World's Fair attracted people from across the country. The Westons, who have arrived at the depot in their horse-drawn carriage, are laden with luggage for their trip. Even the Westons' horse Essex turns his head toward the photographer for inclusion in this photograph. (Courtesy of Janet Adams Larkin.)

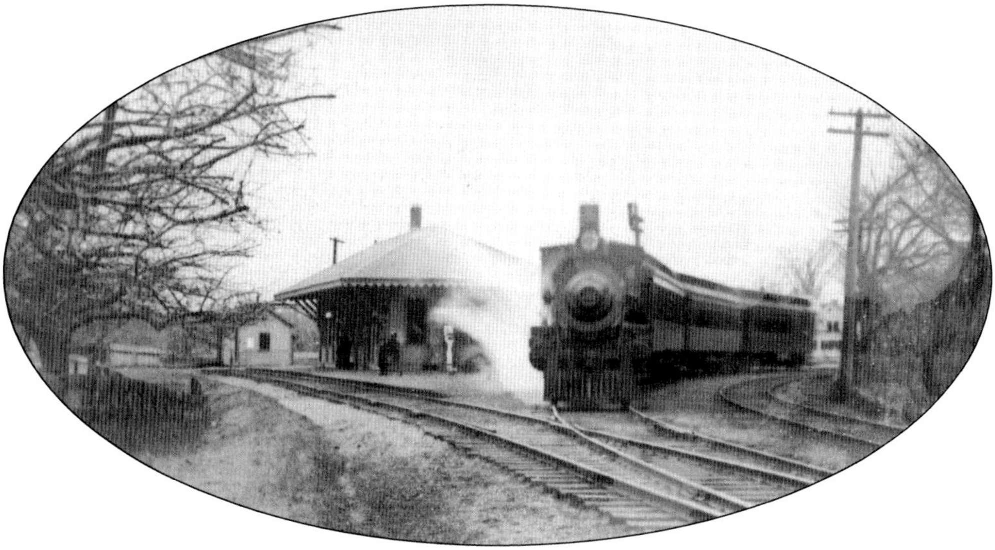

This photograph shows a smoking Boston & Maine train heading north from the Georgetown Depot c. 1875. For 26 years, William Spofford Horner was the stationmaster and freight agent as well as baggagemaster in Georgetown for the Boston & Maine Railroad. After he married Charlotte Morse in 1853, she often helped out in the ticket office during train time, thereby freeing her husband of additional worries and, at the same time, possibly strengthening their marriage. (Courtesy of the Georgetown Historical Society.)

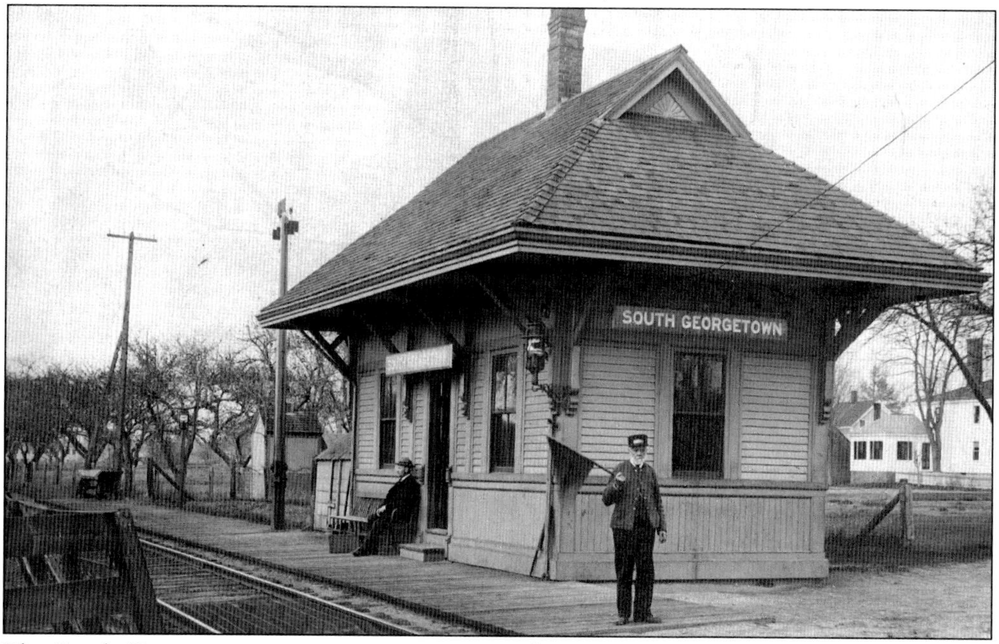

The South Georgetown waiting room was opened in 1879 as a signal station, which meant that a railroad man would have to wave a red flag to signal the Boston & Maine train to stop. In this c. 1890 photograph, stationmaster Charlie Brown waves the flag to the approaching train for the passenger waiting on the bench beside the door to the waiting room. On the right, the house with the cupola is at the junction of Central and Nelson Streets. The depot was demolished in 1942. (Courtesy of the Georgetown Peabody Library.)

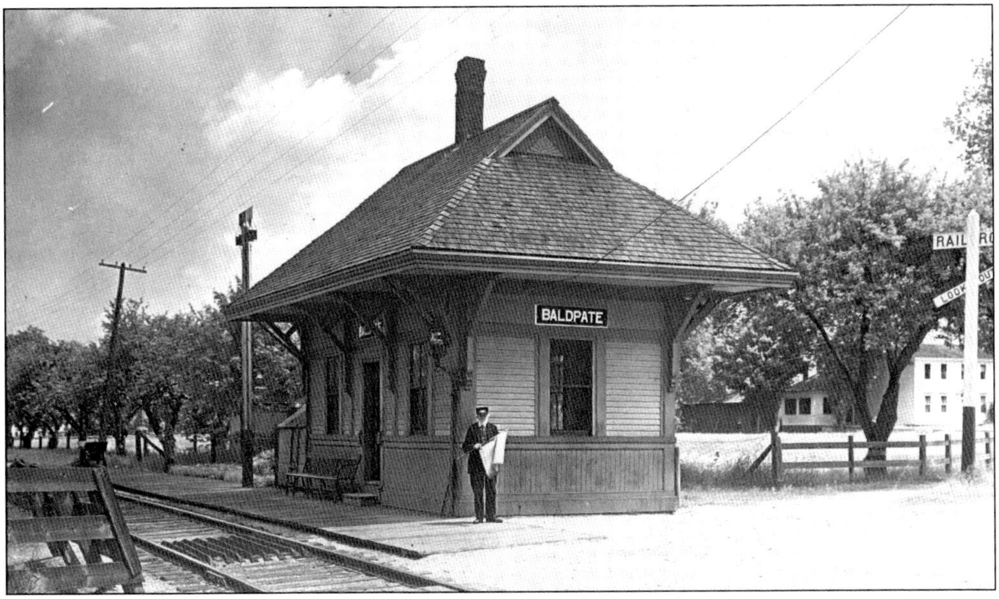

The South Georgetown depot was a remodeled shoe shop that was moved in 1879 from Georgetown Square by John H. Lovering and Samuel Shute. It was named Baldpate in honor of both Bald Pate Hill and the famous Baldpate Inn. Often, the guests arriving at the depot for a stay at the Baldpate Inn would be met by William Bray with his famous yellow-and-black Tally-Ho. Note the railroad crossing sign that warns, "Look Out for Engine," which did not always prevent accidents. (Courtesy of the Georgetown Historical Society.)

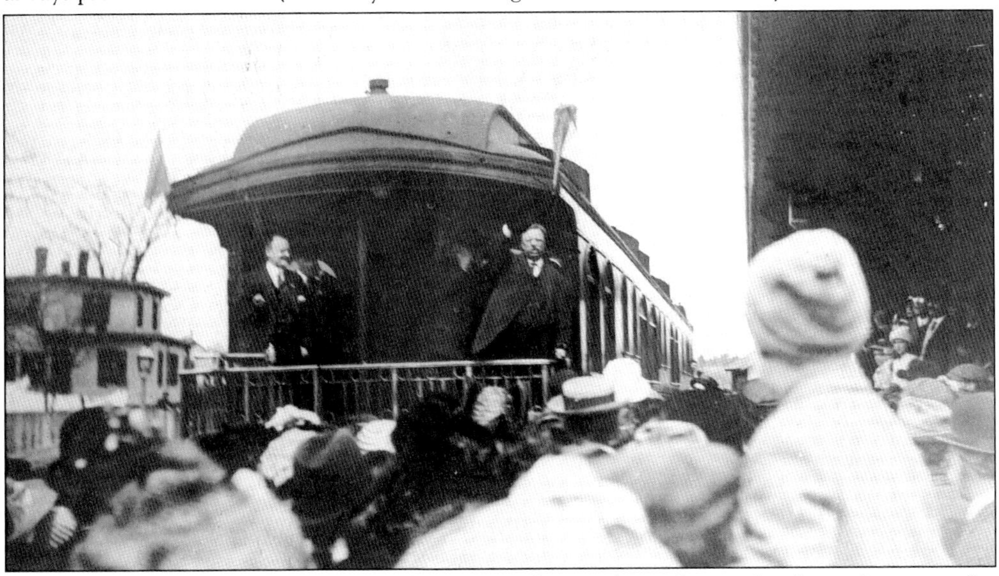

In 1912, Pres. Theodore Roosevelt (1858–1919), on the right, spoke from the rear of a flag-bedecked Boston & Maine Railroad train at the Georgetown Depot. Massachusetts senator Arthur Nason, on the left, accompanied Roosevelt during this railroad trip. Roosevelt had served as president from 1901 to 1909 and was campaigning for the presidency against Woodrow Wilson, to whom he eventually lost. In the foreground, the young boy with the knit stocking cap is Truman Welch, being held by his father, William B. Welch (1864–1925), a clerk at the Pentucket Shoe Store in Georgetown. (Courtesy of Louise A. Richardson.)

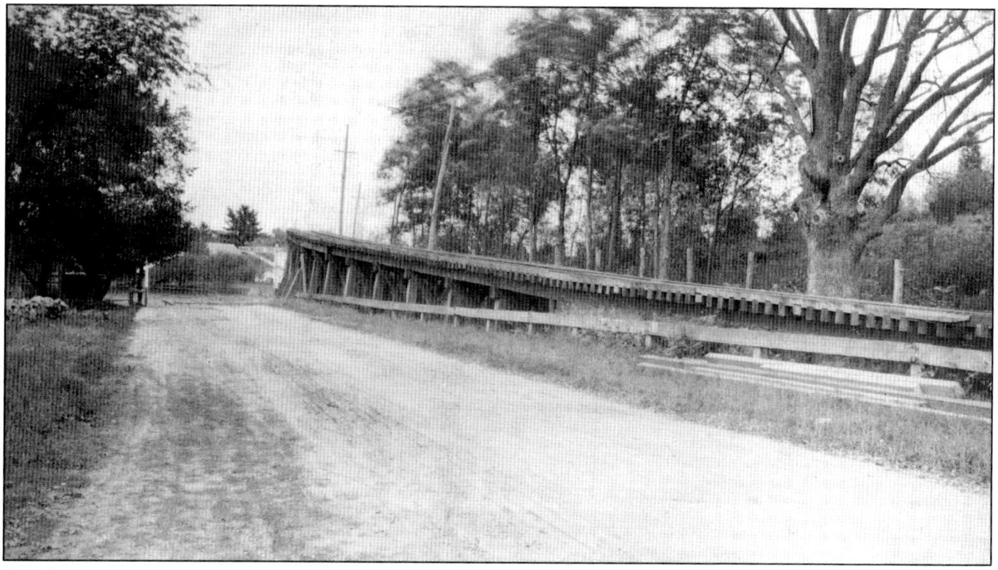

At the insistence of Georgetown officials, a wood trestle to allow streetcars to pass over the Boston & Maine Railroad right-of-way was built (within three weeks) in 1896. A Haverhill, Georgetown & Danvers Railway streetcar would be able to pass high above West Main Street after 1896. The now demolished wood trestle is today remembered by the Trestle Way housing development on West Main Street, which uses a sketch of the long-gone trestle on its letterhead. (Courtesy of the Georgetown Historical Society.)

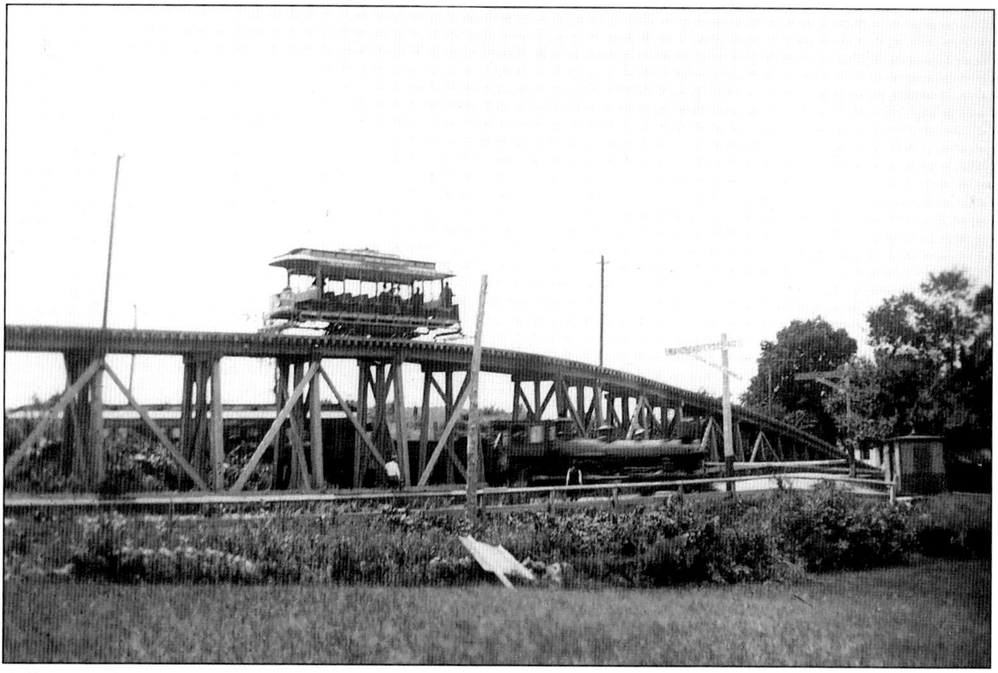

A Boston & Maine train steams under the Weston Trestle in 1913, as a Haverhill, Georgetown & Danvers streetcar passes over it. The wood trestle allowed the streetcars to pass over the tracks without either having to stop. Considered unsightly, the trestle served for less than four decades before it was dismantled. (Courtesy of Homer K. Tapin.)

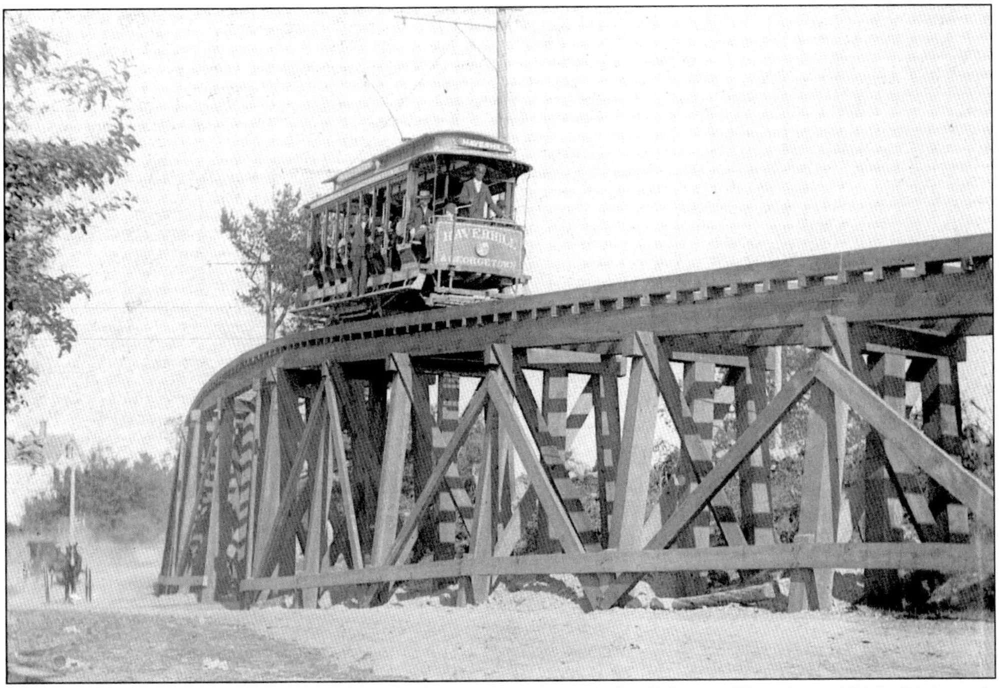

A Haverhill, Georgetown & Danvers streetcar passes over the Weston Trestle *c.* 1905. Although built as a necessary measure to allow the streetcar line to continue on to the square, the trestle soon became a unique feature of the town. (Courtesy of the Georgetown Historical Society.)

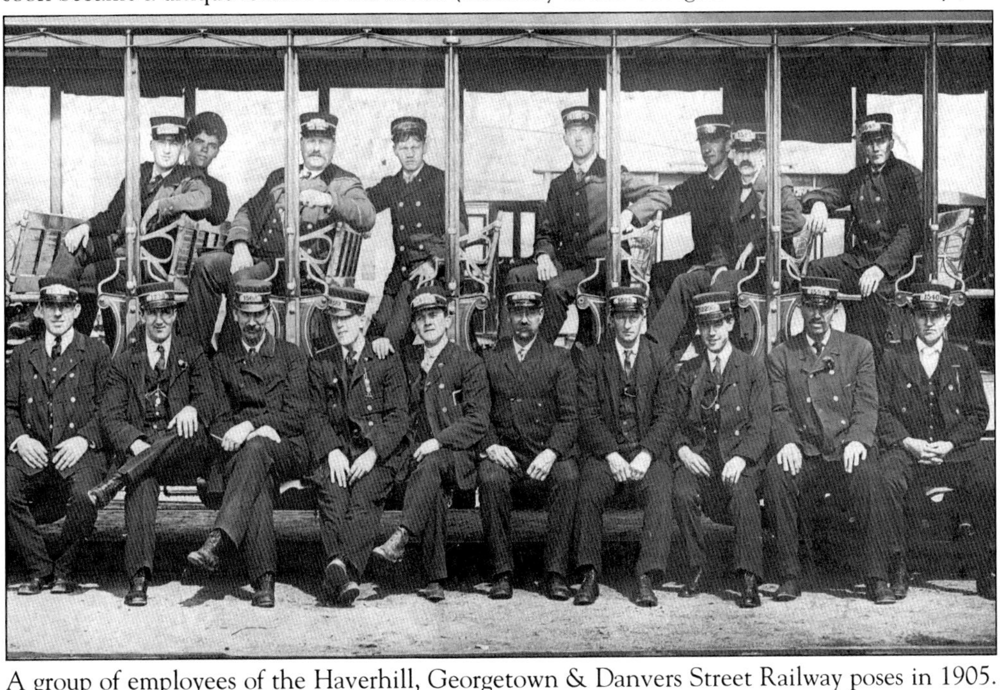

A group of employees of the Haverhill, Georgetown & Danvers Street Railway poses in 1905. On the upper left is Richard B. Larkin, a conductor on this streetcar line and a resident of West Main Street in Georgetown. This open streetcar had wood-and-iron benches and offered a pleasant ride in good weather. (Courtesy of David Morse Larkin.)

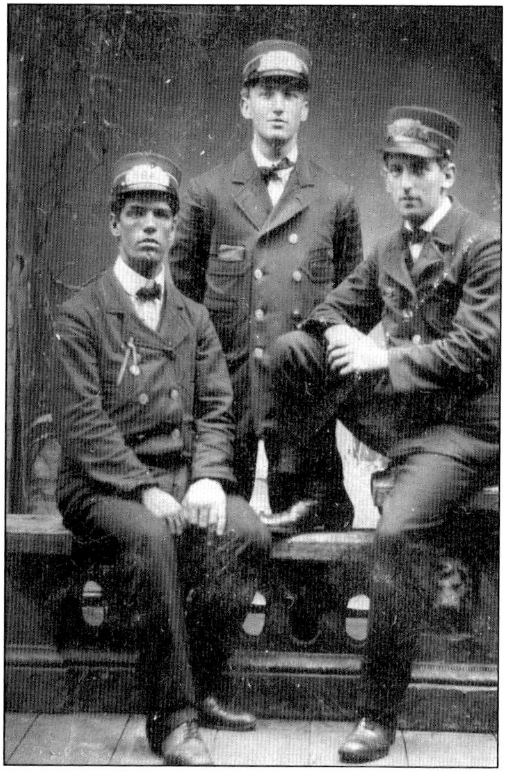

These men were employees of the Georgetown, Haverhill & Danvers Railway. From left to right are Arthur Pearson, Richard B. Larkin (who served as a streetcar conductor), and Fred Rogers. This tintype was taken *c.* 1900 by J.J. Greene at the Sun Beam, Salisbury Beach. (Courtesy of Daniel Cooper Larkin.)

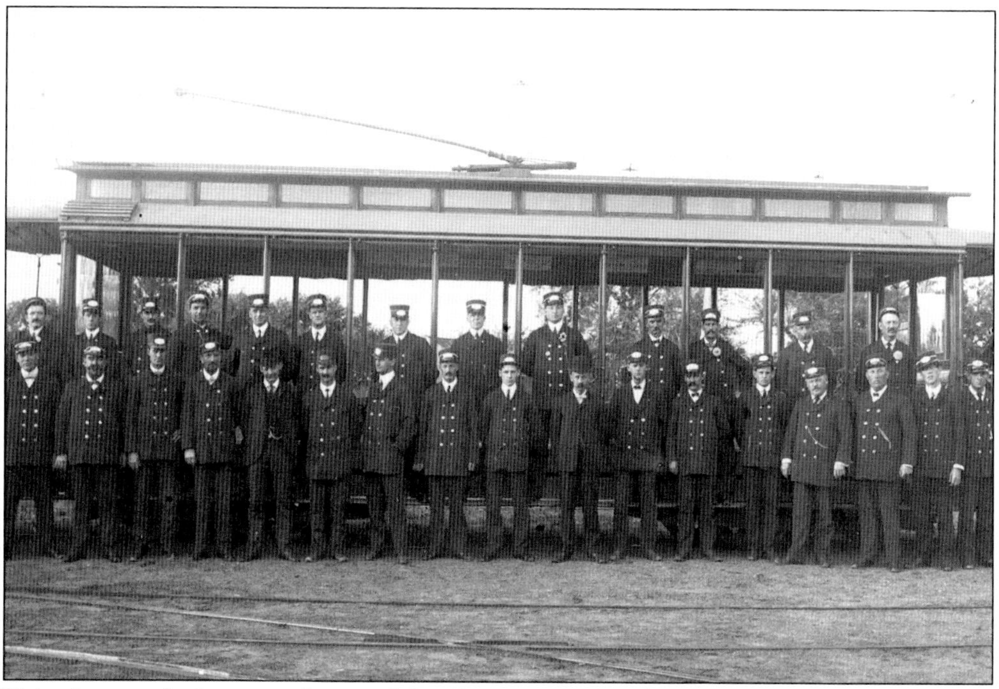

This photograph shows employees of the Georgetown, Rowley & Ipswich Street Railway in 1902. The man in the center with the bowler is superintendent George W. Pratt. His men are lined up with precision in front of an open electric streetcar. (Courtesy of Arthur Paquette.)

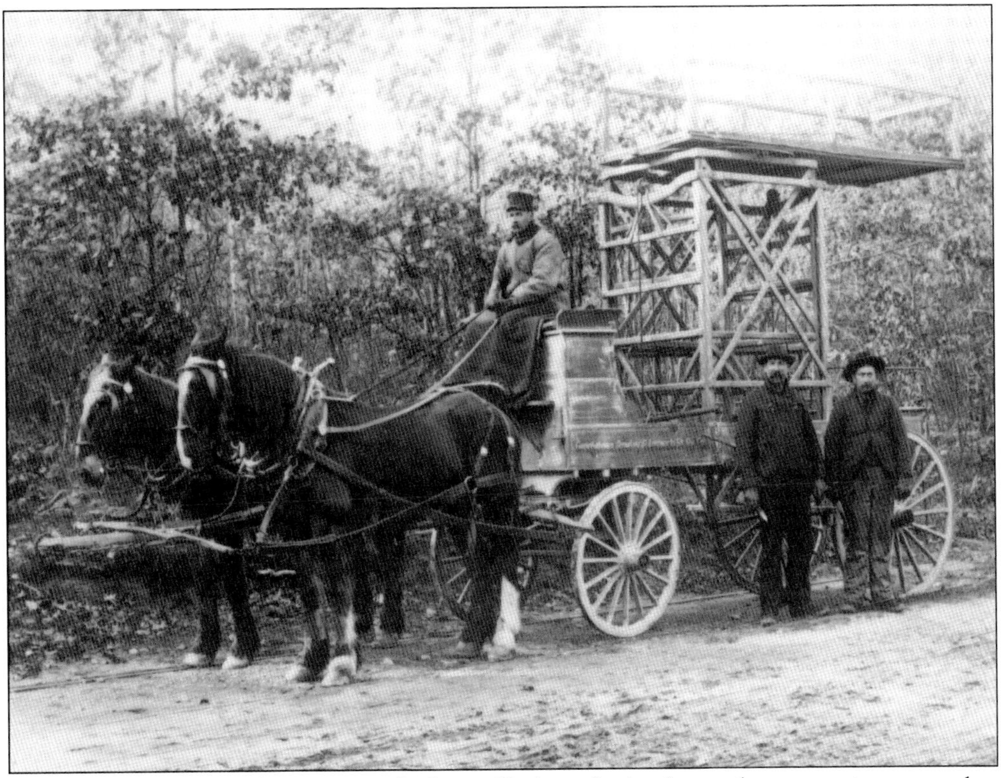

The Georgetown, Rowley & Ipswich Street Railway had a horse-drawn repair wagon that would drive along the railroad beds to ensure that no mishaps would occur due to damaged rails. The workmen pose with the repair wagon *c.* 1905. (Courtesy of Arthur Paquette.)

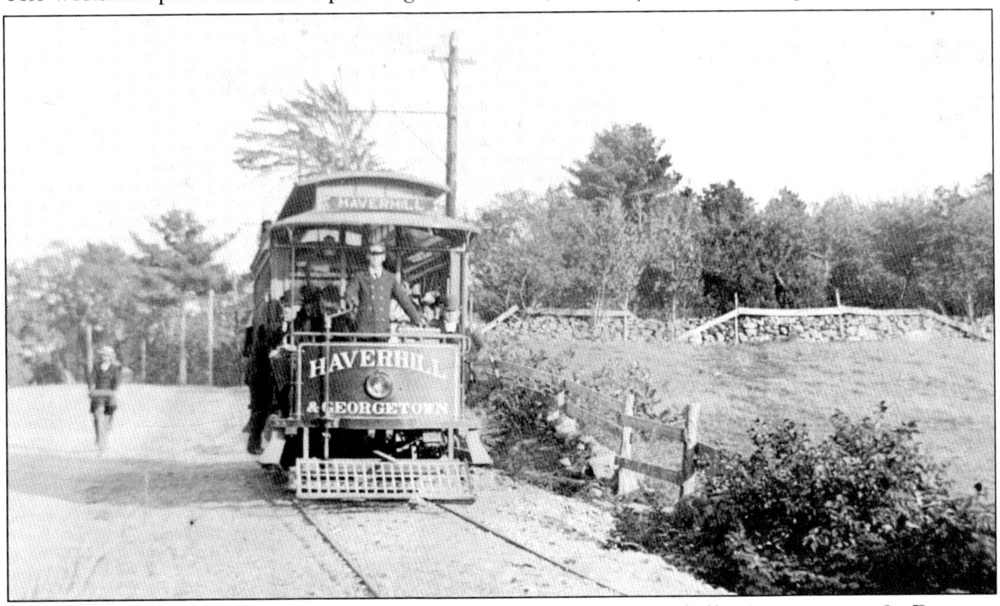

Richard B. Larkin is seen behind the controls of this Haverhill, Georgetown & Danvers Railway streetcar on West Main Street in 1905. On the left, a bicycle rider is diligently trying to keep up with the streetcar. (Courtesy of Louise A. Richardson.)

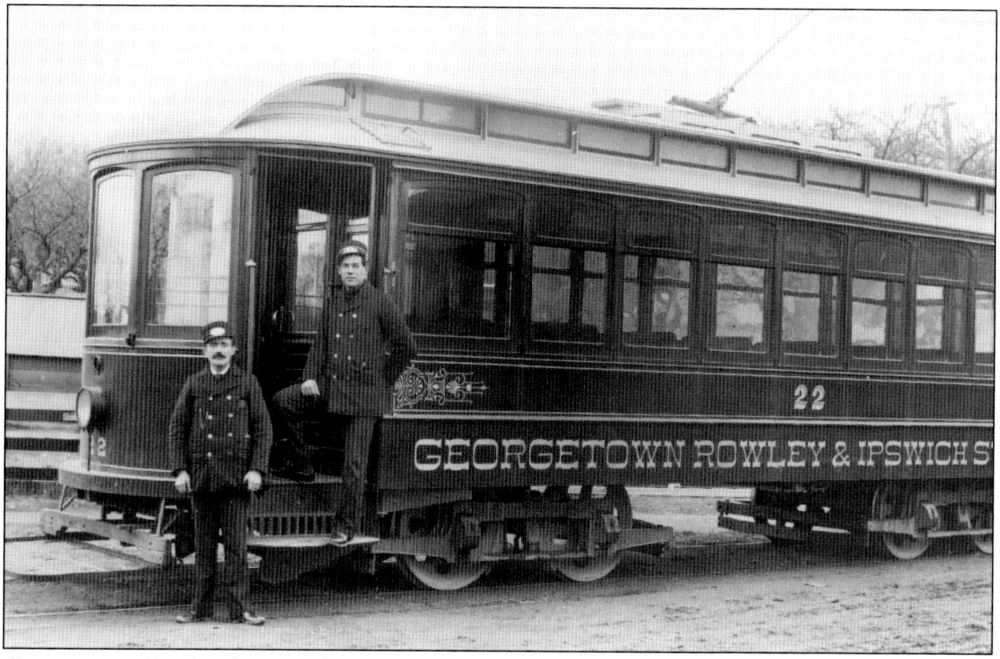

Georgetown, Rowley & Ipswich streetcar No. 22 stops in Georgetown Square in 1900. On the left is Albert Hatfield. Standing on the streetcar's platform is Martin Murphy. (Courtesy of Arthur Paquette.)

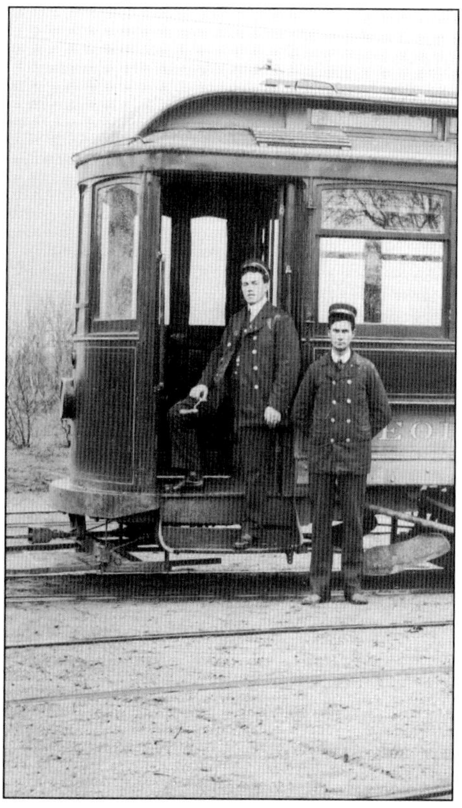

Standing in front of a Georgetown, Rowley & Ipswich electric streetcar are Nathaniel Day (left) and Percy Oliver. The streetcar is stopped near the Byfield Car Barn in 1900. The photographs loaned by Arthur Paquette were taken by Gardner Ramsell, the great-grandfather of Arthur's wife, Kathy. (Courtesy of Arthur Paquette.)

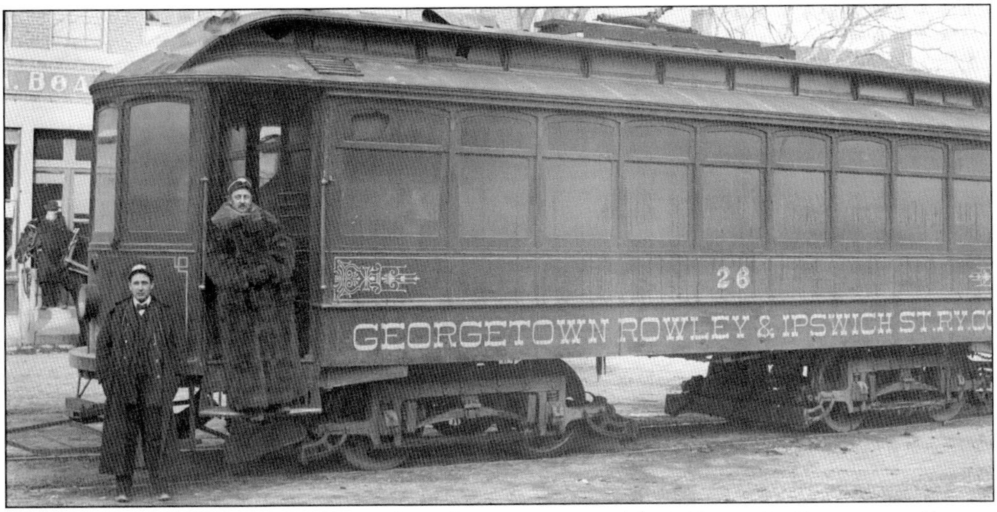

Samuel Larkin (left) and John Kemp (standing on streetcar No. 26) pose in Georgetown Square in front of the M.N. Boardman store in Little's Block in 1900. This photograph was taken the day after a fire destroyed the carhouse and most of the streetcars. Note the smoke-streaked windows of the one streetcar that escaped destruction. (Courtesy of Arthur Paquette.)

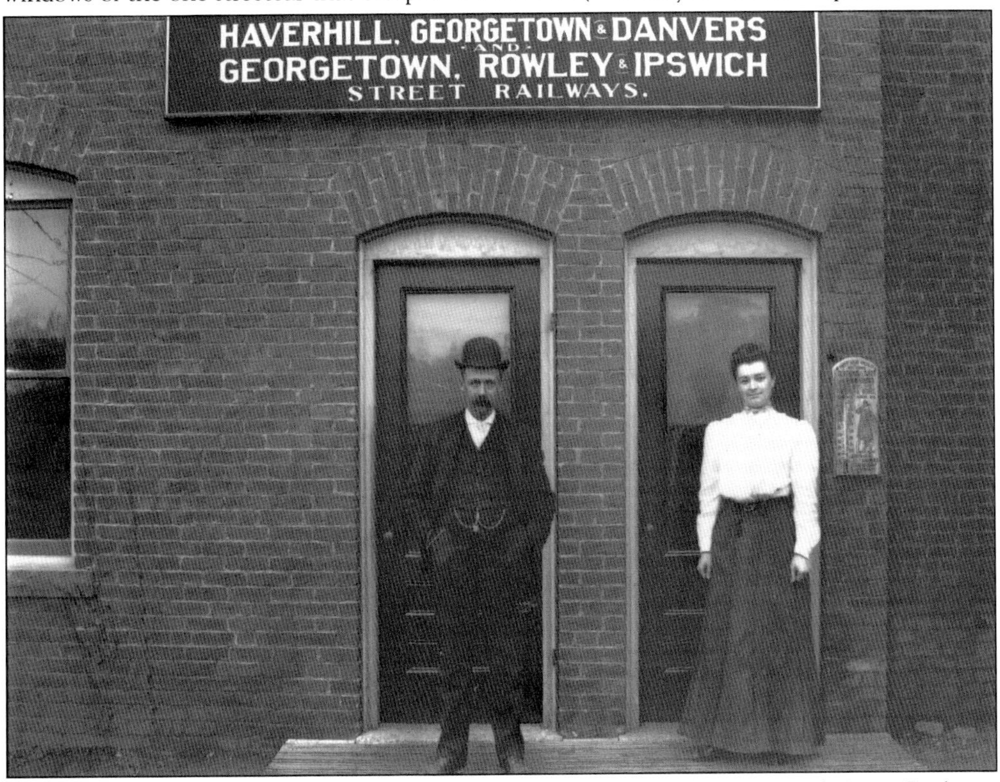

The Haverhill, Georgetown & Danvers and the Georgetown, Rowley & Ipswich Street Railways had their administrative offices in Byfield. Standing in the doorways to the joint office in 1900 are a moustached George W. Pratt (superintendent) and his wife, Janice Pratt (office secretary). The thermometer on the right is an advertisement for Nichols & Morse, owned by N.W. Nichols and Bainbridge Morse, haberdashers in Haverhill. (Courtesy of Arthur Paquette.)

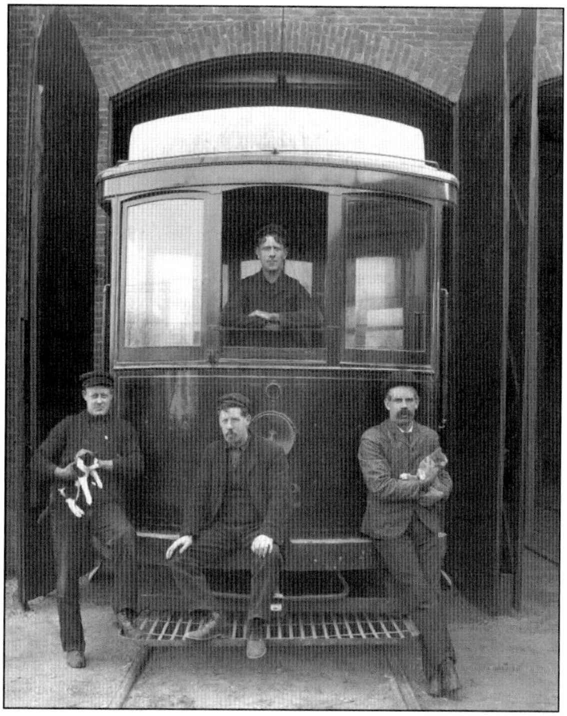

Who said real men can't be gentle? Streetcar workers pose on the front bumper of a Georgetown, Rowley & Ipswich streetcar *c.* 1900. Two of them are holding the company cats, both of which seem to be looking to the right at future prey—possibly the reason they were there in the first place. In the front, from left to right, are B. Carlton, John Kemp, and Wilson Rogers. Fred Rogers is looking out of the window of the streetcar. (Courtesy of Arthur Paquette.)

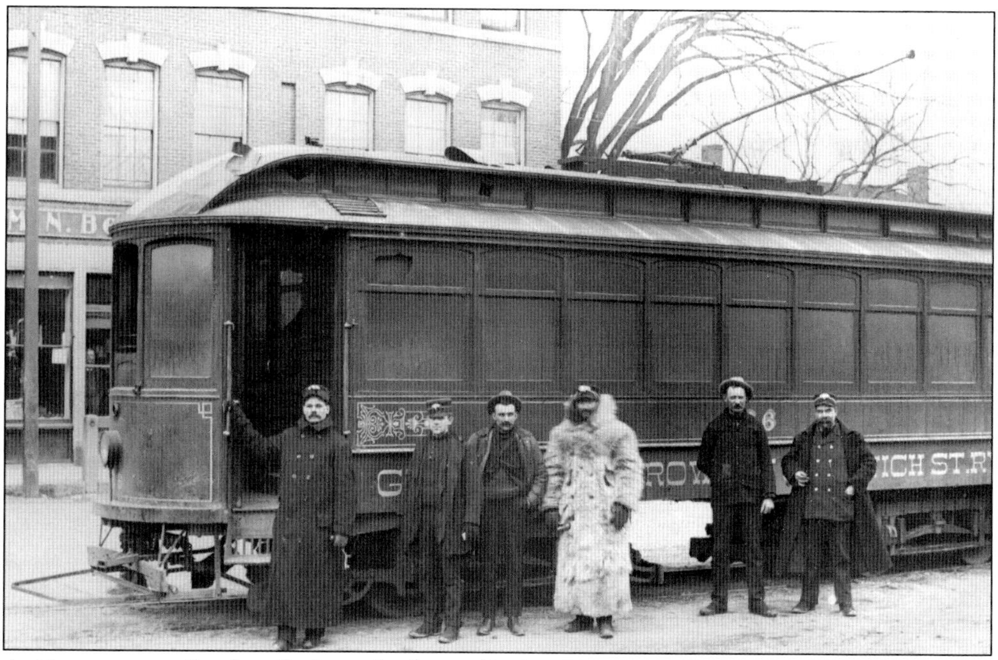

A Georgetown, Rowley & Ipswich Street Railway streetcar (No. 26) stops in front of Little's Block, with the M.N. Boardman store on the left (note the clerk in the doorway), at Georgetown Square *c.* 1900. From left to right are Arthur Thwing, John Riley, Wilson Rogers, Clarence Redmond (swathed in the fur overcoat), Arthur Butterfield (a master mechanic of the street railway line), and Fred Simonds. (Courtesy of Arthur Paquette.)

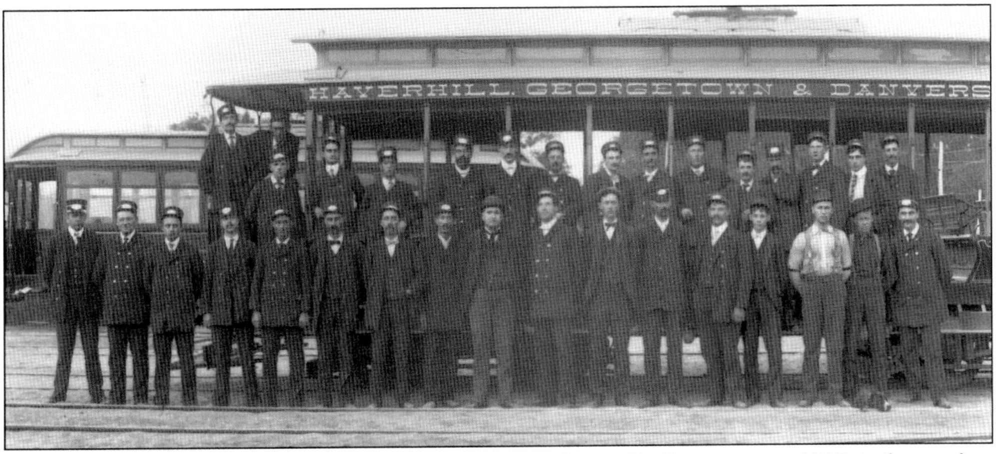

Employees of the Haverhill, Georgetown & Danvers Street Railway pose c. 1900 in front of an open streetcar. From left to right are the following: (front row) Charles Quimby, Martin Herrick, Samuel Larkin, John Morris, Dick Walsh, Ernest Christian, Arthur Irving, Harvey Rogers, Superintendent Hallowell, Martin Murphy, Henry Palmer, Fred Simonds, Charles Benjamin, Dan Johnson, William Sullivan, John Mulhern, and Stephen Lanen; (back row) Albert Hatfield, Arthur Pearson, John Riley, Percy Oliver, Nathaniel Day, Wilson Rogers, Charles Hill, John Kemp, Augustin Peatfield, Benjamin Dresser, Charles Sullivan, John Goodwin, Ned Pearson, Fred Rogers, B. Carleton, and Bert Pickett. (Courtesy of Arthur Paquette.)

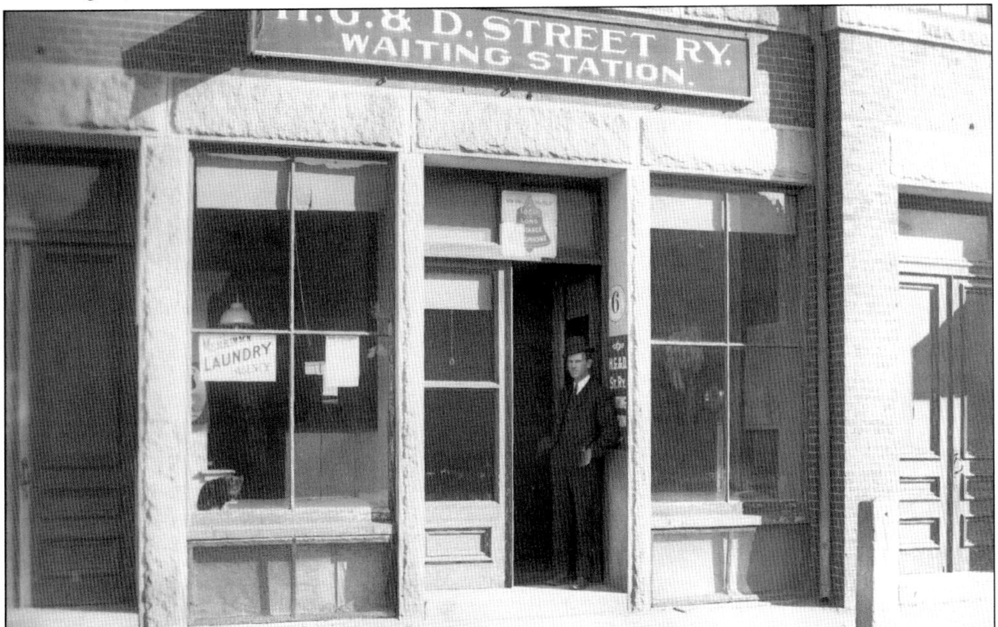

The waiting station for the Haverhill, Georgetown & Danvers Street Railway in Little's Block in Georgetown Square is pictured c. 1900, with John Riley standing in the doorway. The two signs on the left-hand window advertise the Merrimac Laundry Agency and the Rural Letter Carrier. A cat is preening to the lower left. Above the entrance is a sign indicating that there is a public telephone of the New England Telephone & Telegraph Company at this office. In the right window are hanging hands of banana, ripening in the sun. Note the granite horse-hitching post on the right, a poignant reminder of the recent past. (Courtesy of Arthur Paquette.)

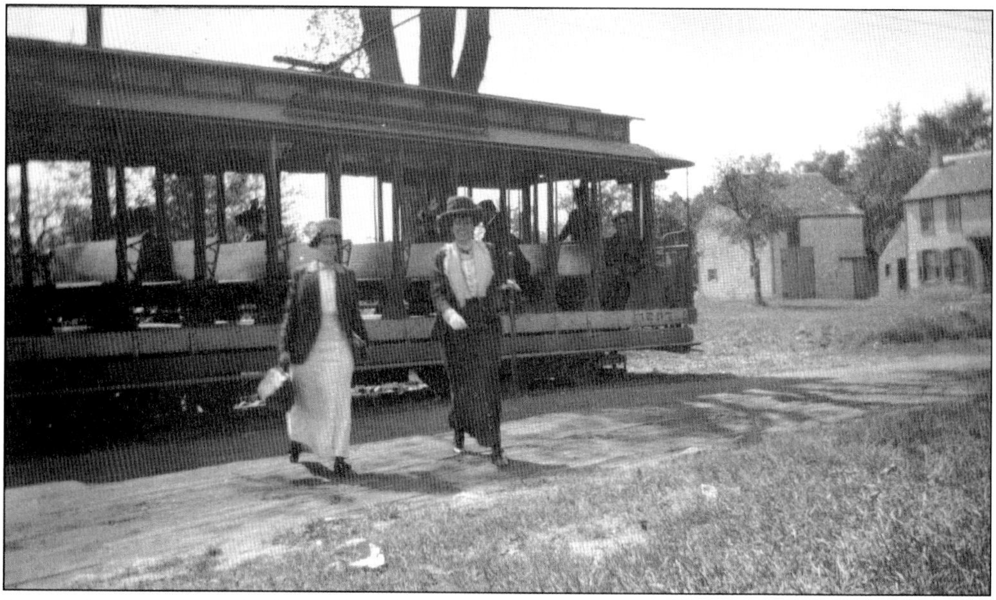

Greta Morse Larkin and a friend disembark from an open streetcar on West Main Street in 1913. On the right is 176 West Main Street, which had the Haverhill, Georgetown & Danvers Street Railway going directly past the house. (From the collection of Bainbridge Morse Larkin Jr.)

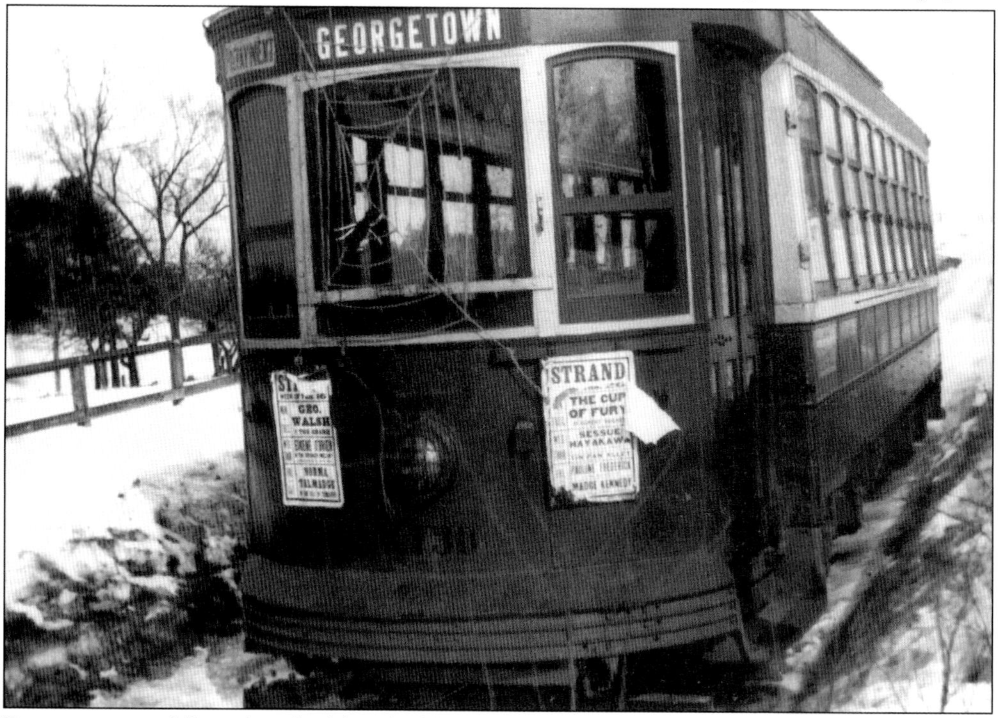

Enormous snowfalls and ice buildup disabled this streetcar for more than four weeks in the late winter of 1920 in front of 170 West Main Street. As a joke, a spiderweb was woven by local prankster Bill Marble and draped over the front window of the streetcar. Thankfully, as spring approached, the streetcar was dislodged and promptly returned to service. (Courtesy of Louise A. Richardson.)

Six

THE 1909 OLD HOME WEEK

Old Home Week was celebrated in Georgetown from July 25 to 28, 1909. The festivities were designed to bring back former residents and the descendants of early settlers to join in the townwide celebrations. In *Souvenir of Old Home Week*, a small booklet published expressly for the event, many important aspects of local history were written for those visiting who might not be as well informed as others.

The booklet said, "We sincerely believe that Georgetown is one of the most attractive of the New England towns; and, while we cannot hope to ever become a great manufacturing center, we do believe that Georgetown offers exceptional advantages for those who seek a quiet village for residences where they may be free from the annoyances of city life." The words *picturesque*, *healthy*, and *well situated* were all used to describe the town, but it was probably more the rapid decrease in population from 2,231 residents in 1880 to 1,958 residents in 1909 that the Old Home Week festivities were aimed at stemming. Planners sponsored walks in town to view the historic houses, the large number of churches, and the industries that offered employment to those who sought it.

The souvenir guide also stated, "A great deal can be said of the healthfulness of our town, and a hundred years ago [1809] Georgetown was spoken of as a place where no one died except from old age." This was quite a claim, but it was further exaggerated by Dr. George Moody, who boasted that the reason for the healthy atmosphere was sulfur. He said that sulphur had a "power of resistance to disease, as the fog and vapor arising from the low land during the damp season contain no malarial poison . . . but have in them a healthful element. Therefore, we would say to those that would like to crown their days with a hundred years, to take up their staff and travel on to Georgetown, and hasten the day of that flourishing metropolis."

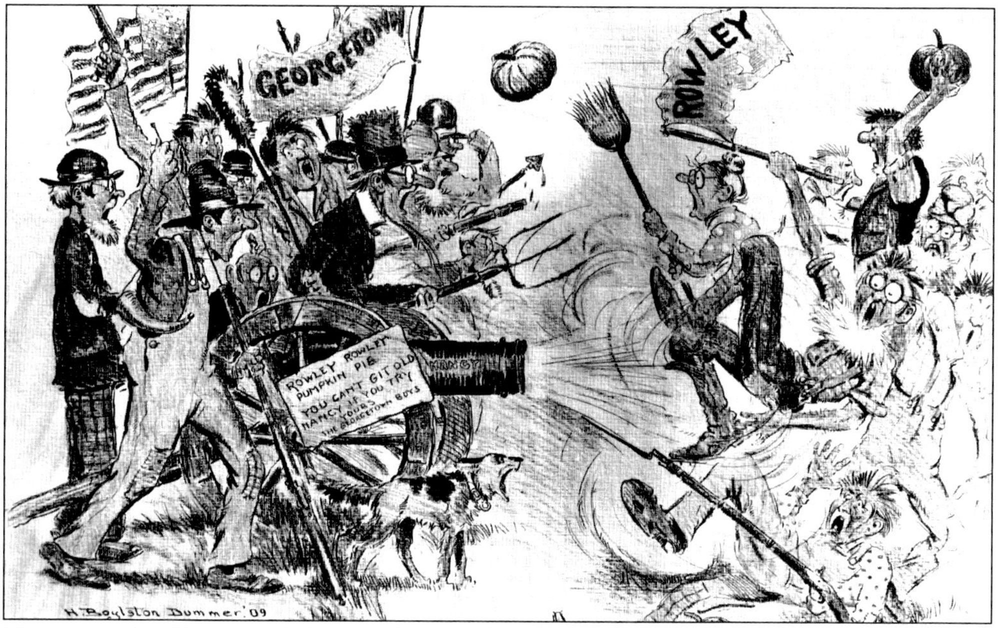

This postcard publicizing Old Home Week in Georgetown shows a contingent of Georgetonians holding high the American flag while igniting "Old Nancy" as they vanquish their pumpkin-throwing and cornbroom-armed rivals from Rowley. Both towns claimed Old Nancy as their own. By firing a cannonball on July 27, 1909, it allowed the cannon to speak, albeit deafeningly, once again. A placard boasted, "Rowley, Rowley Pumpkin Pie, you can't git Old Nancy if you try!" (Courtesy of the Georgetown Historical Society.)

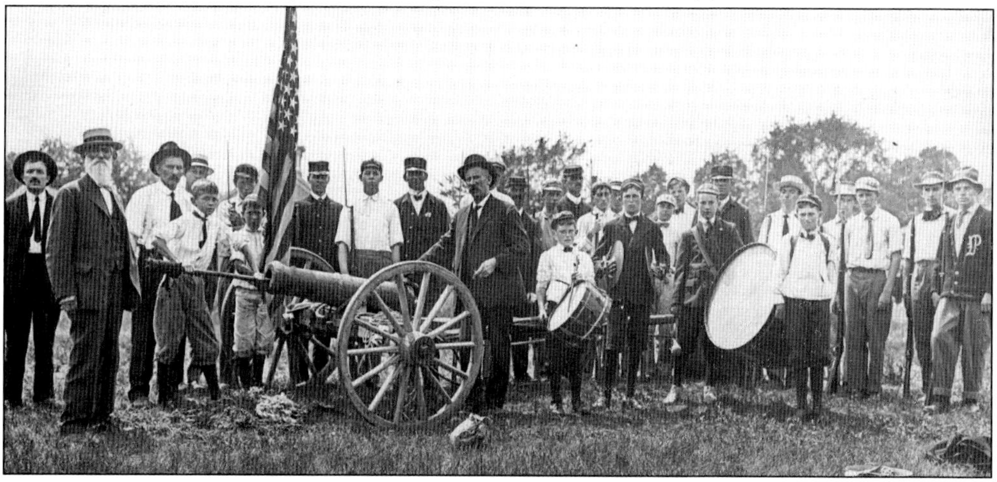

These Georgetonians gather to fire Old Nancy on July 27, 1909, as part of the festivities. It seemed as if the appearance of Old Nancy brought out every man in town, from elderly bearded gentlemen to young boys. Sixteen young men formed a guard to protect the cannon, which had not seen the light of day since 1888, when it had been overhauled under the direction of F.M. Edgell. The machine work was done by Stephen Osgood and Daniel Hale, and the blacksmithing was done by D.W.M. Morrill. To the beat of drums, and in the shadow of the American flag, the four-pounder was fired in 1909 for the first time in more than 20 years and created a loud discharge that brought an even greater cheer. (Courtesy of the Georgetown Historical Society.)

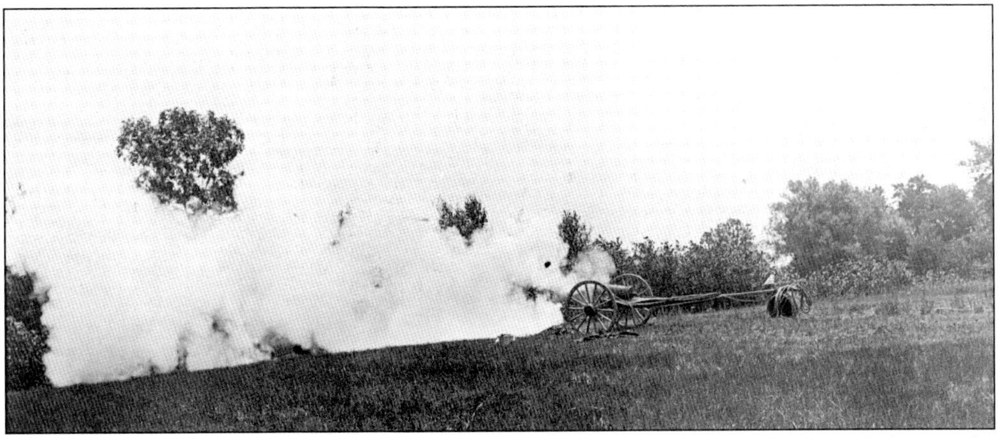

Old Nancy (named for the British brig *Nancy*, on which it had been placed during the Revolutionary War and captured off Cape Ann in 1775) fires a cannonball with profuse amounts of smoke accompanying the ear-deafening discharge. In 1888, when Old Nancy was fired to commemorate the 50th anniversary of the incorporation of Georgetown, the firing of the cannon broke many a window in town by its loud discharge. For many years, the cannon was buried "under a pile of carpets" in the cellar of Stephen Osgood, where it remained protected from Rowleyites until it resurfaced in 1909. (Courtesy of the Georgetown Historical Society.)

As time rolls on in after years, parents will lisp in children's ears
Of the time when Rowley was in tears for a cannon.

—Anonymous

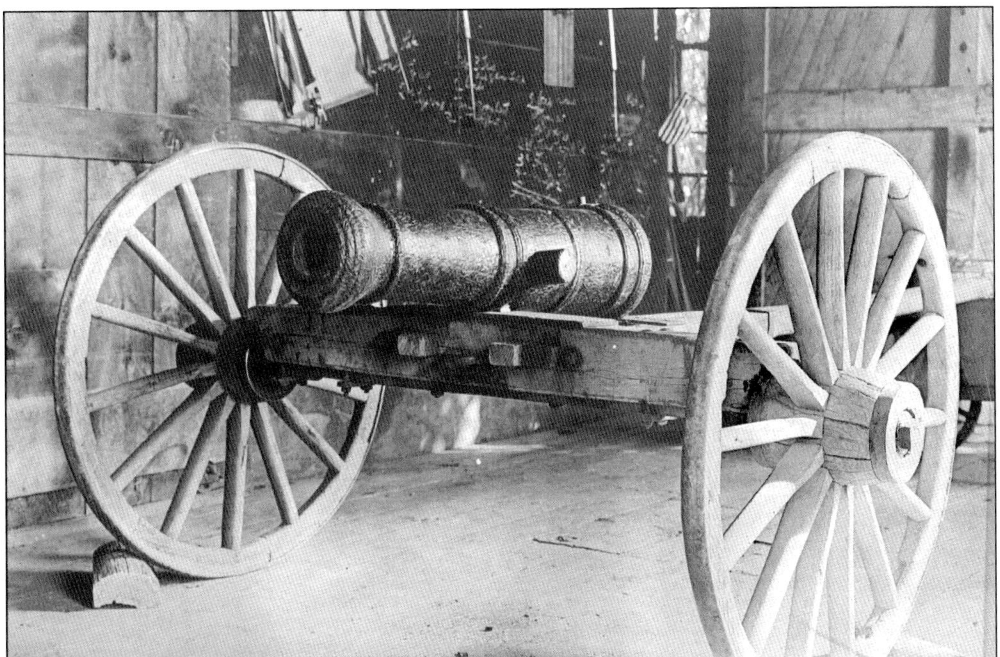

This close-up of Old Nancy clearly proves that it did not show any trace of its great age. A four-pound cannon from the Revolutionary War, it was stolen from Rowley in the early 19th century and protected by proud Georgetonians. Today, the noble cannon greets visitors to the Georgetown Memorial Town Hall. (Courtesy of the Georgetown Historical Society.)

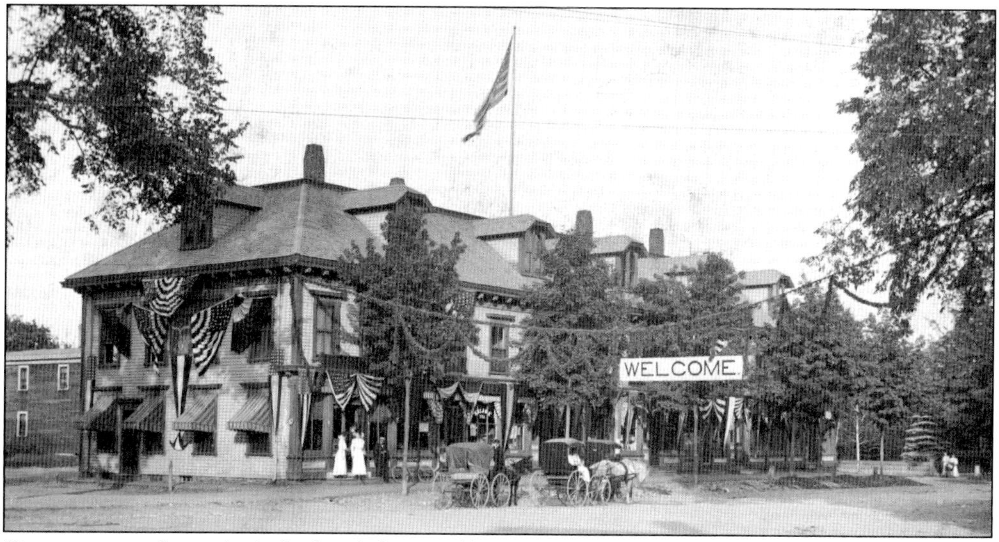

Georgetown is shown bedecked with flags and bunting for Old Home Week, which was celebrated from July 25 to 28, 1909. A large Welcome banner is suspended from a smilax-decorated wire stretched across East Main Street. The Union Block is decorated with bunting, with an American flag flying high over the building. (Courtesy of the Georgetown Historical Society.)

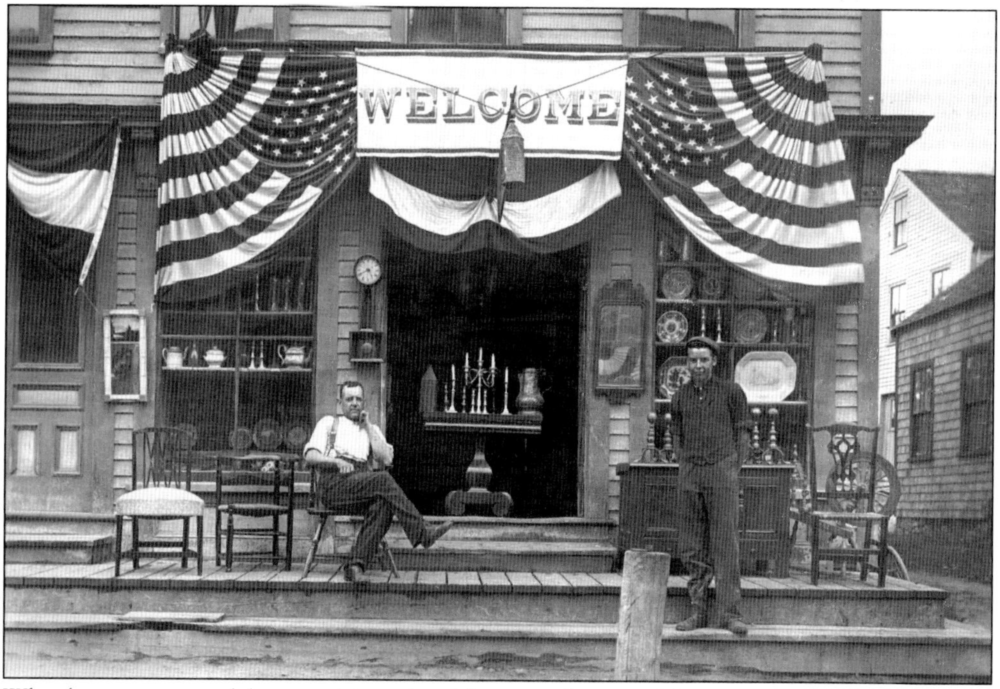

What better way to celebrate a visit to the old ancestral town of Georgetown than to stop at the bunting-decorated Spaulding's Antique Shop in the Phoenix Block and purchase an antique? Here, proprietor Wilbur Spaulding sits comfortably while Thomas Hurd stands in front of the long-gone antique shops of old. A Federal chair, an early corner chair, and a Chippendale chair can be seen on the front porch. A banjo clock hangs to the left of the doorway, and a Chippendale mirror is on the right. One can only wish for antique shops from the days of old. (From the collection of Albert E. Meader.)

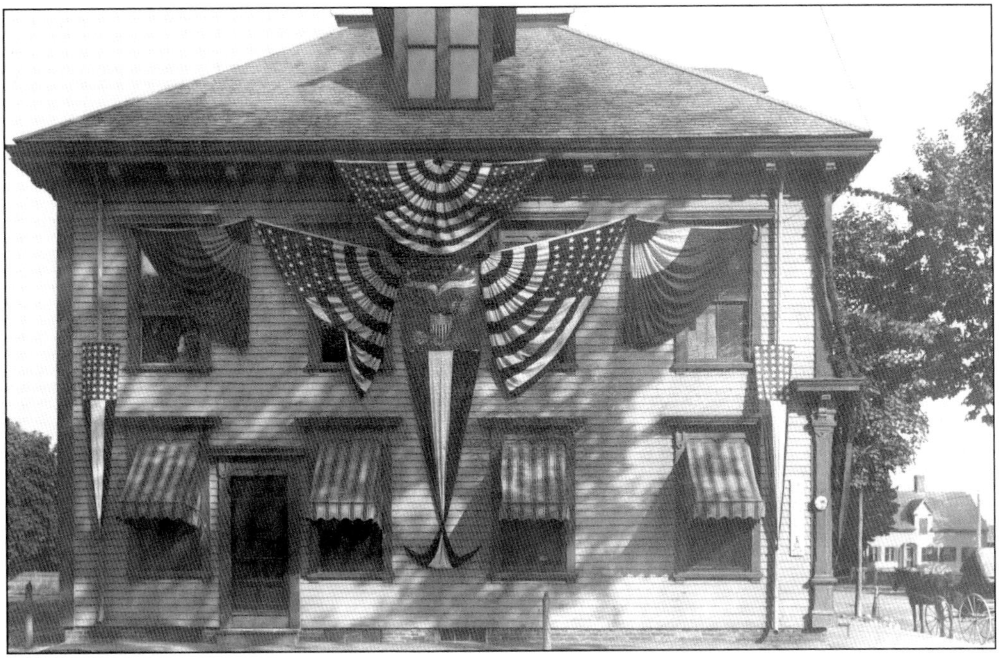

The artistically draped bunting seen here was on the Georgetown Square end of the Union Block. The Union Block, which today remains virtually intact, is an important part of the streetscape of Georgetown Square. (Courtesy of the Georgetown Historical Society.)

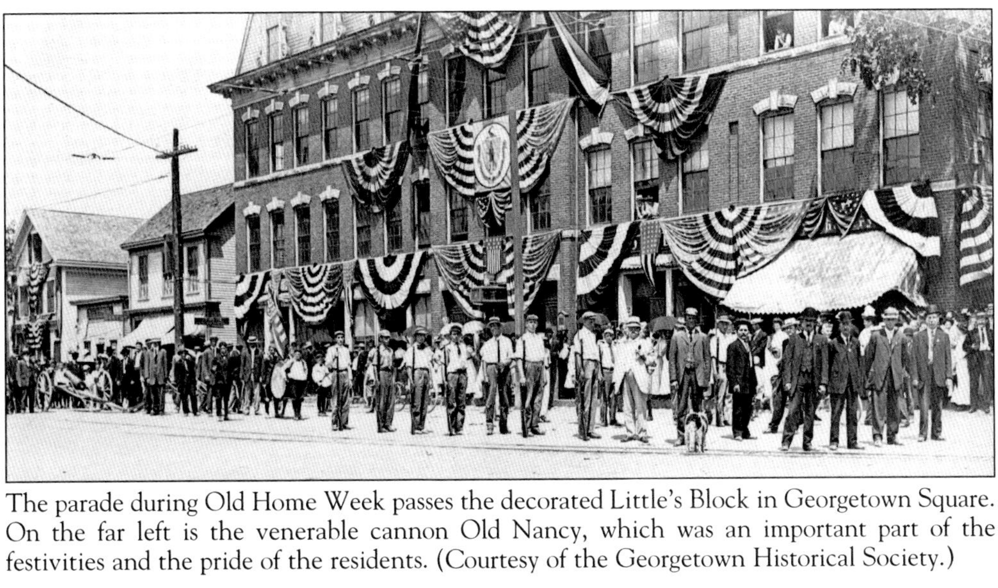

The parade during Old Home Week passes the decorated Little's Block in Georgetown Square. On the far left is the venerable cannon Old Nancy, which was an important part of the festivities and the pride of the residents. (Courtesy of the Georgetown Historical Society.)

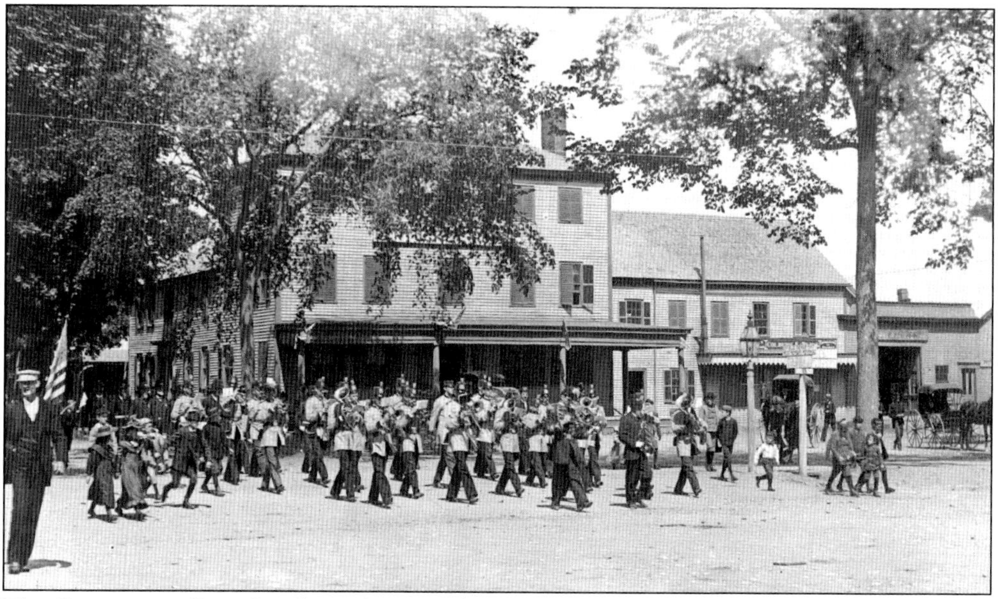

The Georgetown Brass Band parades past the Pentucket House in Georgetown Square. Note all the youngsters following the band—something like a 20th-century version of the pied piper. (Courtesy of the Georgetown Historical Society.)

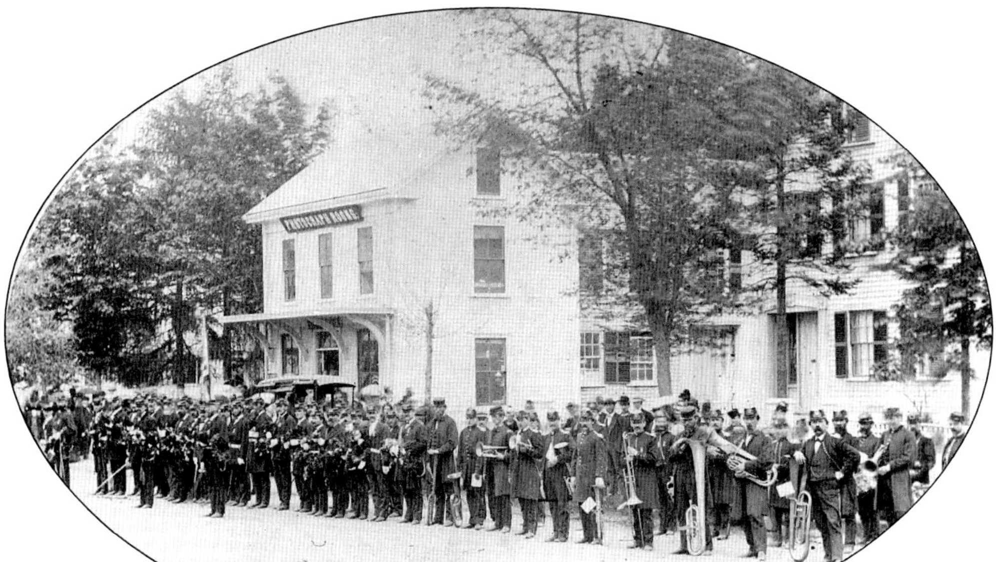

The Georgetown Brass Band and members of the Grand Army of the Republic (GAR) pose in front of the photography studio of S.C. Reed at 14 Central Street. The Georgetown Brass Band participated in the Old Home Week festivities in 1909 (leading the parade through Georgetown) and in many other town festivities. (From the collection of Albert E. Meader.)

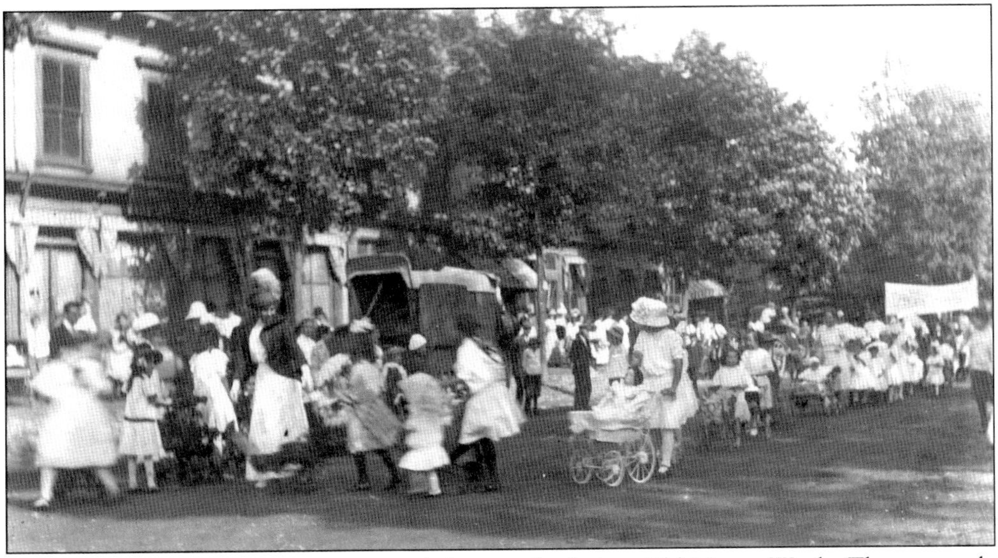

A doll carriage contingent was part of the parade during Old Home Week. These smartly dressed girls with their mothers march down East Main Street as they pass the Union Block, some with their doll carriages. (Courtesy of the Georgetown Historical Society.)

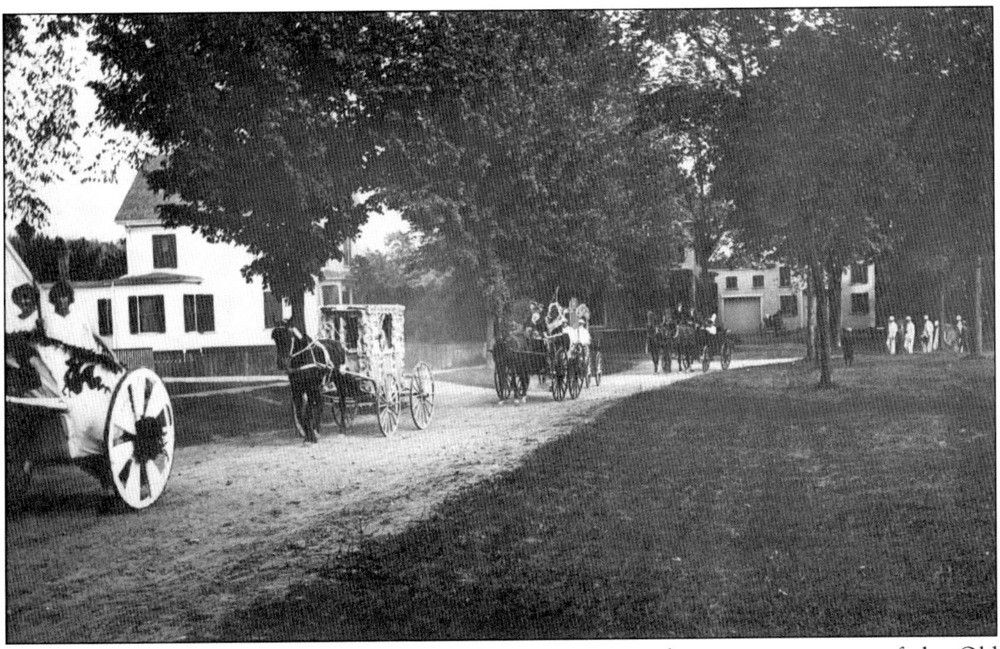

Decorated with crepe paper and ribbons, these carriages and wagons were part of the Old Home Week parade. They are traveling along Pleasant Street, with Lincoln Park to the right. (Courtesy of Homer K. Tapin.)

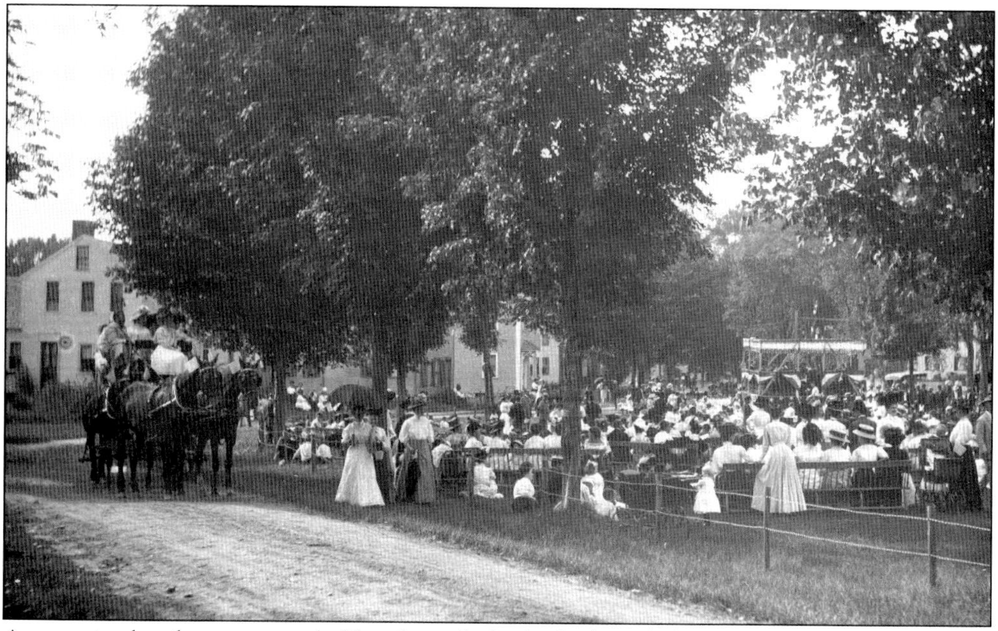

An evening band concert was held on Lincoln Park, the lawn behind the Georgetown Peabody Library. The Baldpate Inn's Tally-Ho can be seen on the left, arriving with passengers who are destined for the concert. (Courtesy of the Georgetown Historical Society.)

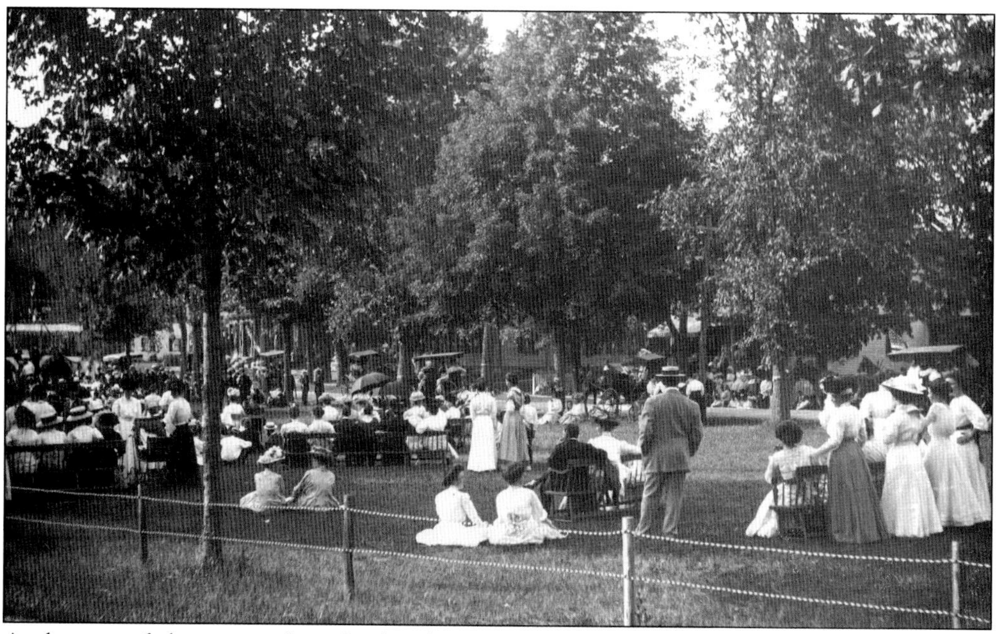

A close-up of those attending the band concert shows well-dressed Georgetonians settling down for an enjoyable summer band concert at the end of the Old Home Week festivities. (Courtesy of the Georgetown Historical Society.)

Seven

Business and Industry

Georgetown's greatest industry has thus far been the shoe industry, with dozens of shops and ten-footers throughout the town. Hundreds of thousands of pairs of shoes and heels have been produced. By 1840, some 30 people in the southern part of town worked in the shoe industry. After Paul Pillsbury invented the first shoe pegs used in the shoe industry and Stephen Little made the first pegged shoes, the cordwaining business took on new meaning and importance, as shoes were used as barter for West Indies goods. In addition to the currying and tanning of leather necessary for boots and shoes, it was also used in the manufacture of saddlebags, harnesses, and horse collars. The need to ship the manufactured shoes would lead to the opening of a shoebox shop where the boxes were made from wood.

Georgetown was primarily an agrarian community until the early 20th century. Along with gristmills and cooper shops, some small businesses produced milled wood, snuff, molasses, and saltpeter, but these small-scale operations had little impact on the economy. With the use of steam power, however, such mills as the Spofford Saw Mill, the Weston Saw Mill, and the Weston Cider Mill all took on greater meaning, as the production was increased tremendously. In fact, local lumber was used not only to build houses in the area but also to repair the USS *Constitution* and for shipping to the shipyards of Essex and Newburyport. The early invention the sewing machine used in the clothing business and the ingenious invention by David Haskell of an attachment to the sewing machine ensured that the ready-made clothing business continued successfully.

The cutting of ice on Pentucket and Rock Ponds began as early as 1853 and continued for a century, providing blocks of ice for iceboxes, the predecessor to the electric refrigerator. With woolen mills and Atwood's Bitters (a "cure-all" for those with perpetually poor health), these businesses and industries spread Georgetown's name throughout the country.

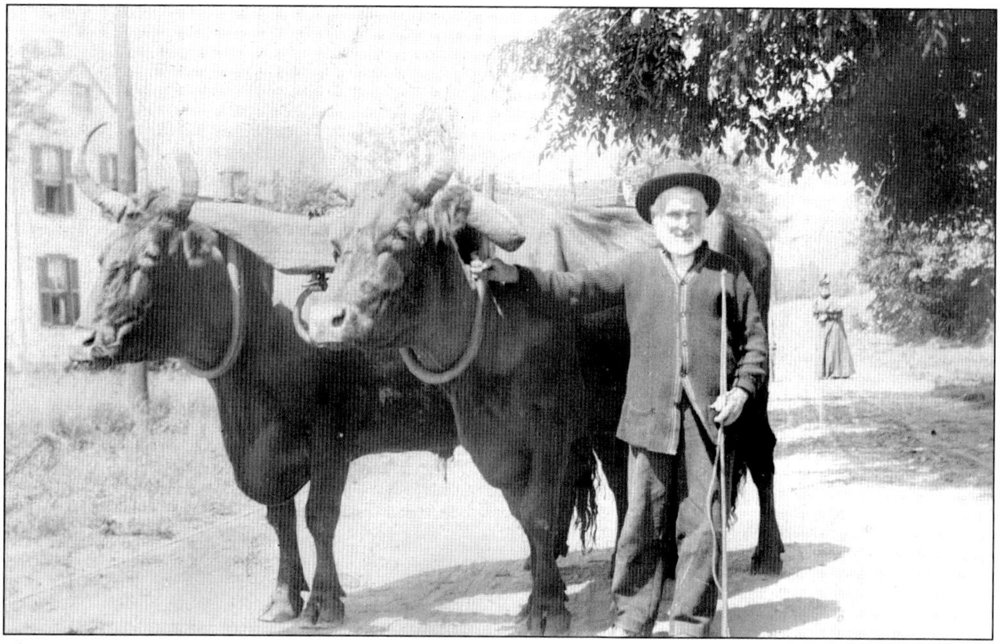

Flint Weston (1807–1898) is shown in 1896 at the age of 89, still an active farmer, with two of his yoked oxen near his house and farm on West Main Street. In the 20th century, the Weston Farm was subdivided. The roads laid out through the former farm, east of Pentucket Pond, included Pine Grove, Spofford, and Weston Avenues; Bartlett Drive; Dodge Street; and Flint, Robert, and Chaplin Roads. (From the collection of Thelma Larkin Richardson.)

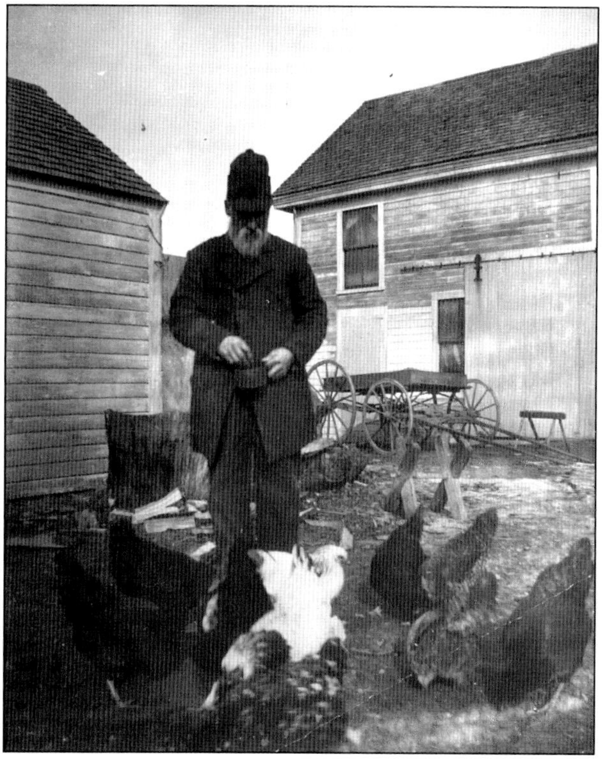

Charles Rich Weston is seen feeding the chickens in front of his barn at 163 West Main Street. This daily chore has today mostly gone by the board, but it was necessary a century ago to ensure that eggs were laid by happy, well-fed chickens. The wagon in the background was built by Charles's brother John Burden Weston, who was a well-known wheelwright in Georgetown in the mid-19th century. (Courtesy of Louise A. Richardson.)

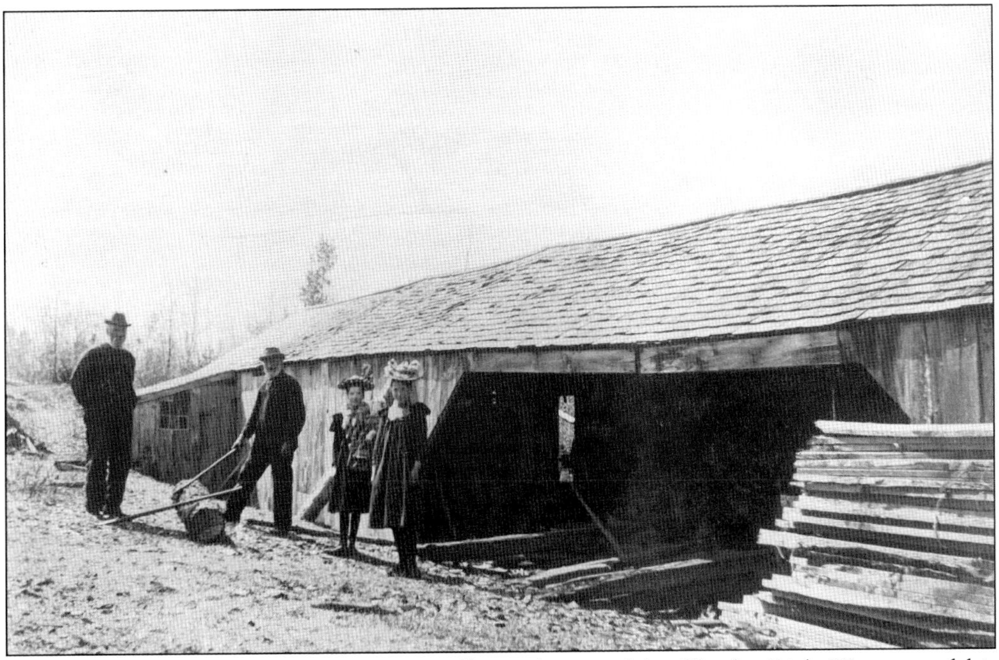

The Weston Saw Mill was a one-story mill jointly owned by Charles Rich Weston and his cousin George Spofford Weston. Located on Andover Street near the Boxford line, it was an important mill in town, as most buildings were built of wood. Standing in front of the mill c. 1900 are, from left to right, Charles Rich Weston, George Spofford Weston, Pauline Newell, and Nellie Maginnis Dummer. (From the collection of Bainbridge Morse Larkin Sr.)

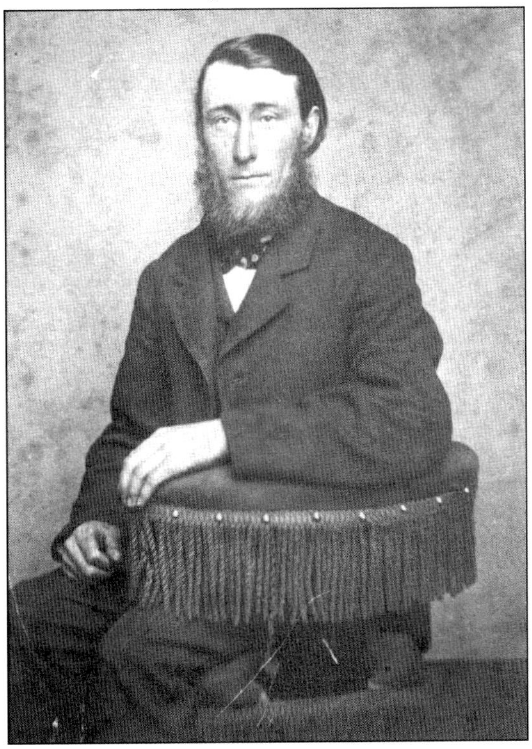

George Spofford Weston was a co-proprietor of the Weston Saw Mill on Andover Street. Weston lived at 185 West Main Street near Pentucket Pond. In the early 18th century, the Harriman and Plummer Saw Mill was located on Rock Pond Brook, and here the timbers and boards for the first meetinghouse in New Rowley were milled in 1729, as sawmills were an important part of the development and building of houses. (Courtesy of Louise A. Richardson.)

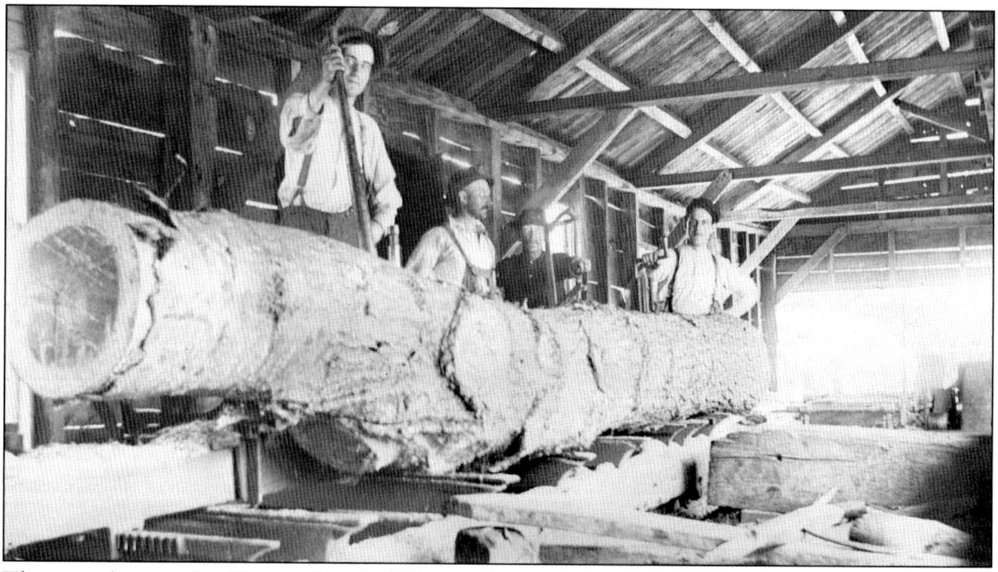

These workers in the Weston Saw Mill have a large tree trunk on the up-and-down saw, which would cut the trunk into even-sized boards. The Weston Saw Mill was purchased by Henry Ford from Ida Weston Morse for his museum, known as Greenfield Village in Dearborn, Michigan. It was dismantled, and each piece was numbered for reerection once the railroad flatcars reached Michigan. Today, the Weston Saw Mill is an attraction at Greenfield Village and preserves a piece of Georgetown history, albeit 1,000 miles away. (Courtesy of Louise A. Richardson.)

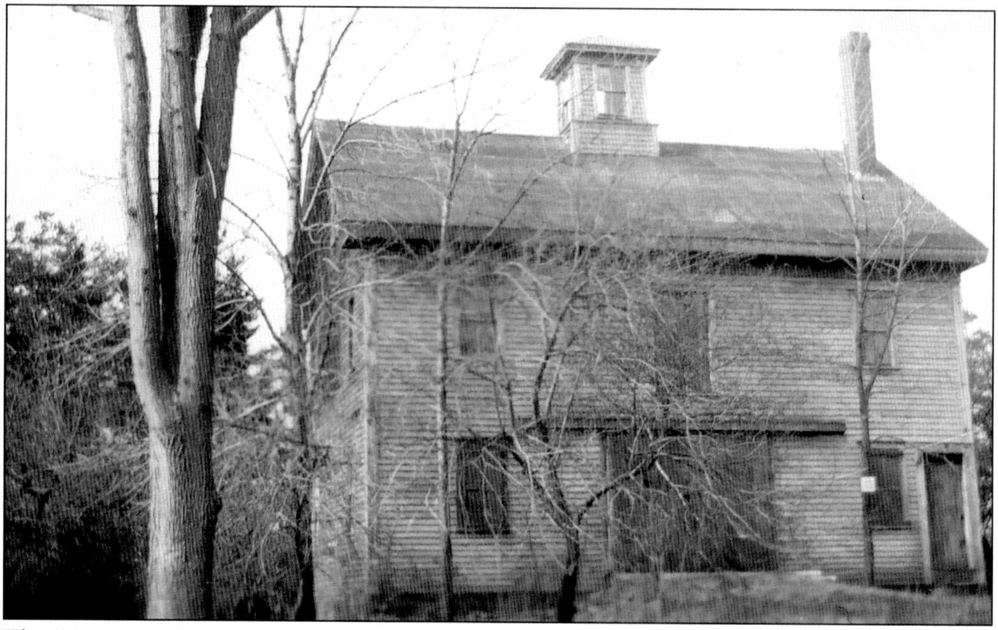

The Weston Cider Mill was at the corner of West Main Street and Rock Pond Avenue and was where apples were pressed for cider, which was often allowed to ferment for hard cider, or vinegar. Seen here in 1898, the wood mill was owned by Orin Weston and his brother Flint Weston. The Weston Cider Mill was operated by steam power and was opened in 1876 between their properties, on West Main Street. The cider mill was demolished in the 1930s. (Courtesy of Louise A. Richardson.)

S.C. Reed opened a photographic studio on Central Street in Pentucket Square in the 1860s. Here, in the shadow of the Peabody Memorial Church tower, patrons could sit for "Life-Size Portraits and every Style of Picture known to the Photographic Arts, executed in a superior manner," as was written on Reed's trade card. Reed was to photograph Georgetown's public buildings, residences, and residents. He took this photograph of his own studio, with his wife in the doorway and three of his friends, *c.* 1870. (Courtesy of Louise A. Richardson.)

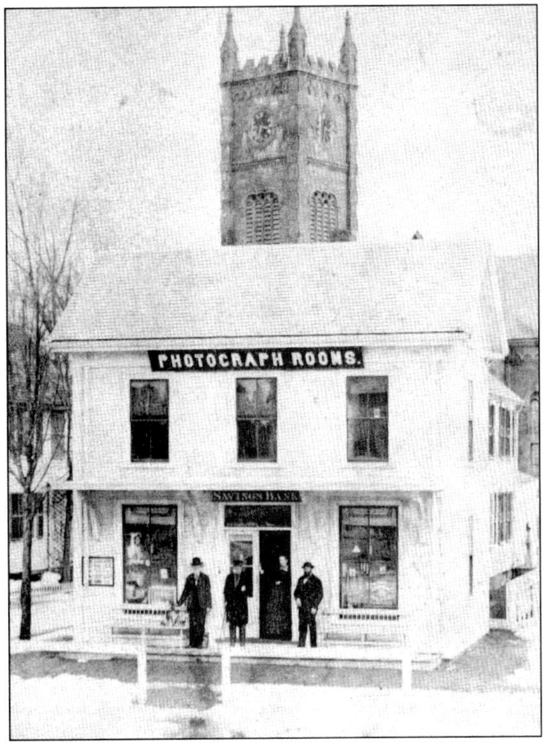

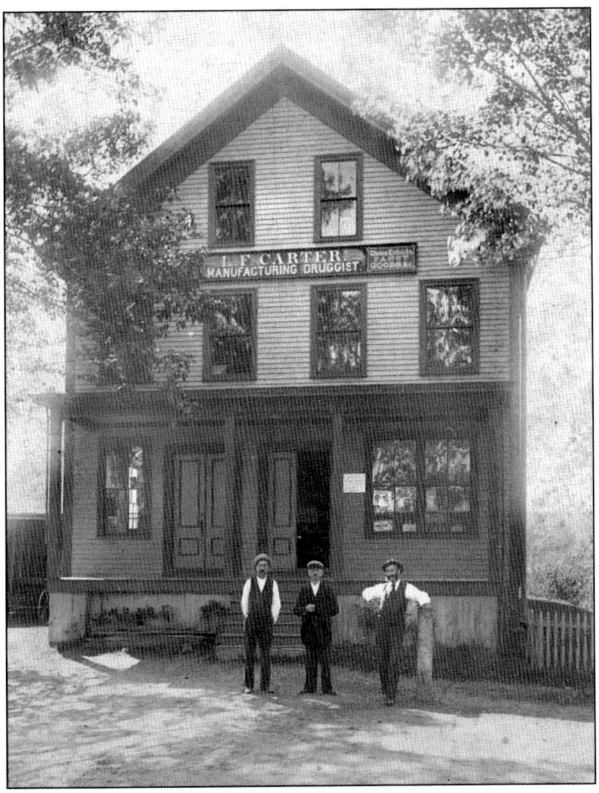

Luther F. Carter was a manufacturing druggist on East Main Street who sold Carter's Elixir of Life. Carter sold "choice extracts and fancy goods" in his shop and continued the manufacture of Atwood's Bitters, a standard patent medicine that had been started by Moses Atwood in 1844. Herbal bitters were added to gin and were sold as a patent medicine in the 1850–1870 period without offending the temperance movement. A portion of the building was also used by Oscar Martin, who had a wood-heel shop where he made parts supplied to other shoe shops. (From the collection of Albert E. Meader.)

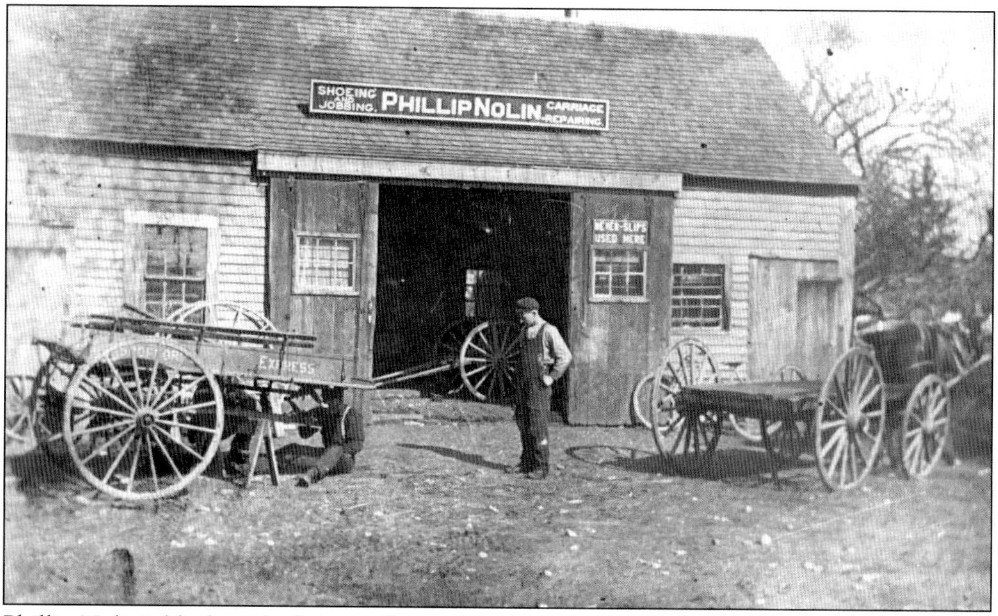

Phillip Nolin's blacksmith shop was located at the corner of North and Pond Streets. In this photograph, a fellow blacksmith watches proprietor Phillip Nolin working under a cart of Spofford's Express. Often, the blacksmith would shoe horses and repair metal of all sorts. (From the collection of Albert E. Meader.)

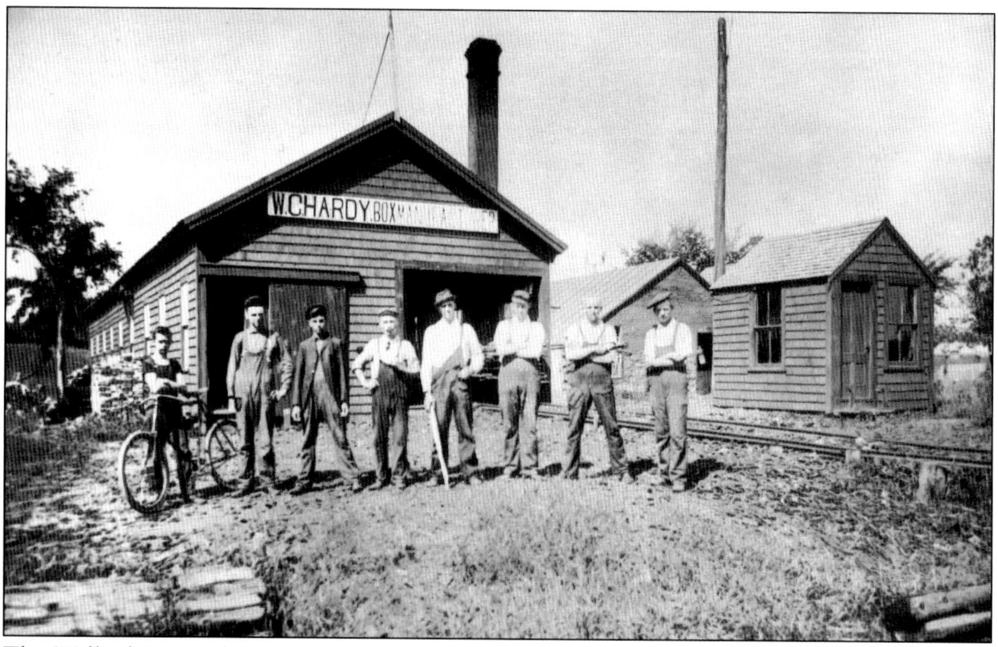

The Willard C. Hardy Box Factory on Railroad Avenue produced shoeboxes in shared space with the Preble Shoe Factory at the corner of Clark and School Streets. In this photograph, workers pose in front of the shedlike factory, with a spur of the railroad on the right. Shoeboxes were first manufactured in Georgetown by Moses F. Carter in the years just before the Civil War and proved a lucrative business, considering the vast number of boots and shoes manufactured locally in the 19th century. (From the collection of Albert E. Meader.)

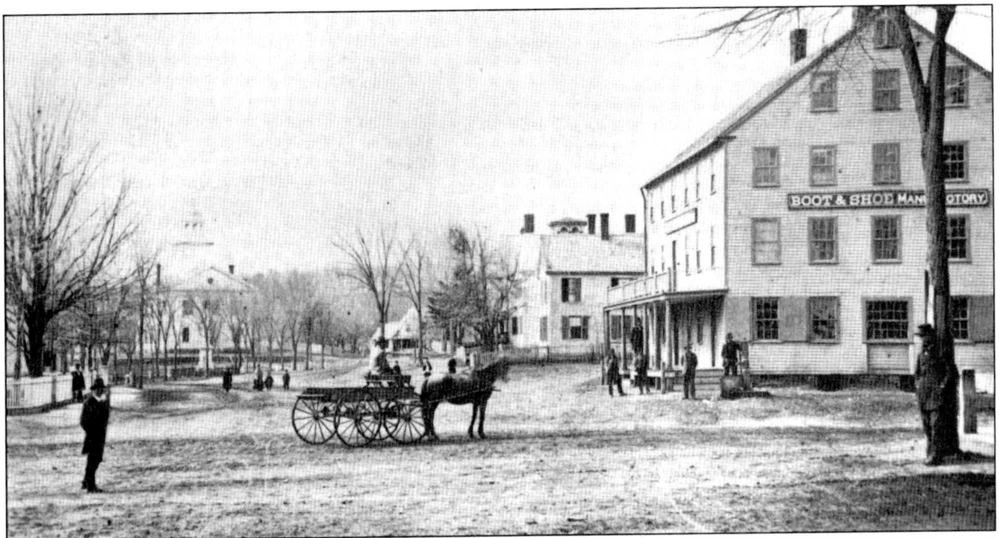

Pentucket Square in 1875 was dominated by the town house, seen on the left behind the Civil War Soldiers' Monument. On the right, at the corner of West Main and Central Streets, is the Little & Tenney Boot & Shoe Manufactory in the Phoenix Block. The building just beyond is that of B.A. Tenney. Stephen Little claimed to have made the first pegged shoes from Paul Pillsbury's invention of a shoe-pegging machine. A gas station occupies the site today. (Courtesy of Homer K. Tapin.)

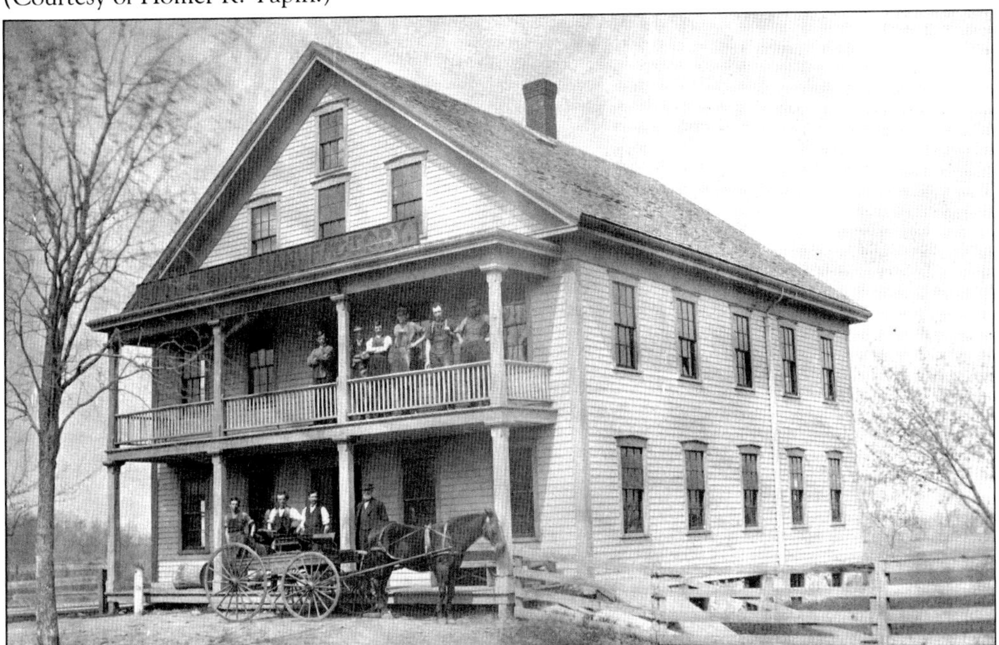

Chaplin's Shoe Shop was built *c.* 1860 at 154–156 Central Street. Henry P. Chaplin Sr. had workers who specialized in the manufacture of miner's shoes in the 1860–1880 period. Pictured from left to right are the following: (first floor) Charles Scates, Joe Scates, Jim Fuller, and Henry P. Chaplin Sr.; (second floor) George Bray, Charles Millett, Gus Hood, Martin Hoyt, Jim Carroll, and David D. Mighill. The former shoe shop was converted to an apartment house *c.* 1930 and still stands. (From the collection of Albert E. Meader.)

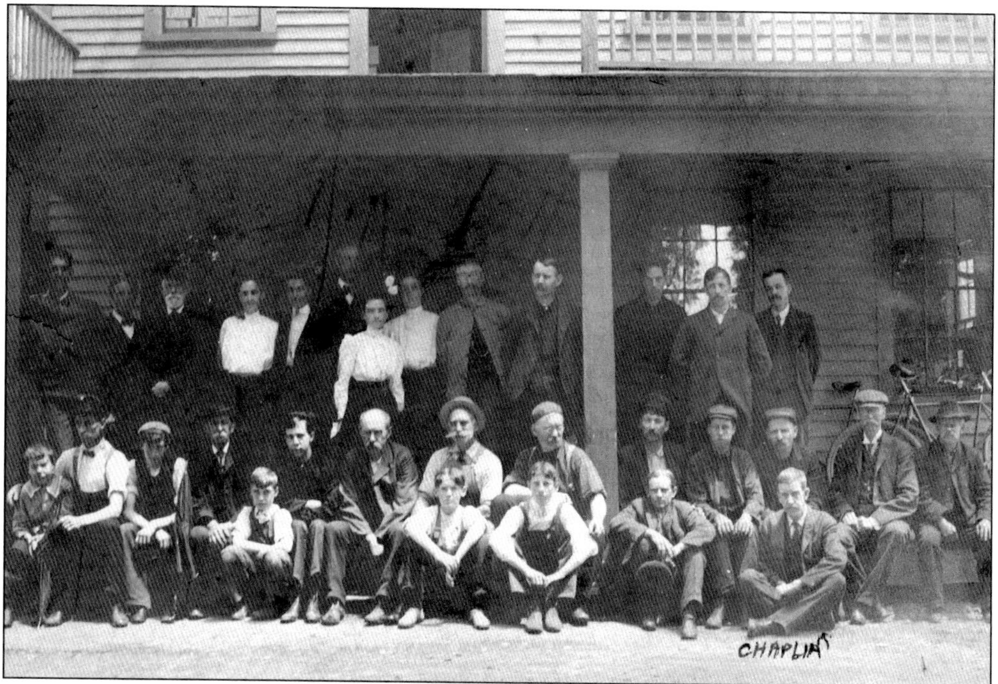

In this *c.* 1895 photograph, Henry P. Chaplin Jr. is seated on the ground on the far right in front of his family's shoe shop at 154–156 Central Street. In 1846, the 419 men and 237 women working in the shoe shops in Georgetown produced 381,198 pairs of shoes and 29,260 pairs of boots. Five decades later, that number was double. Chaplin's Shoe Shop made a varied stock of shoes from miner's shoes to those of the latest styles for both men and women. (Courtesy of Ruth Flanders Tyrie.)

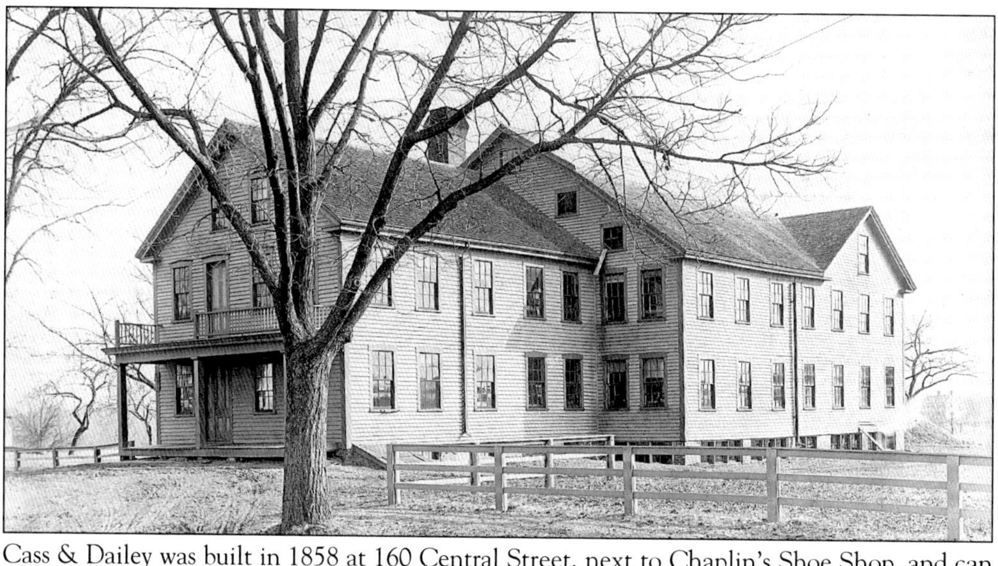

Cass & Dailey was built in 1858 at 160 Central Street, next to Chaplin's Shoe Shop, and can be clearly distinguished by the number of attic windows in the front gable (two at Cass & Dailey and one above three at Chaplin's). The telescopic shoe shop had additions on the rear but was destroyed by fire in 1922. Today, the site is occupied by a private residence. (Courtesy of Homer K. Tapin.)

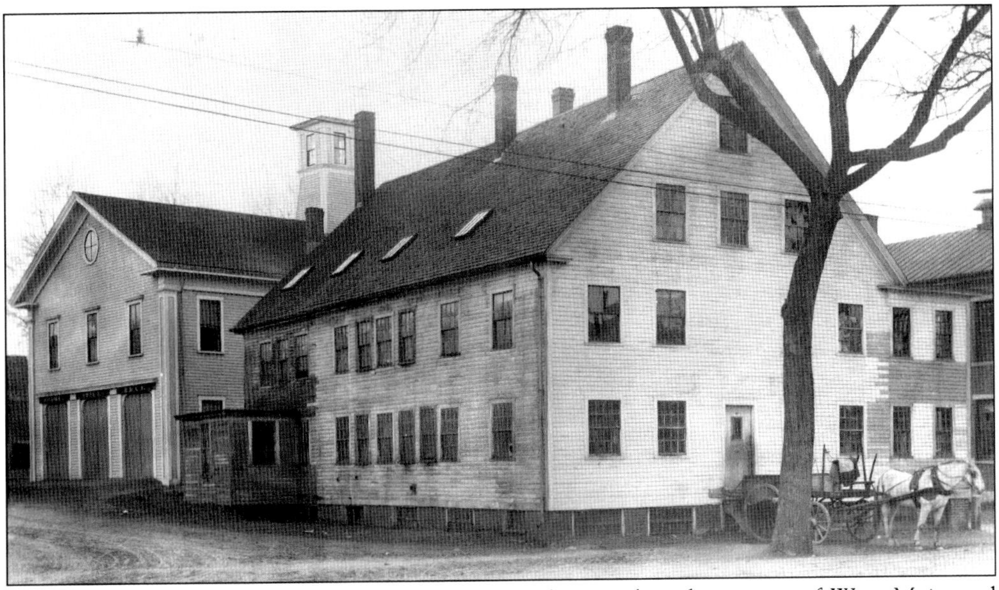

The A.B. Noyes Shoe Shop was built in 1820 and opened at the corner of West Main and Middle Streets as one of the many shoe shops in Georgetown during the 19th century. Alfred B. Noyes and his partner David Holmes, who died in 1868, specialized in miner's footwear and later sold the property. It later became Roberts' Shoe Shop and then Pickering's Hardware Store (often referred to as "the white shop" because of its paint color). It is now Scala's Antique Shop. On the left is the Central Fire Company. On the far right is School No. 4, now used as the Noack Organ Company. (Courtesy of the Georgetown Historical Society.)

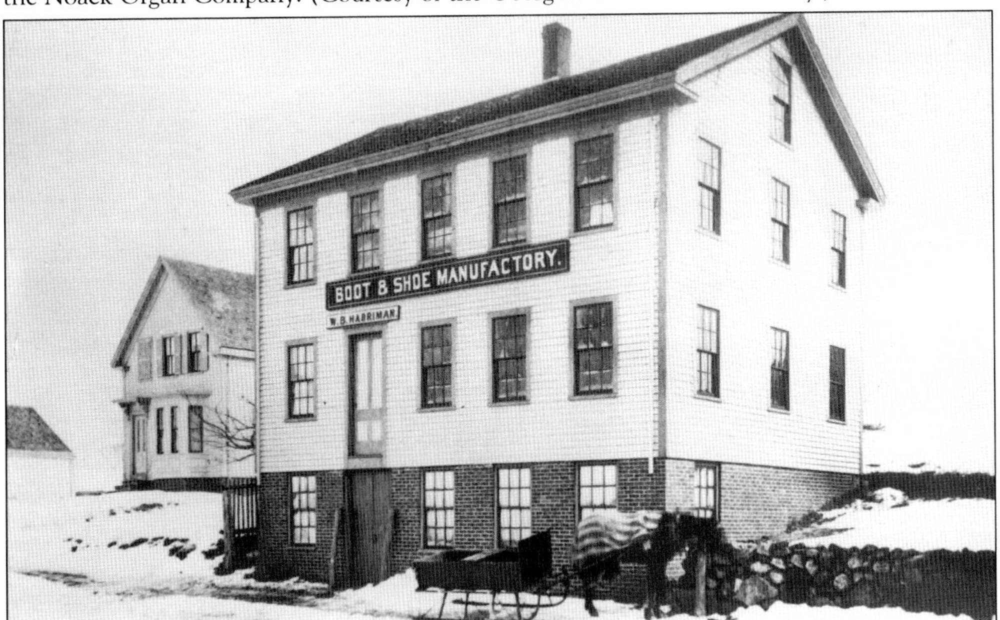

The W.B. Harriman Boot & Shoe Manufactory was located next to 94 Elm Street. The total cost of the lumber to build this wood shop c. 1870 was said to be only $300. Note the blanket-covered horse that is harnessed to a sleigh awaiting its driver, who is probably inside the shop. (From the collection of Albert E. Meader.)

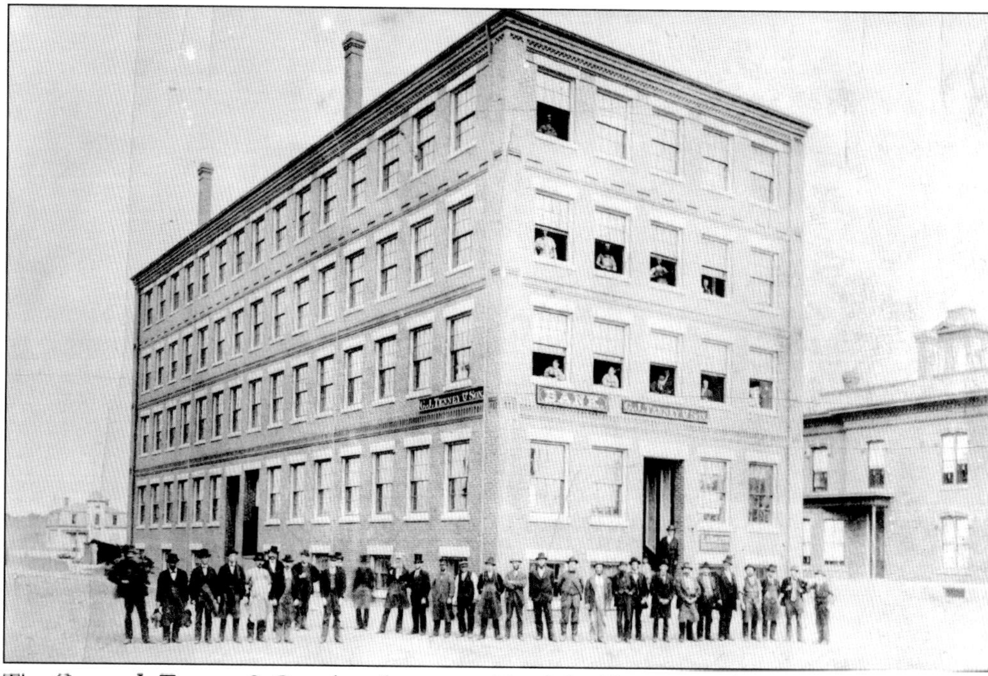

The George J. Tenney & Son shoe factory and bank building, at Park and East Main Streets, was built of red-brick and granite in 1875. It was destroyed a decade later in the conflagration that destroyed much of Georgetown Square. George Jewett Tenney (1805–1896) was the son of Squire Amos Tenney, who was a shoemaker as early as 1812. The Tenney factory is pictured here with many of the shoe workers in front of the building and also looking out of the windows. Local builder Alfred J. Tidd later owned the property. (From the collection of Albert E. Meader.)

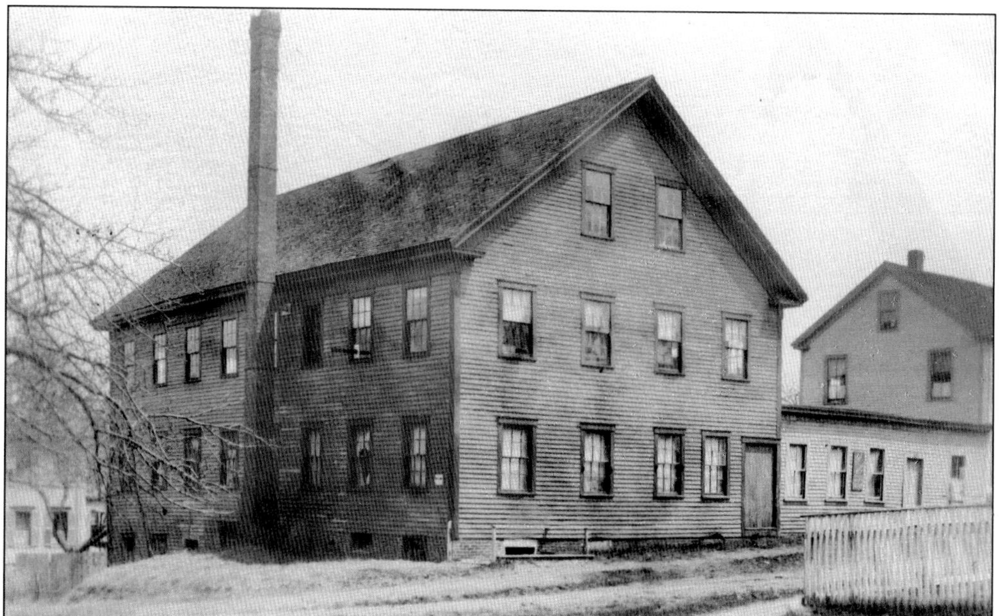

The Preble Shoe Factory, located at the corner of Clark and School Streets, later became the well-known Spaulding Antique Shop. (Courtesy of the Georgetown Historical Society.)

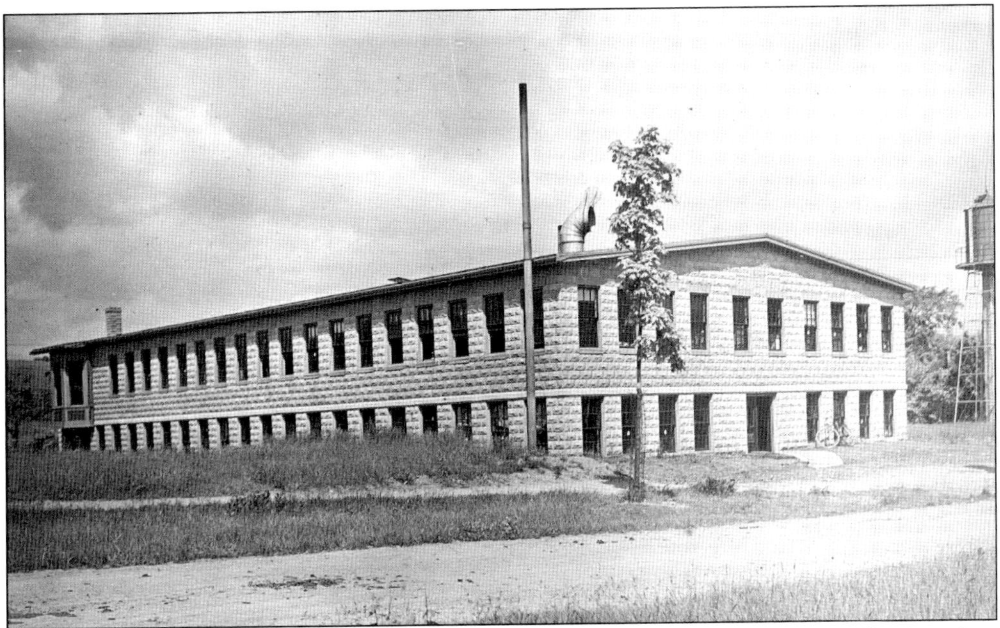

The Fred Baker Shoe Factory was built of cinder blocks at 201 Central Street. The first shoe factory was destroyed by fire in 1917. A new structure was built on its site and was occupied by the Coronet Leather Finishing Company. The factory was demolished in 1999, and townhouses were built on the site. (Courtesy of the Georgetown Historical Society.)

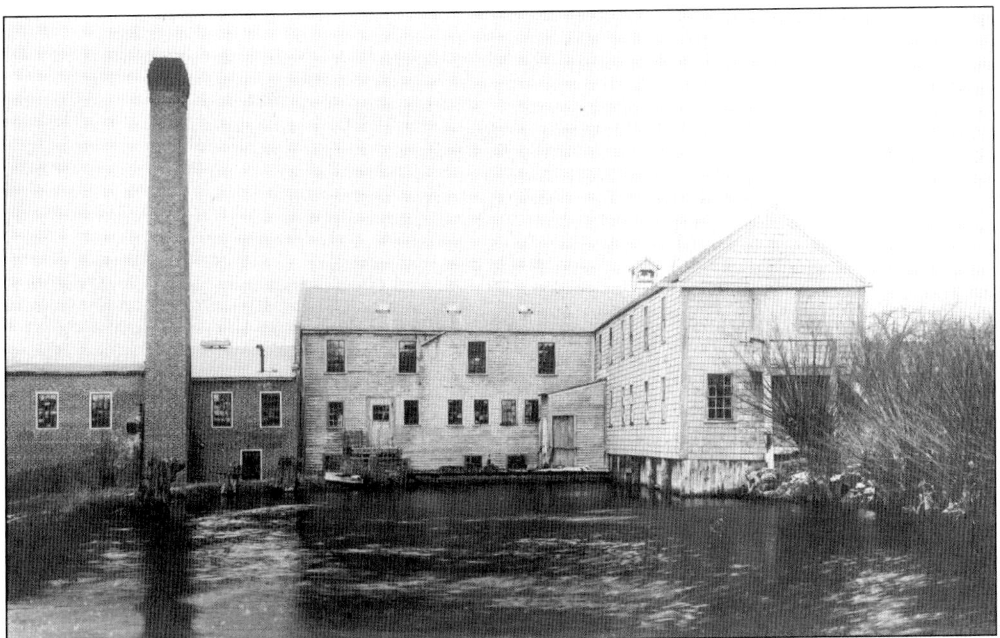

The Cashmere Woolen Mills were located on Pentucket Pond, on the north side of Mill Street between Penn Brook and the Parker River. Wool was scoured after having been sheared from sheep and was then passed through a fulling mill, where the wool was shrunk, thickened, and shipped to a weaving mill. Cashmere is finely carded wool that is softer than normal wool and is therefore more expensive. (Courtesy of the Georgetown Historical Society.)

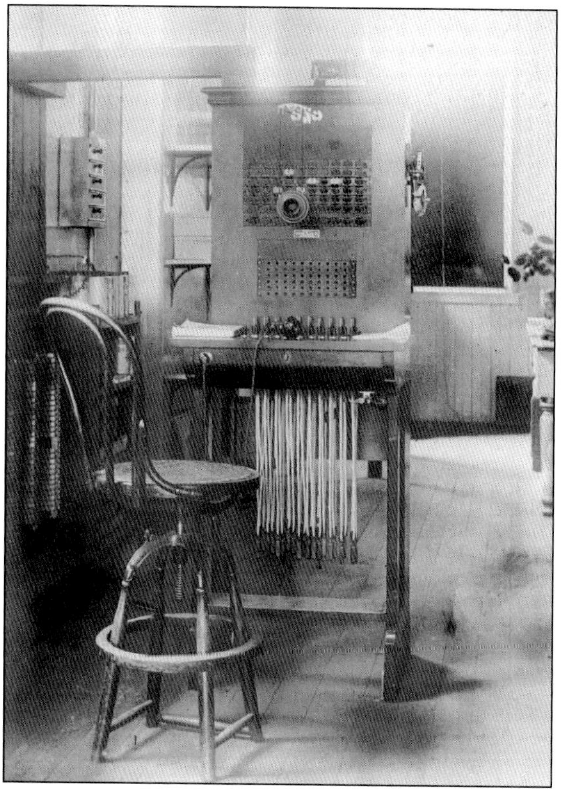

The first Georgetown American Telephone & Telegraph switchboard was located in a corner of Justin White's Shoe Store in Little's Block. Here, the switchboard had numerous plugs, which would be used to connect customers. This switchboard served those who subscribed in Georgetown but also had two lines that could be connected to Haverhill. (Courtesy of the Georgetown Historical Society.)

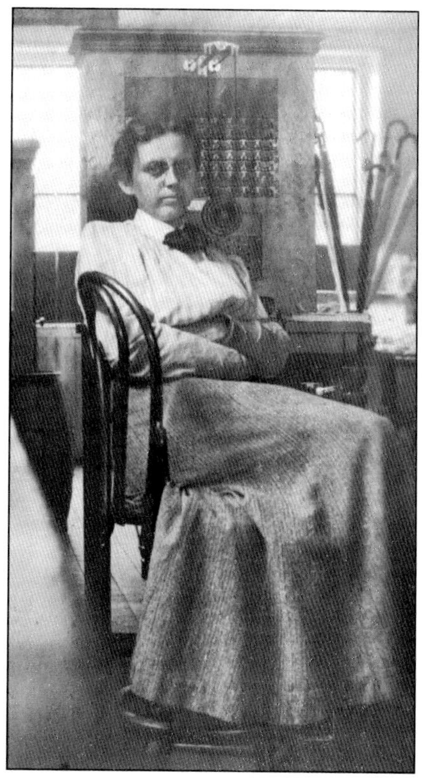

Harriet Olive Harriman (later Mrs. Calvin Pingree) was the first telephone operator in Georgetown. The telephone switchboard was later moved to the *Georgetown Advocate* office on Middle Street after Harriman married Calvin Pingree, editor of the weekly newspaper. Here, Mrs. Pingree relaxes at her switchboard while waiting for the next telephone connection request. (Courtesy of the Georgetown Historical Society.)

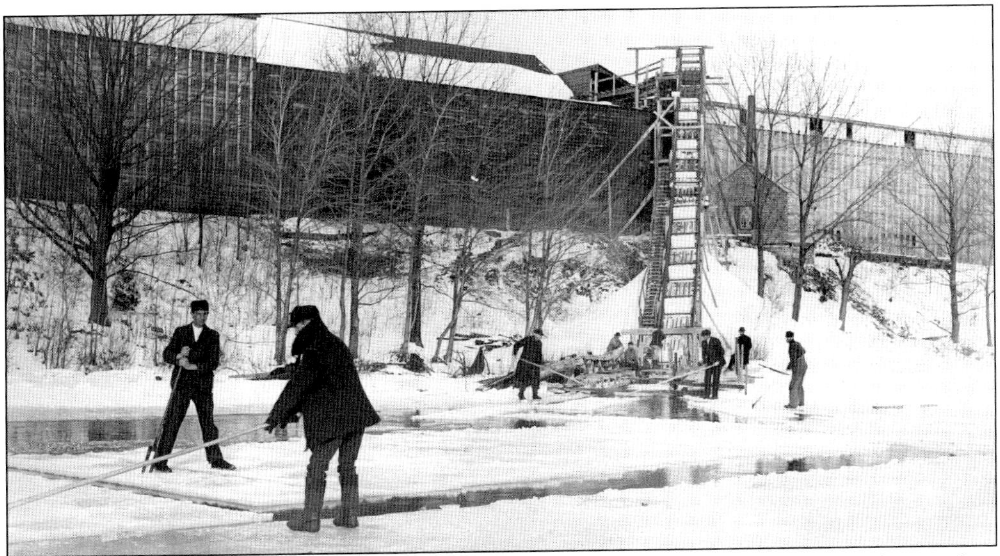

Ice was harvested in Georgetown as early as 1853 by marking the ice with a horse-drawn edger and then cutting it with saws into square blocks. The ice was stored in an icehouse with sawdust between the layers to prevent melting until it was either used locally or shipped to Boston. The conveyor belt shown in the center was roughly four stories high and led to the icehouse. The icehouses on Pentucket Pond were made of tapered wood, with sawdust used as insulation between the walls. (Courtesy of the Georgetown Historical Society.)

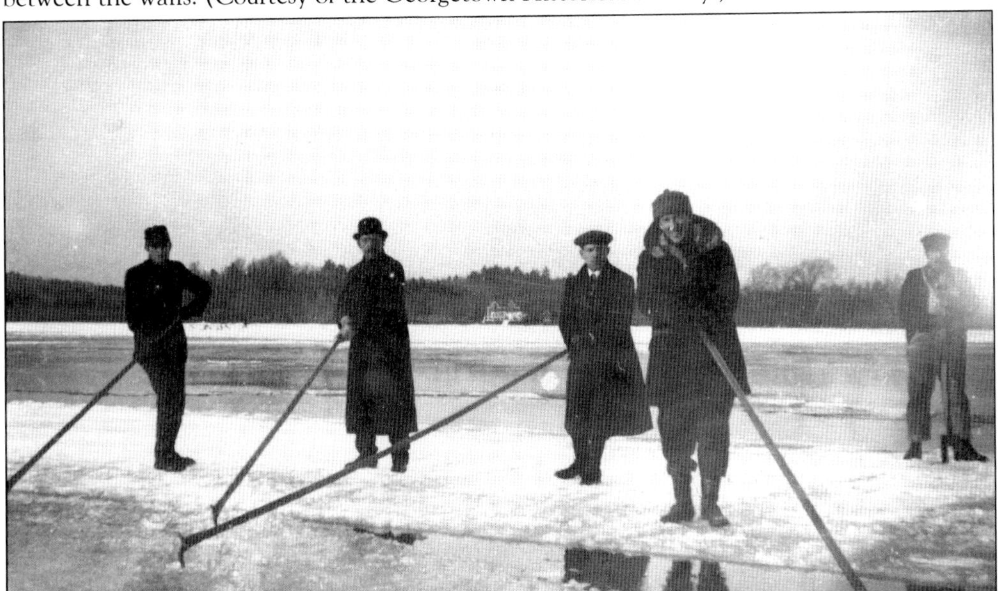

A group of men directs a float of ice blocks along a channel on Pentucket Pond. These uniformly sized ice blocks, of which an average of 2,400 could be cut per day, would be floated down a channel cut through the ice and pushed with long hooks. The blocks would be brought into the icehouse by a chain conveyor fitted with lags. These icehouses were operated by Sherman Nelson, John A. Hoyt & Son, Edward Lee, Wallace Adams, David Hemeon, the Elliott Brothers, and Little & Tenney. (From the collection of Albert E. Meader.)

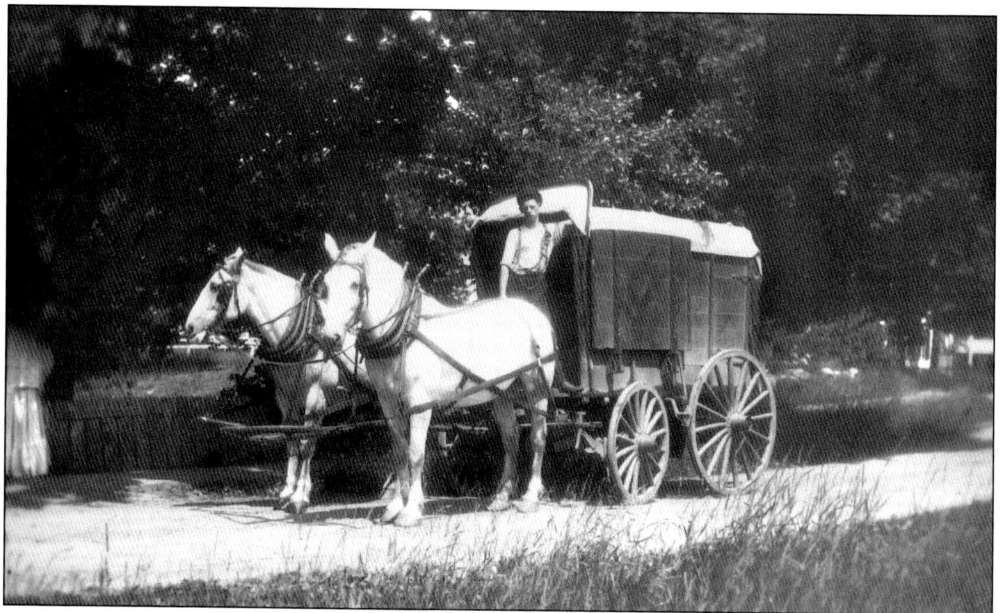

A horse-drawn ice wagon stops in Georgetown c. 1900. Ice was first cut commercially by Frederic Tudor (1783–1864), a Boston merchant known as the "ice king" of Boston. Tudor had followed the lead of Lord Timothy Dexter of Newburyport, who would ship cut ice to warm-weather ports and reap a tremendous profit from the ice that had not yet melted. Although the ice on Pentucket and Rock Ponds was not really cut for commercial purposes until the 1850s (when started by Little & Tenney on Pentucket Pond and by the Abbott Brothers on Rock Pond), it would continue until World War II for use in iceboxes. (From the collection of Albert E. Meader.)

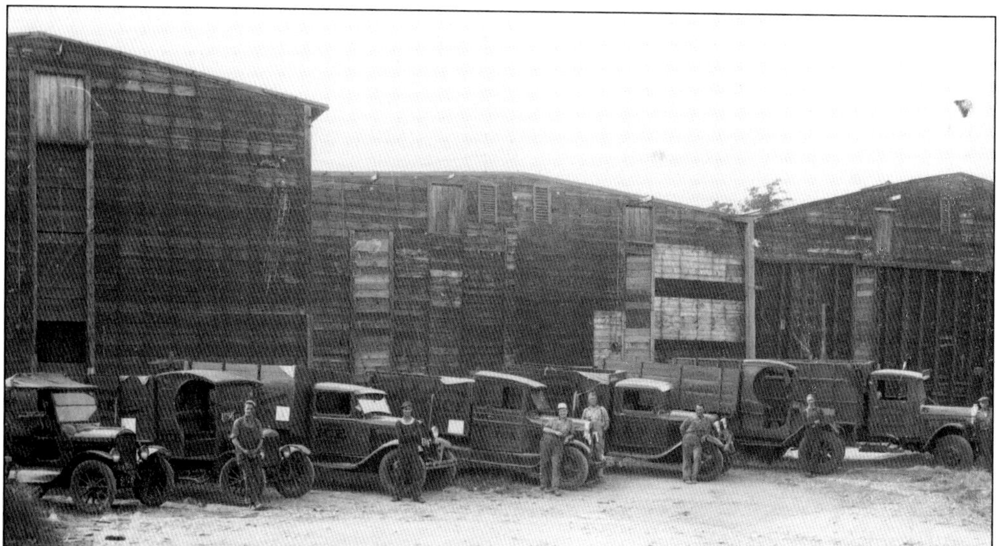

The motorized vehicles of the Pentucket Ice Company are shown with their drivers in 1934. David D. Hemeon, proprietor of the Pentucket Ice Company, was an ice dealer at 237 Central Street, and his employees would deliver cut ice by truck to homes and businesses, which ensured that the ice did not melt as rapidly as when delivered by horse and wagon. (From the collection of Albert E. Meader.)

Eight

Georgetown Architecture

Georgetown's architecture begins with the Brocklebank House, which is the oldest house in town and now serves as the headquarters of the Georgetown Historical Society. In the broader sense, however, architecture has been described as the science of designing and constructing buildings. We often view architecture as an important aspect of our daily lives. The style and design of town buildings, schools, places of worship, and residences are unique examples of an architect's and our own personal expression and therefore influence the way we view our town.

Georgetown is fortunate in the wide spectrum of architecture. The town features First Period houses, such as the Dickinson-Pillsbury-Witham House, the Brocklebank-Nelson-Beecher House, and the Hazen House. It is also home to mid-20th-century houses, such as the Adams family's Techbuilt house (built in 1962 on Central Street) and the more recent development of new houses on Central Street in South Georgetown. Combining many 18th-century Colonial houses with an even greater number of 19th-century Federal and Greek Revival houses, the range of styles is remarkable.

Through the efforts of the Georgetown Historical Commission, an attempt at the systematic identification and the designation of houses in town has been undertaken. These individual architectural survey forms, which are available for review at the Georgetown Peabody Library, identify significant houses, schools, and churches that are important contributing factors to the town and its streetscapes. With the assistance of the Massachusetts Historical Commission, future historic districts might be identified and designated to ensure that the contributing architectural aspects are preserved for our descendants. In this vein, this photographic history was written in the hopes of assisting the reader in the identification and exploration of the wide array of architectural styles represented in town and to expand upon the known history and development of this fascinating place called Georgetown.

The Art of Building faithfully portrays the social history of those people
To whose needs it ministers but cannot get beyond those boundaries.

—Calvert Vaux

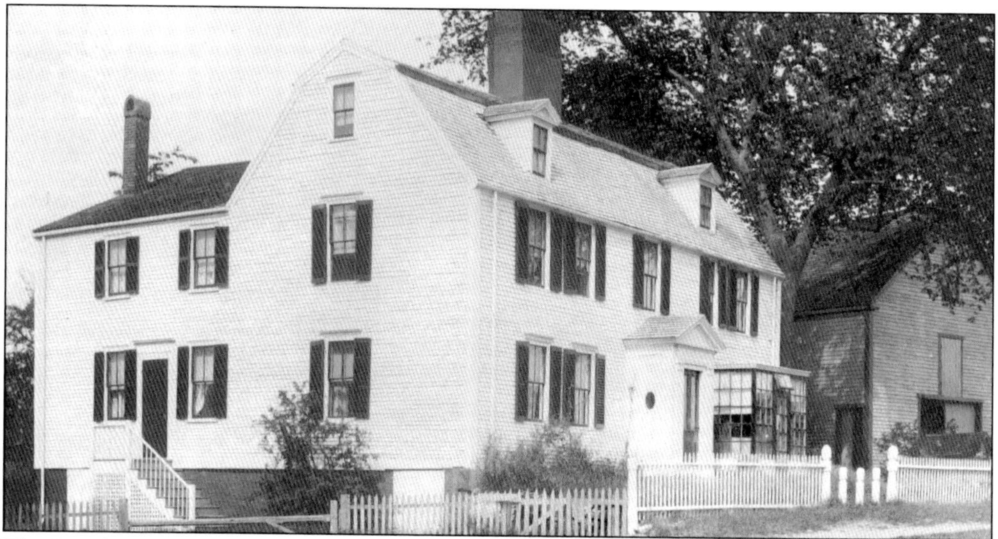

The Brocklebank-Nelson-Beecher House is reportedly the oldest house in Georgetown. It was reputedly built in 1660 and was remodeled *c.* 1740. Lived in by generations of descendants of Samuel and Hannah Brocklebank, it also served as the White Horse Tavern in the mid-18th century under innkeeper Dudley Tyler. The house later became the parsonage to the Old South Church. From 1858 to 1880, it was the home of the Beecher family and was used as a stop on the Underground Railroad, transporting slaves from the South to eventual freedom in Canada. The house was remodeled by the Spofford family, who added the large glass window on the right, which was used as an exotic plant room. A similar house is the John Adams House (*c.* 1725), at 93 West Main Street. (From the collection of Albert E. Meader.)

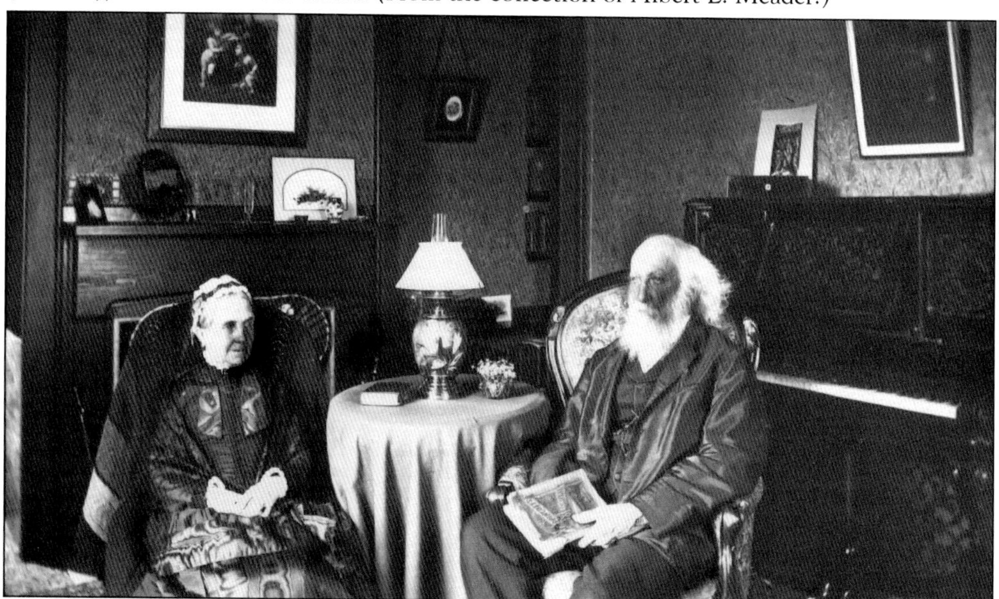

Sarah Leland Coffin Beecher and Rev. Charles Beecher are shown in the back parlor of the parsonage of the Old South Church in 1890. Owned by the Georgetown Historical Society, the parsonage is now the Brocklebank Museum. It is interesting to note that Reverend Beecher is not holding a copy of the Bible but rather an edition of *Lippincott's Magazine*, a popular monthly journal in the late 19th century. (Courtesy of Homer K. Tapin.)

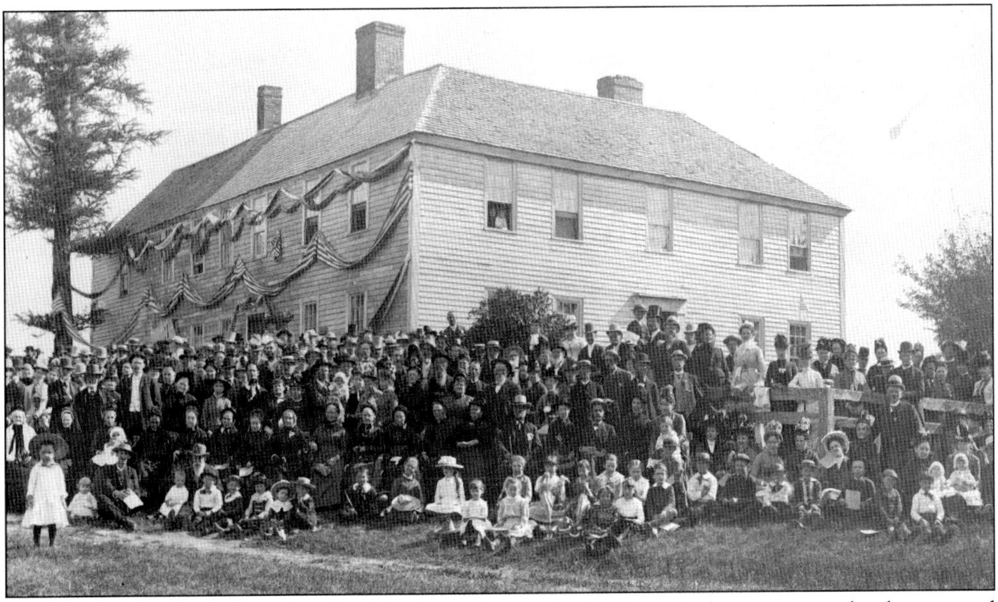

The Spofford House, on Spofford Hill, is shown in 1885 with bunting on the house and generations of descendants of John Spofford posing in front. In 1909, in conjunction with Old Home Week, another Spofford family reunion was held in Georgetown. The descendants dedicated a boulder with a bronze tablet near the corner of Andover and West Streets. The inscription was written by Harriet Prescott Spofford: "On this hill in 1669 John Spofford descendant of Orme and Gamelbar with his wife Elizabeth Scott founded the race of Spoffords in America. A race respected for integrity, courage, generosity and intelligence." (Courtesy of the Georgetown Historical Society.)

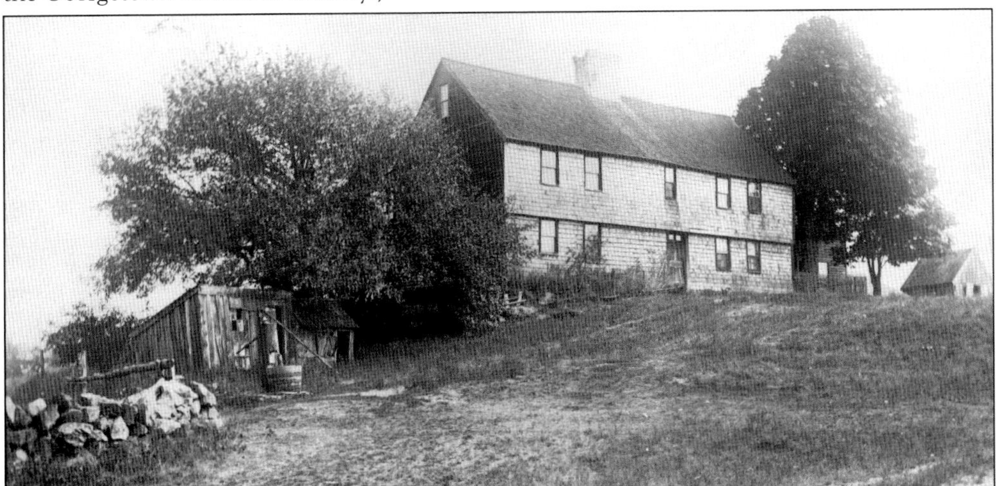

The Dickinson-Pillsbury-Witham House was built c. 1692 by James Dickinson and still stands at 170 Jewett Street. Typical of First Period houses, it has an overhanging second story and oak summer beams. After 1801, the house was owned by Paul Pillsbury, a noted inventor who received a patent for a corn sheller, which stripped the kernels of corn from the ears. Pillsbury also invented this country's first shoe-pegging machine, which revolutionized the shoe industry and led to the large number of shoe mills in Georgetown in the mid-19th century. (From the collection of Albert E. Meader.)

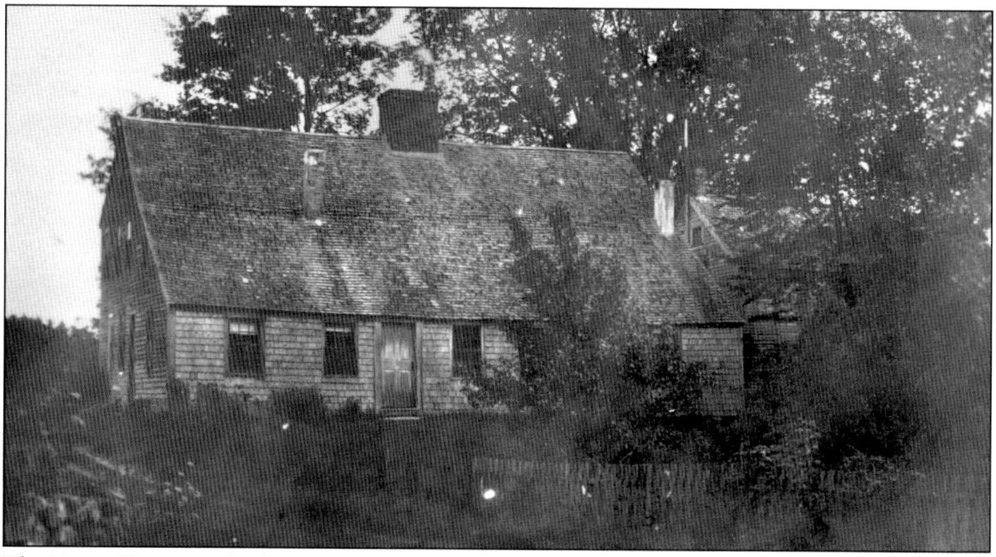

The Hazen House was built *c.* 1711 at 225 East Main Street. Built by Samuel Hazen, the house still retains a large parcel of land below Penn Brook. The house is a typical First Period house, having been built as a center-chimney saltbox house with a lean-to. First Period houses in New England usually extend from the initial settlement of Puritans to the Massachusetts Bay Colony in 1630 to 1730. The houses have distinctly medieval architectural features that builders from England used in their construction in New England. (Courtesy of the Georgetown Historical Society.)

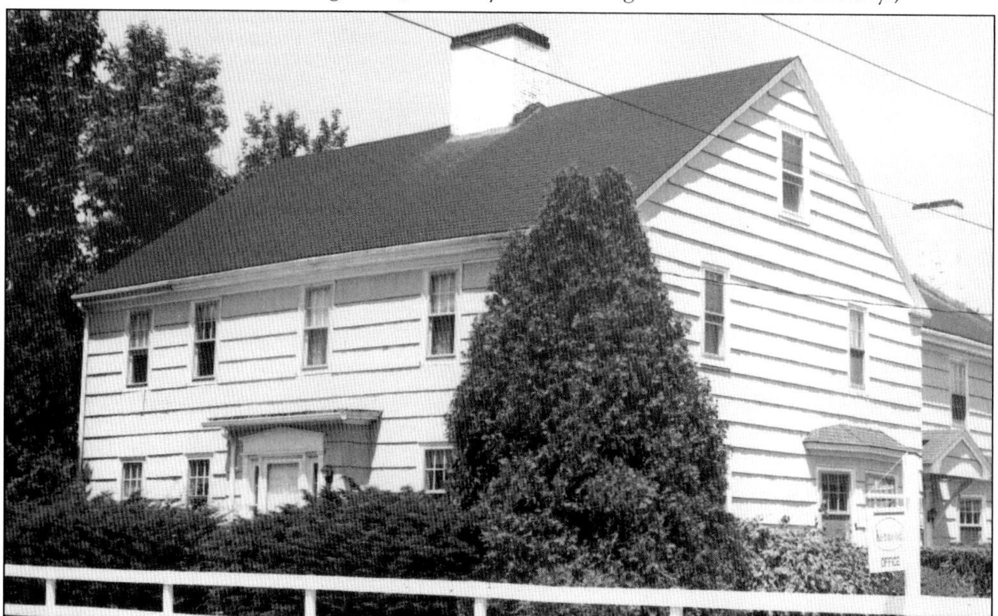

The Thurston-Spofford House was built *c.* 1725 and stands at 241 Andover Street on Spofford Hill. It is a First Period house with a center chimney and a five-bay facade. Although it has later features, such as a Greek Revival doorway and siding, it still gives the impression of an early-18th-century house. Today, the property is known as the Andover Hill Farm, which once had an impressive herd of 100 Guernsey and Holstein cows when it was owned by Paul Muscovitz. (Courtesy of the Georgetown Historical Commission.)

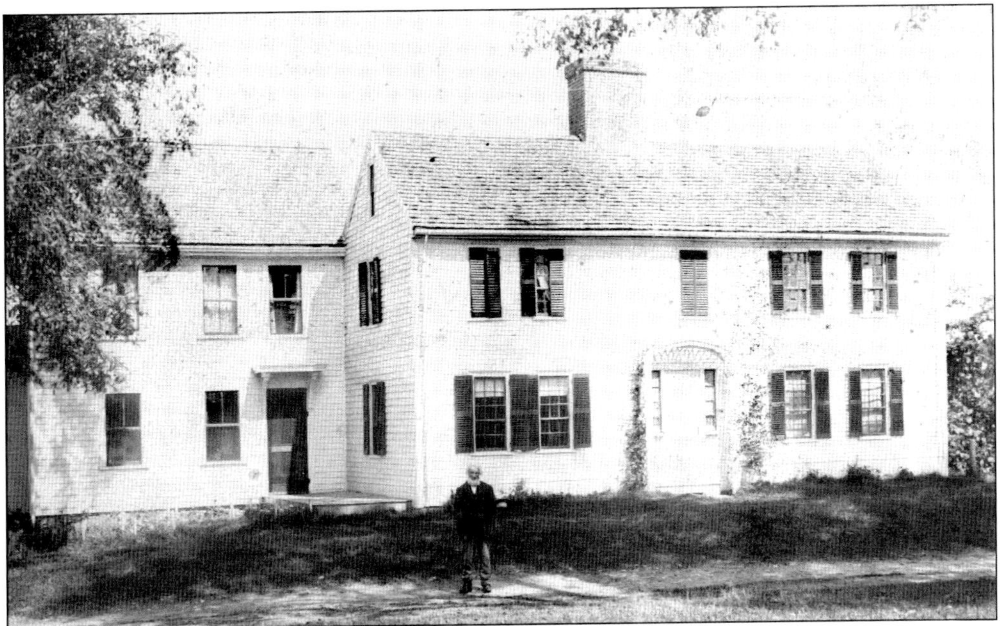

The Flint Weston House is pictured in 1896, with Flint Weston standing in front. His wife was Caroline Hardy Weston. At the time of this photograph, the house had been remodeled since it was built *c.* 1732 by John Harriman on Hampshire Lane in Federal City, near Pentucket Pond. Part of the house was moved by oxen across the ice of Pentucket Pond to its eventual site at 175 West Main Street. Another house of this period is the Joseph Nelson House (built in 1738), located at 81 Elm Street in Georgetown. (Courtesy of Louise A. Richardson.)

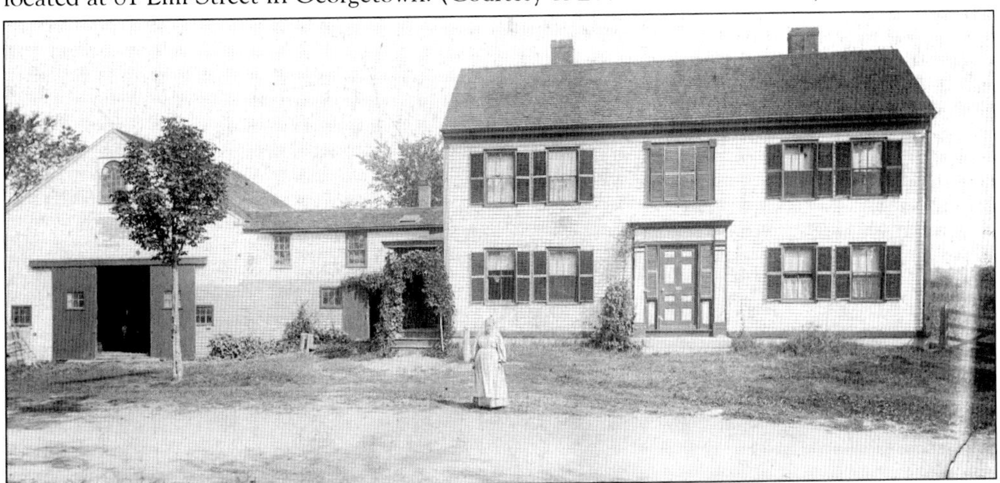

The Captain Orin Weston House was built at 185 West Main Street upon his marriage in 1835 to Lavinia Spofford. A late-Federal house, it also had early examples of the Greek Revival style in the door entablature and the tripart window directly above. Standing in front of the house is Lavinia Spofford Weston (1799–1894), a noted poetess who even in old age was, according to *The History of Essex County*, "actively engaged in composition, equally in vigor the production of her early years." On the left is the barn with a gable-arched window that was taken from the First Baptist Church in Georgetown, which was sold to Captain Weston when a new meetinghouse was built in 1829. The house was later the home of their son George Spofford Weston, co-owner of the Weston Cider Mill, across the street. (Courtesy of Louise A. Richardson.)

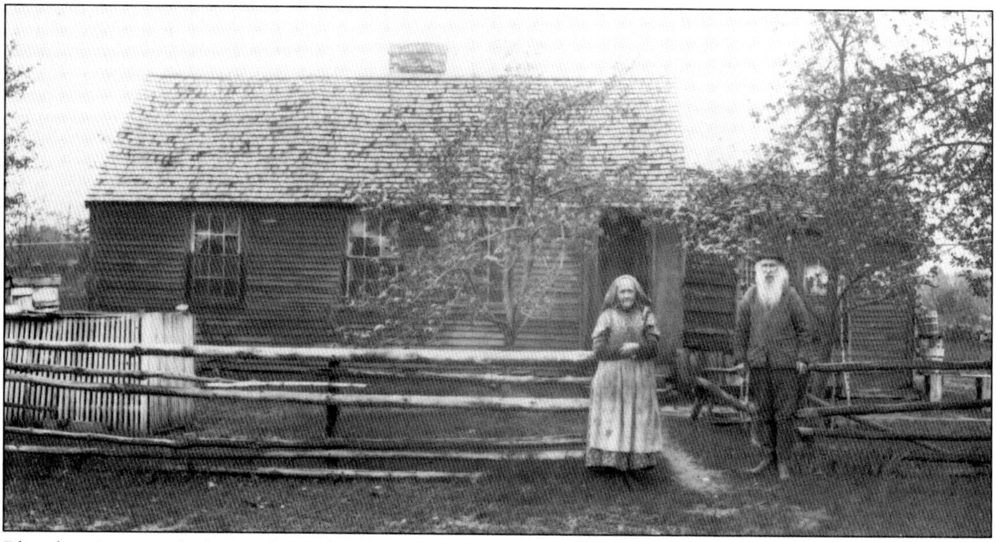

Phoebe Ann and Aaron Kneeland pose in front of their home at 115 Thurlow Street. The Kneelands, in 1899, had been married a mind-boggling 71 years and would eventually celebrate their 75th wedding anniversary. Aaron Kneeland worked as a custom shoemaker (or cordwainer, as it was originally known) until he was 95. The house was a small, one-story building where the Kneelands raised 12 children and had a ten-footer, which was his shoe shop on the right. Similar to this house is the Jeremiah Dodge House, built c. 1750 and moved from Bailey Lane across the ice on Rock Pond to 153 West Main Street in Georgetown. Judith Dodge Peabody (1770–1830) was born in this house when it was located on Spofford Hill. (Courtesy of Arthur Paquette.)

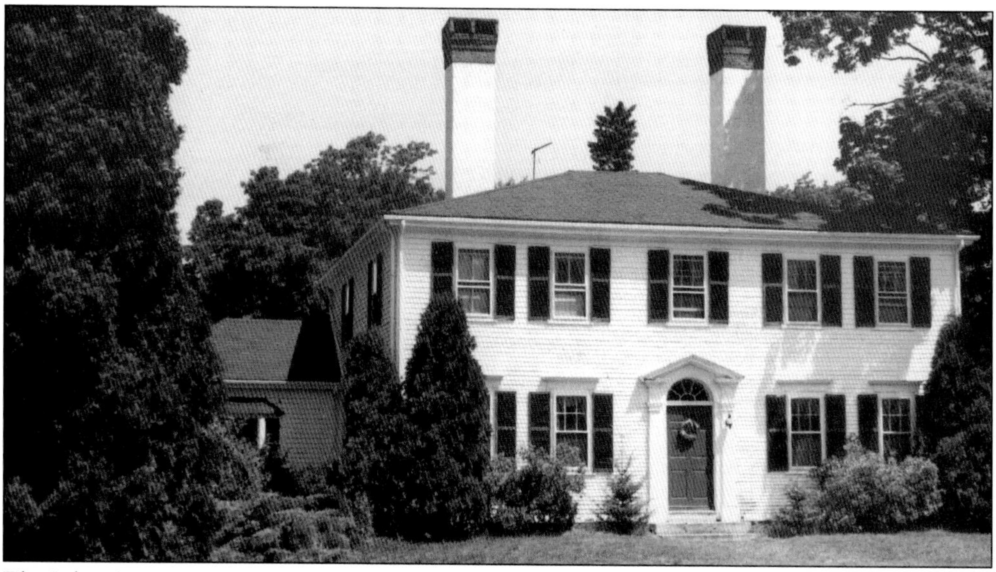

The John A. Lovering House is probably the most elegant Federal house in Georgetown. It was built c. 1800 at Lovering's Corners (the junction of Central and Nelson Streets) at what is now 237 Central Street. This impressive five-bay facade and low-hip-roof house is offset by a pair of tall brick chimneys, giving it a prominence as one passes along the street. Another impressive house is the Captain Benjamin Adams House (302 Central Street), which was the first house in Georgetown to be painted white. (Courtesy of the Georgetown Historical Commission.)

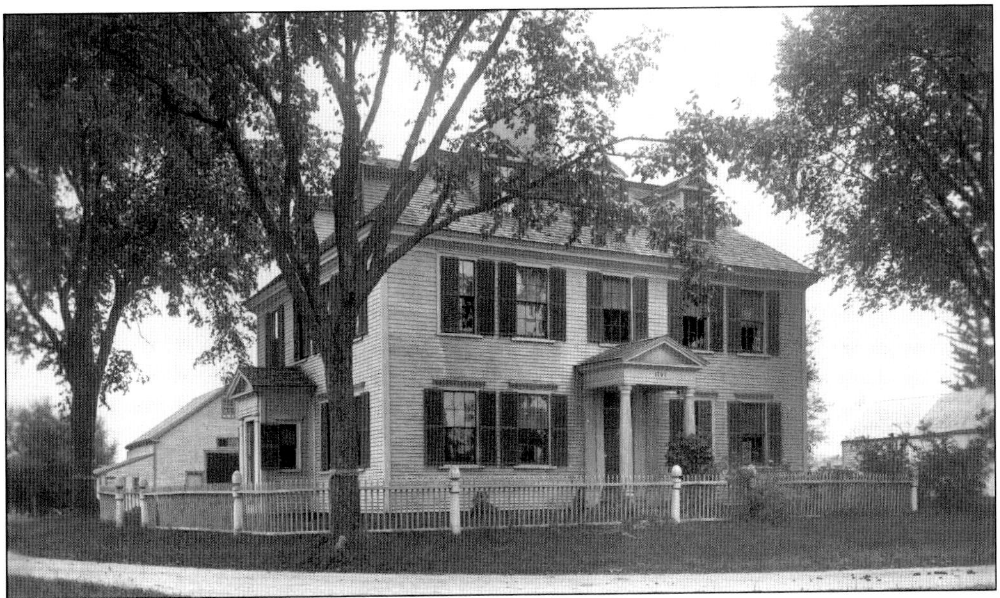

The Nathaniel Nelson House was built in 1797 at 8 Elm Street and is an impressive example of late-Georgian architecture. A square, five-bay facade is offset with a pedimented porch, which is supported by two Doric columns surmounting plinth bases. The hip roof is punctuated by three pedimented dormers, all the while maintaining overall symmetry. The house was built by Nathaniel Nelson, a prominent Newburyport banker, adjacent to the Old South Church at the corner of East Main Street. It is purported that gold from Nelson's Newburyport bank was hidden in the cellar chimney during the War of 1812. (From the collection of Albert E. Meader.)

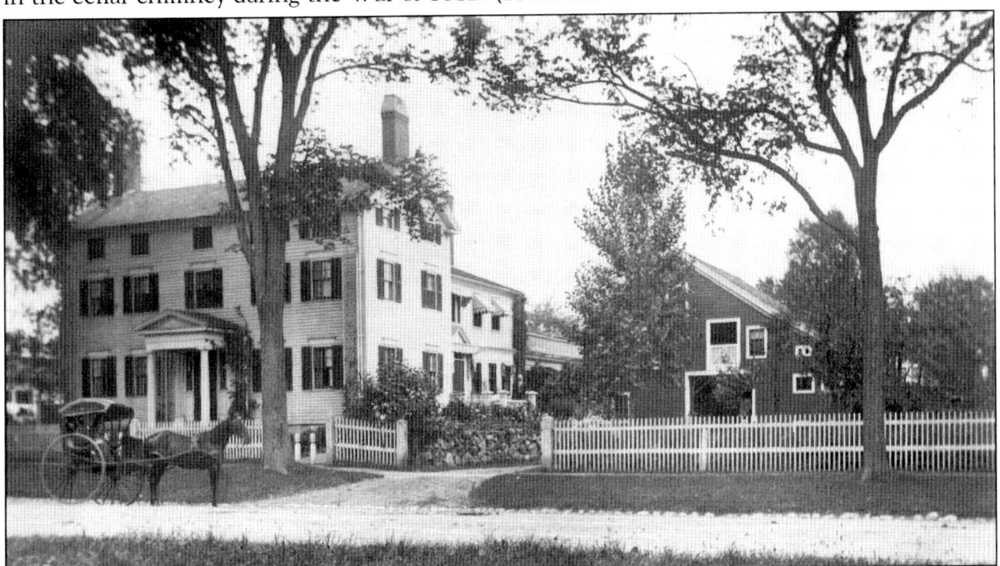

The Coker-Hoyt House, an elegant three-story Federal structure, was built *c.* 1800 on East Main Street. For many years, it was the residence of Dr. Edward Hoyt, successor to Dr. Ralph C. Huse, who can be seen in his one-horse shay on the left. This three-story, five-bay-facade style of house was more common in Salem and Newburyport than in Georgetown. Today, the house has been converted to the Georgetown branch of Fleet Bank. (Courtesy of the Georgetown Historical Society.)

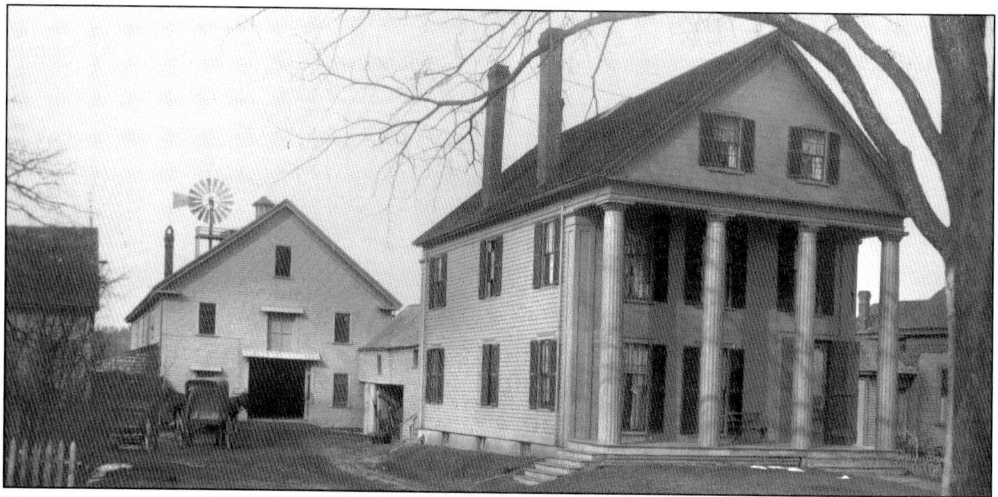

This temple-fronted, Greek Revival house was built by Josiah Adams in 1835 at 5 Elm Street as a store, with Adams Hall above. The four reeded Doric columns support a frontal gable that has two windows in the pediment. Many Greek Revival houses were copied directly out of Asher Benjamin's book *The Practical House Carpenter*, which was one of the first books published in this country with architectural plans and details. With floor-length windows, intact shutters, and a Doric colonnade, this is an important house of the period. Purchased in 1849 by the Old South Church for use as a vestry, the house was used after 1931 as a showroom for the reproduction furniture crafted by the Everett Spaulding Company. (From the collection of Albert E. Meader.)

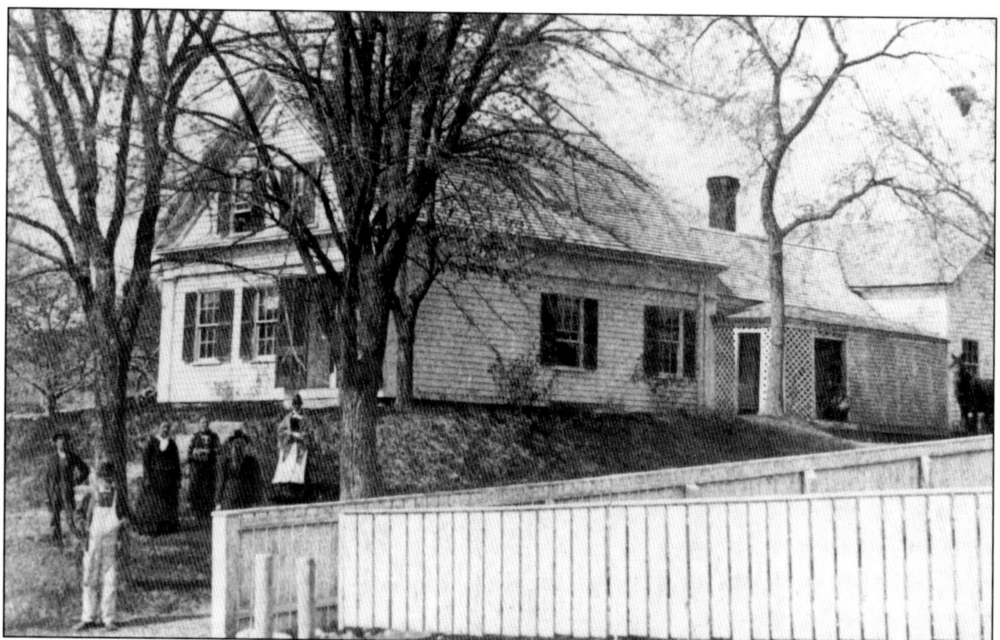

This charming Greek Revival house was built *c.* 1840 by the Hill family on East Main Street in Marlborough Village on a gentle slope. Members of the family pose in front of the house *c.* 1860, and even the horse can be seen on the far right. Although not architecturally impressive, these small Greek Revival cottages were more common than the grand, architect-designed houses of the same period. (Courtesy of Homer K. Tapin.)

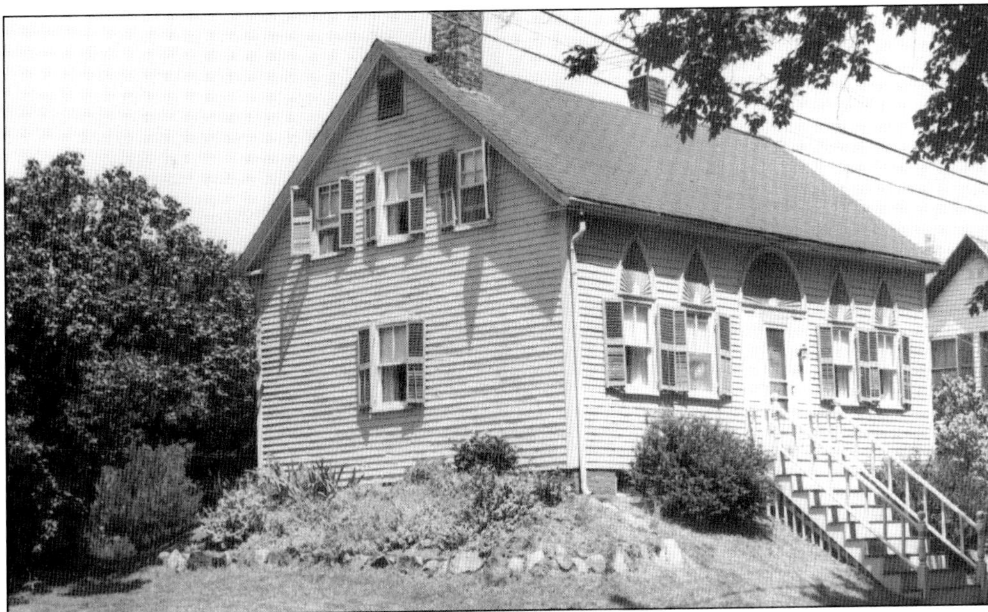

The Clark House, a late–Greek Revival cottage at 23 Middle Street, was built c. 1840, with interesting lancet-shaped louvered fans above the facade windows and a demilune fan above the entrance—all giving the cottage a decidedly Gothic Revival aspect. Clark Street was named for the family that lived in this cottage. A similar house—but with demilune rather than lancet-shaped louvered fans above the facade windows—is the c. 1840 house at 33 Library Street, overlooking Harry Murch Park. (Courtesy of the Georgetown Historical Commission.)

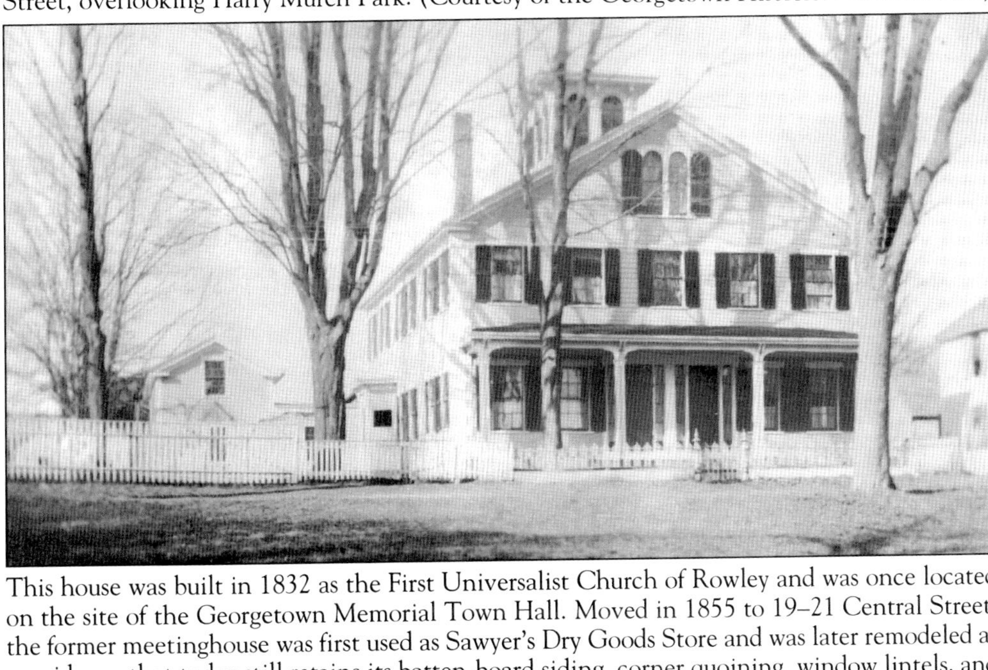

This house was built in 1832 as the First Universalist Church of Rowley and was once located on the site of the Georgetown Memorial Town Hall. Moved in 1855 to 19–21 Central Street, the former meetinghouse was first used as Sawyer's Dry Goods Store and was later remodeled as a residence that today still retains its batten-board siding, corner quoining, window lintels, and shutters. This house is among the most prominent houses in the Italianate style in Georgetown, and its four-sided bracketed cupola creates a sense of elegance (and great views) to the remodeled meetinghouse. (Courtesy of the Georgetown Historical Commission.)

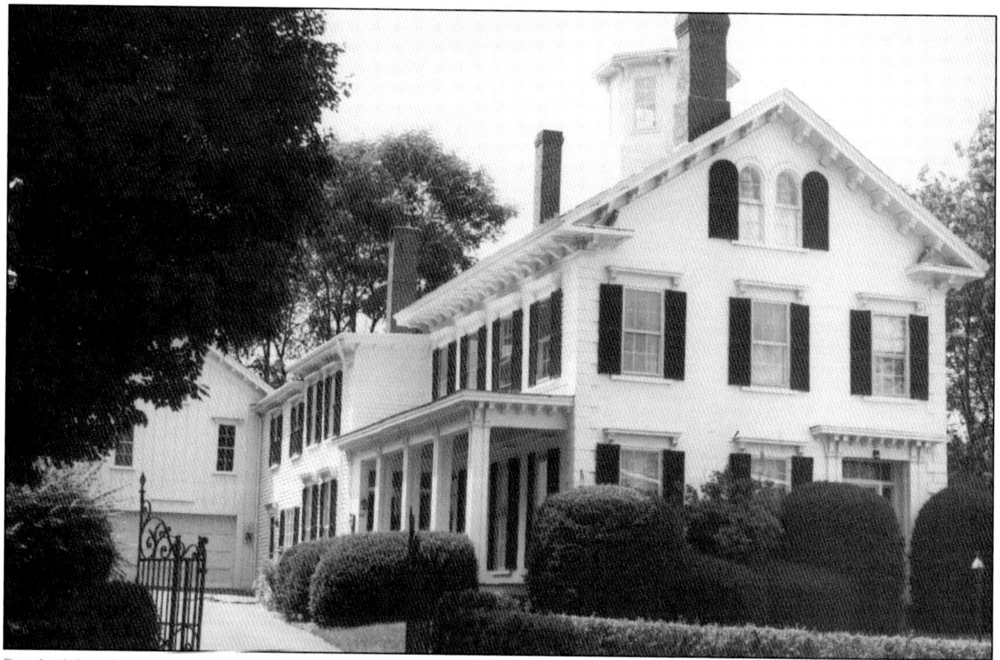

Probably the most impressive and meticulously kept mid-19th-century house in Georgetown is this c. 1860 Italianate house at 67 Central Street. With corner quoining and a facade sheathed in flush boards, the well-detailed house is further embellished with heavy bracketing, a side porch with squared columns, and a bracketed octagonal cupola. The barn was sheathed in vertical batten-board siding and retains its original siting at the end of the carriage drive. In all, this house, its barn, and the well-planted grounds offer an example of how attractive a historic house can be when maintained in this manner. (Courtesy of the Georgetown Historical Commission.)

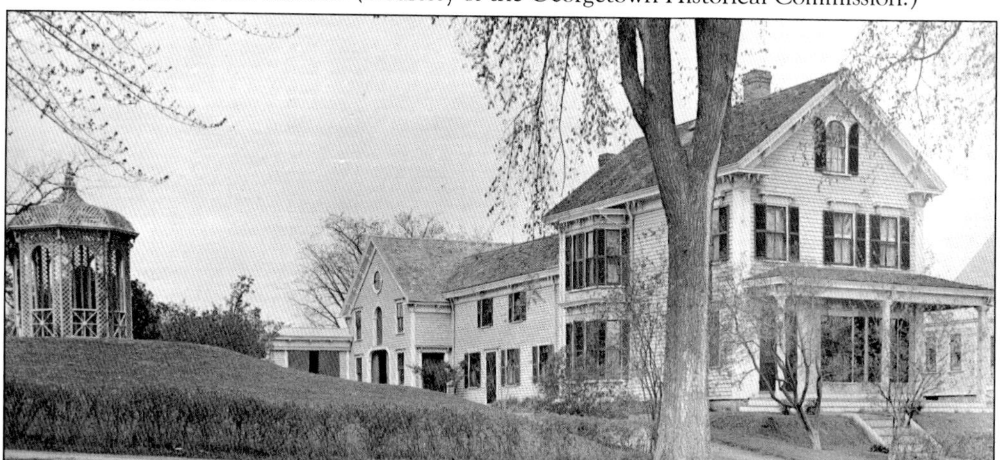

The former rectory to Old St. Mary's Church was purchased in 1881 by Rev. Edward L. McLure (who served as pastor from 1878 to 1887) from the G.W. Boynton family. Built c. 1860 on Central Street, the Italianate house had a side lawn embellished with an octagonal latticework summerhouse. Due to the distance between the church at the corner of East Main and Elm Streets and the rectory, an oratory was created in one room for parishioners. Today, this is the site of the shopping center where Center Pharmacy (now CVS) is located, just south of the police department and the Central Fire Company. (Courtesy of the Georgetown Historical Society.)

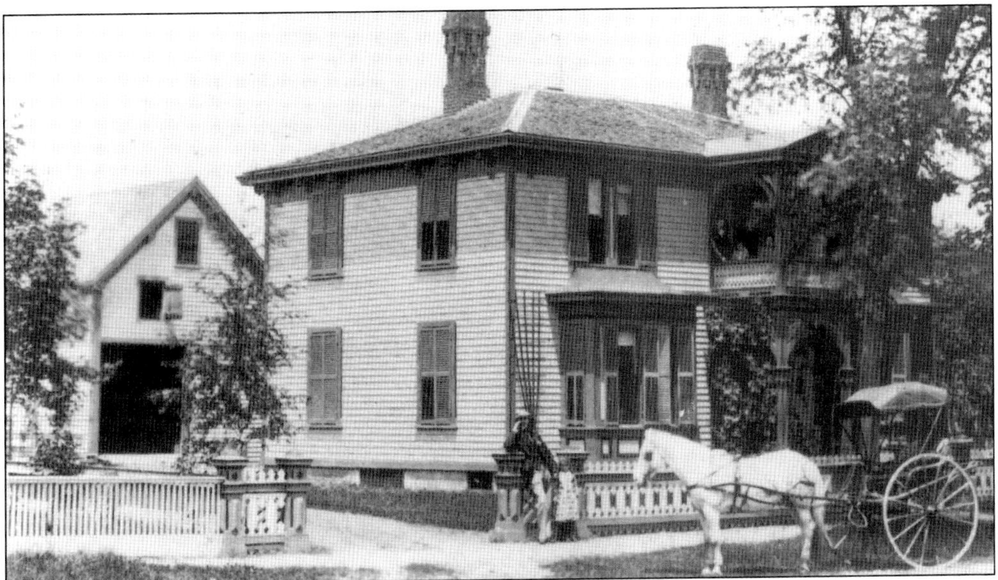

A one-horse shay is stopped in front of the house of Dr. Richmond B. Root at 24 North Street, opposite Pleasant Street. Built c. 1820 by Greenleaf Spofford as a simple Federal house, it was greatly remodeled in 1874 when Dr. Richmond Root purchased it and added scrollwork, fretwork railings, a Stick-style balcony on the second floor, and heavy bracketing along the cornice eaves. Dr. Richmond Root was the son of Dr. Martin Root (originally of Root's Corners in Newbury) and was the second of three generations of his family to serve as a highly respected local physician. Richmond Root's son, Dr. Raymond R. Root, lived at 7 Pleasant Street, near Lincoln Park. (Courtesy of Homer K. Tapin.)

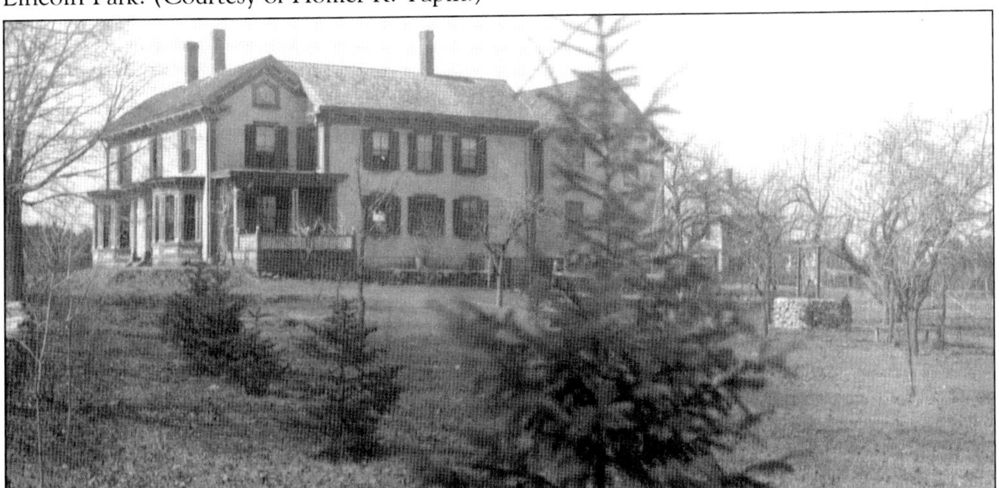

The house at 117 West Main Street was a double-bay Victorian with a large ell in the rear. Part of it was moved to its present location from Federal City and remodeled c. 1870. Typical of Italianate houses (in this case a remodeling of an earlier house), it had orioles flanking the front entrance. It was the home of Rev. Bartlett Hardy Weston (1840–1932), Georgiana Dodge Weston (1856–1929), and daughters Marion and Ruth. Reverend Weston, a graduate of Dartmouth, taught at numerous West Coast schools and was later the headmaster of Atkinson Academy. Weston later served as a missionary among the Sioux Indians at Santee Agency, Nebraska. (Courtesy of Louise A. Richardson.)

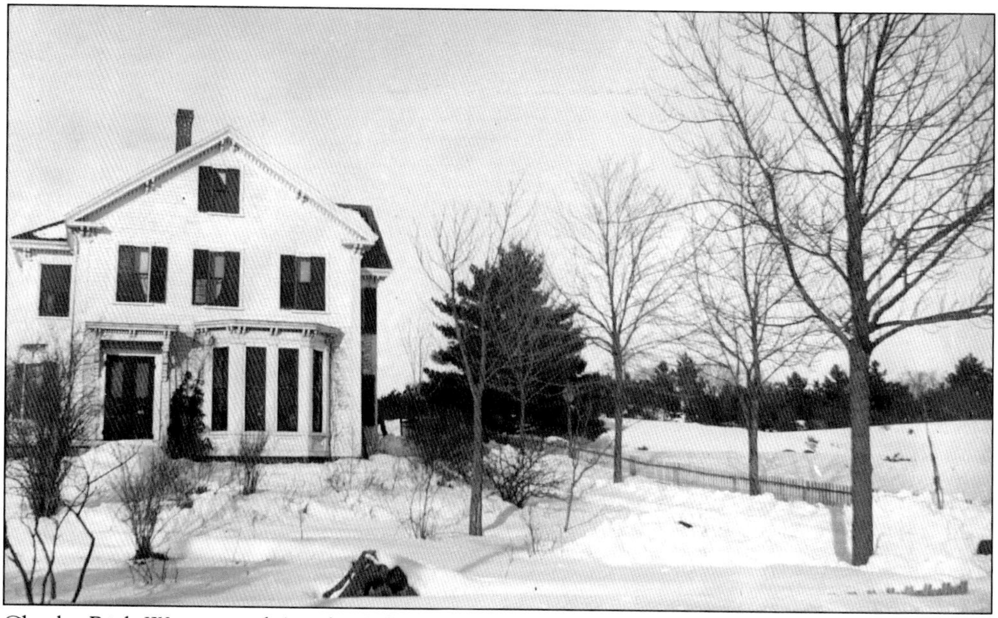

Charles Rich Weston and Amelia Adams Weston built this Italianate house at 163 West Main Street. A simple, wood-framed house, it has a large bay window to the right of the front door. It was otherwise a straightforward Victorian house. In the rear of the property was a stable where Essex, the family horse, was stabled. (Courtesy of Louise A. Richardson.)

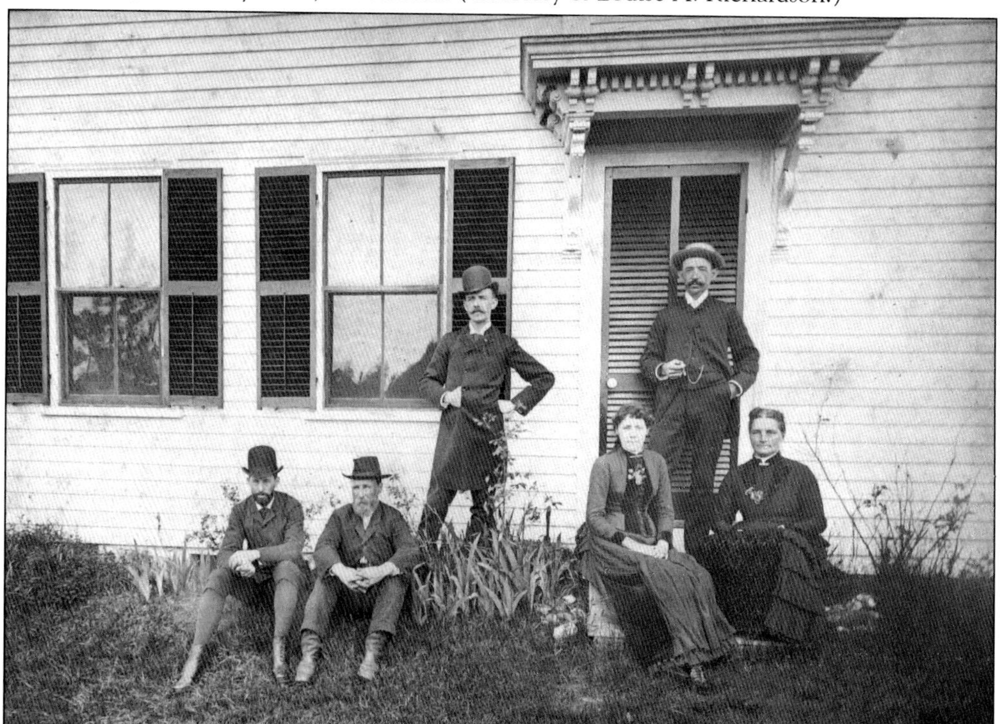

Members of the Weston family pose in 1885 on the side of 163 West Main Street. The only embellishment to the side of the house was the double-bracketed lintel above the doorway. (Courtesy of Louise A. Richardson.)

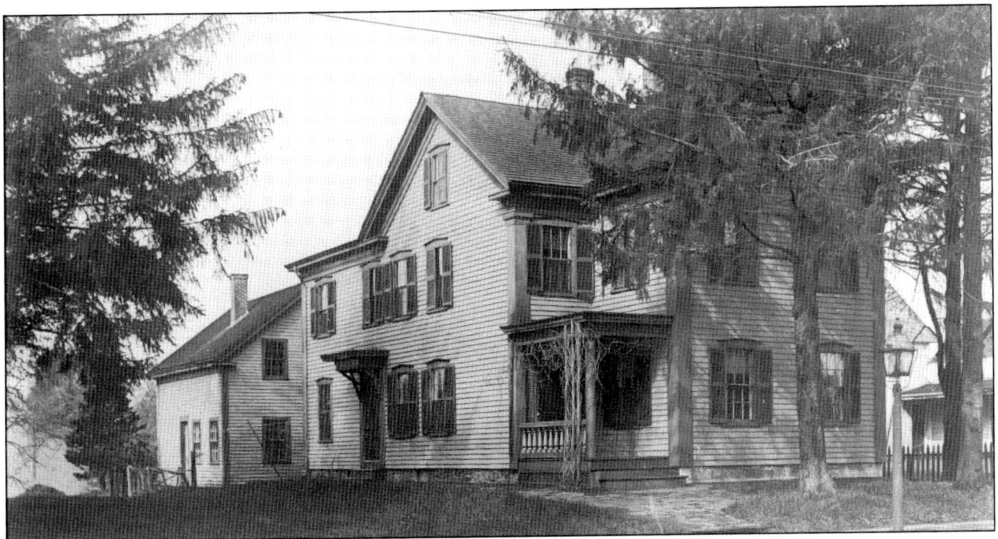

Orlando Barnard Tenney (1816–1899) built his house in 1874 at 52 West Main Street. Judge Tenney served as a justice of the peace and as a trial justice for four decades, having been appointed in 1857. He also served as the first librarian of the Georgetown Peabody Library and as a state representative and town moderator. He was among the most respected of Georgetonians. (Courtesy of the Georgetown Historical Society.)

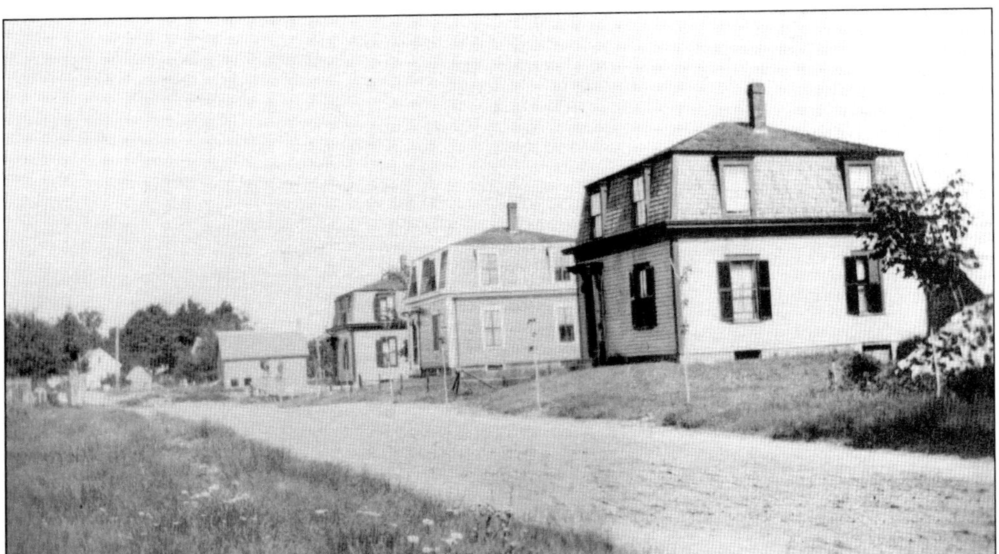

These mansard-roofed cottages were built on Boardman Street off North Street c. 1870. Following the Civil War, houses were often built with fashionable mansard roofs, which had been introduced in France in the early 17th century by architect Francois Mansard. By 1870, the mansard roof was used as often on mansions as it was on one-story cottages. (Courtesy of the Georgetown Historical Society.)

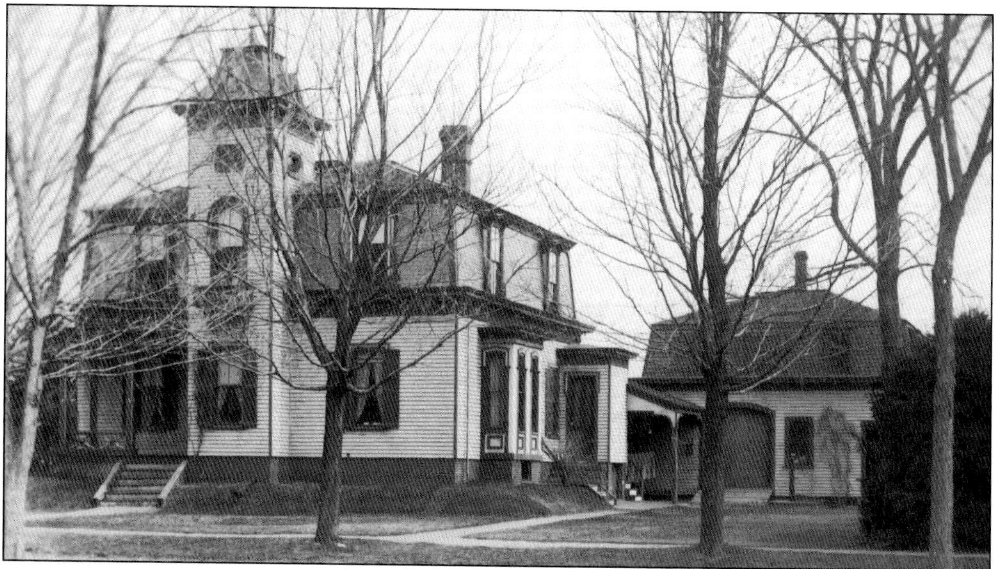

The Brewster House was built in 1872 by wealthy shoe manufacturer Walter M. Brewster at 14 Pleasant Street, opposite Lincoln Park. A small Second French Empire cottage, it was given an even grander aspect by the addition of a two-story, mansard-roofed tower. With rounded windows, oval windows, and pedimented dormer windows, this fanciful and architecturally eccentric house still retains its unique character after having been converted to the Merton E. Roberts Jr. & Conte Funeral Home. (From the collection of Albert E. Meader.)

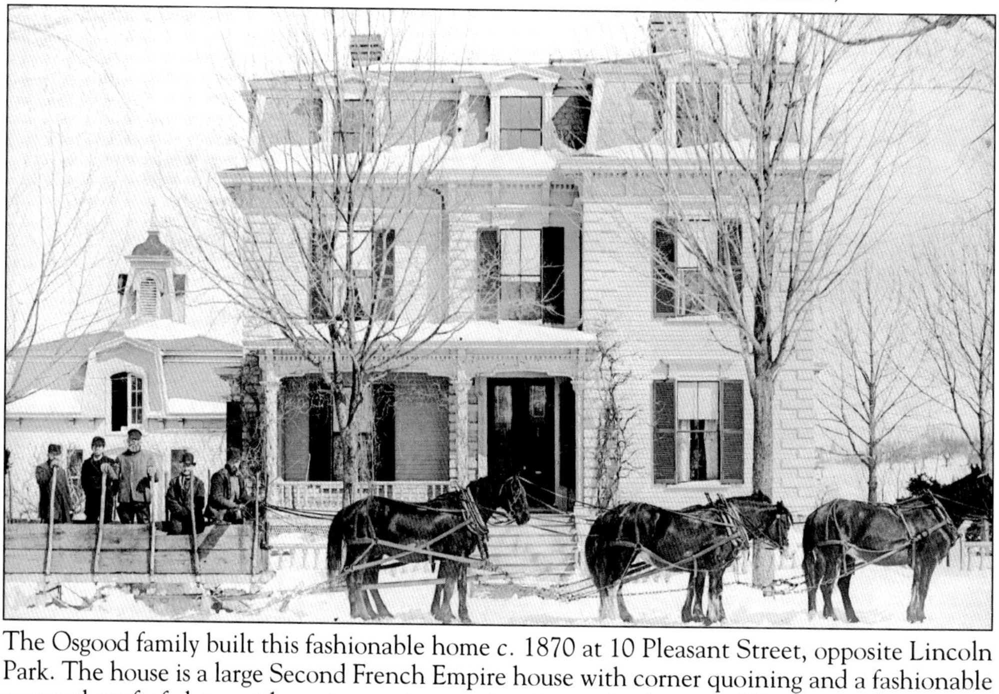

The Osgood family built this fashionable home *c.* 1870 at 10 Pleasant Street, opposite Lincoln Park. The house is a large Second French Empire house with corner quoining and a fashionable mansard roof of slate, with an impressive carriage house in the rear. (Similar to the carriage house roof is that on 55 West Main Street, also built *c.* 1870.) In this 1892 photograph, a team of six horses has been harnessed to a pung, which will roll rather than plow the recent snowfall along the streets of Georgetown for sleighs. (From the collection of Albert E. Meader.)

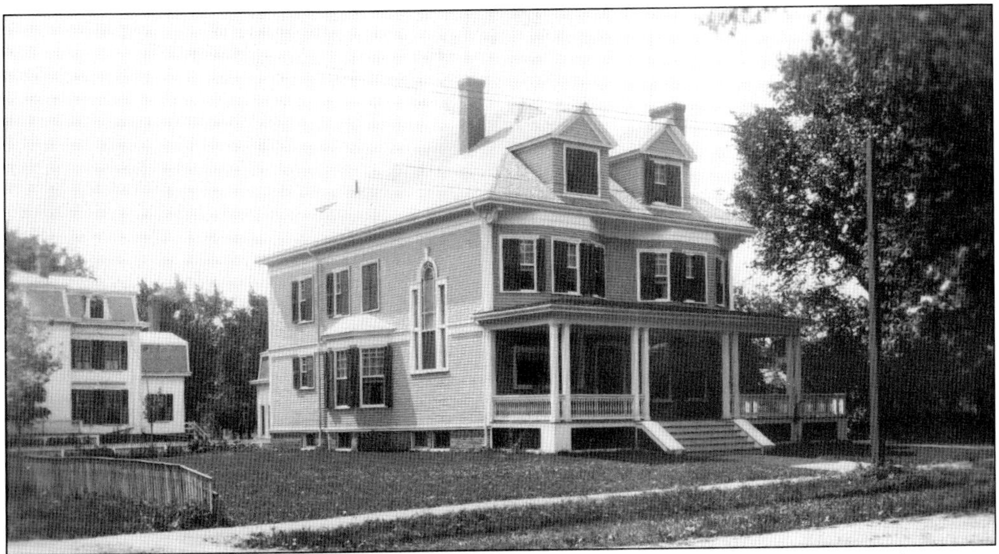

This impressive Colonial Revival house was built in 1900 by the Harriman family at the corner of North and Pleasant Streets. A high-style house, it had a double swell-bay facade with a dormered hip roof. Note the elongated Palladian stair-hall window on the side and the paired porch columns, all of which were impressive high-style Colonial Revival details. On the left is the rear of Dr. Raymond R. Root's house, on Pleasant Street. (From the collection of Albert E. Meader.)

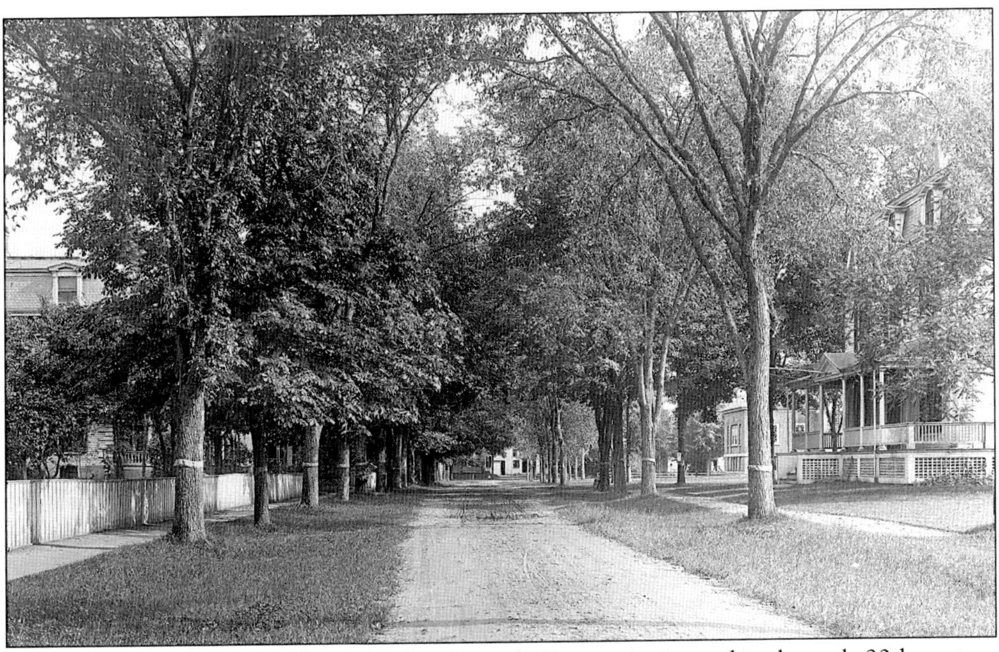

Pleasant Street, which runs from North to Lincoln Streets, is pictured in the early 20th century and obviously lives up to its name. With houses set back from the street and mature shade trees, this was truly a pleasant street. To the center right, a corner of the Georgetown Peabody Library can be seen. (Courtesy of the Georgetown Historical Society.)

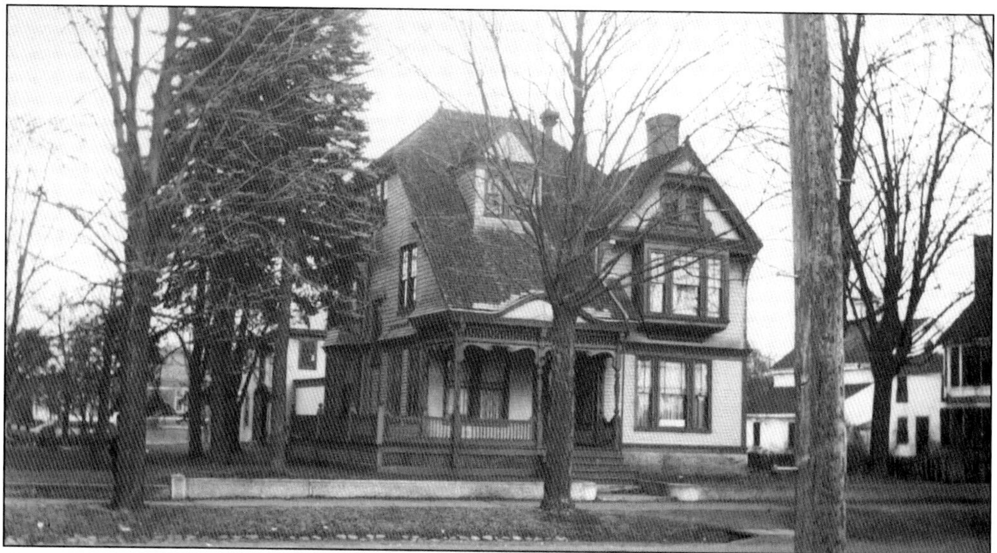

The George Jewett Tenney House was built in 1886 on East Main Street near Park Street following a disastrous fire that destroyed much of Pentucket Square. This Queen Anne house is quite distinctive, in that it is an asymmetrical Victorian house with a sloping hip roof, a corner piazza with an eyebrow swell, and a projecting three-part flat oriole on the second floor below the frontal gable. This house has now been converted to apartments. (Courtesy of Homer K. Tapin.)

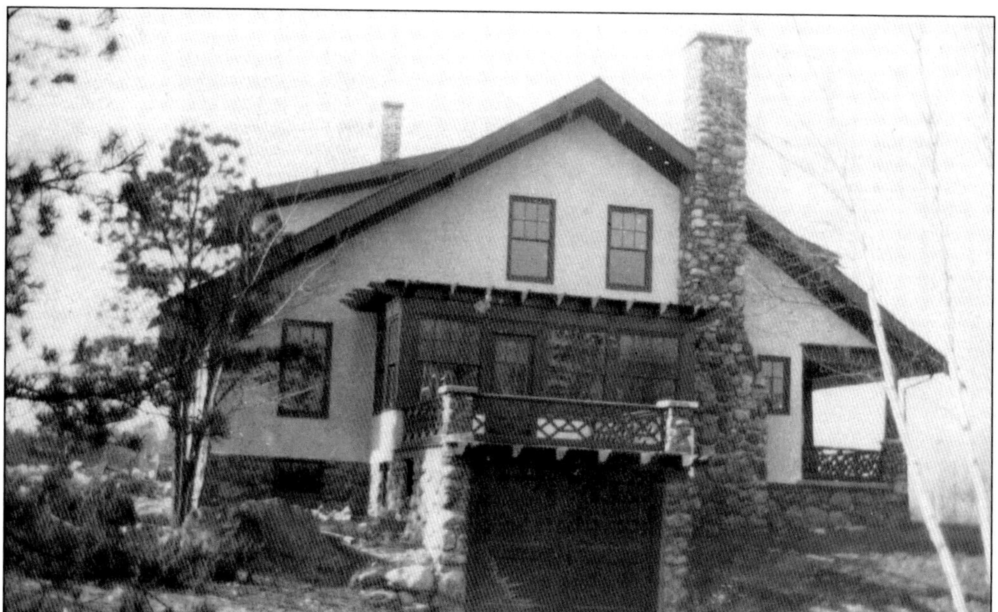

This Craftsman-style bungalow was built in 1915 by Dr. Richard B. Larkin and Greta Morse Larkin at 170 West Main Street. It was later the home of Thelma Larkin and Rollo A. Richardson. The bungalow has a long sloping roof, with random fieldstone used for the foundation, pier supports, and chimneys. The bracketed overhanging roof of the porch and the Chinese Chippendale–inspired balustrades add great distinction to this Arts and Crafts house. (Courtesy of Louise A. Richardson.)

Nine

The Baldpate Inn and Hospital

The house that became the Baldpate Inn was built in 1724 and stood on the south side of Bald Pate Hill, in the West Rowley section of town. Originally the home of Dr. George Mighill, it remained the residence of Mighill descendants until 1894, when Paul Nelson Spofford (son of Paul Spofford of the New York firm Spofford & Tileston) purchased the house and adapted it as the Baldpate Inn. A wealthy man, he hired Mr. and Mrs. William Bray in 1894 to manage the inn. According to *The History of Essex County*, "its success was due to the efforts of its managers. . . . It was their hospitality, good food and hard work which brought the inn fame." The innkeepers offered not only old-fashioned hospitality but also "charming walks, drives over fine roads, the finest to be found in Essex County, with boating, fishing and lawn tennis furnishing the means for an abundant out door recreation."

In the early 20th century, the Baldpate Inn was the also the scene in early October of the annual foxhunt of the Myopia Hunt Club. The club members would have an early breakfast at *Indian Hill Farm*, the estate of the Ben Perley Poor in West Newbury, after which the fox hunt would commence, with riders and hunting dogs perusing the fox through the Essex County countryside. After the hunt, members would dine at the Baldpate Inn. One of the most famous guests of the Myopia Hunt who dined at the Baldpate Inn was Edward, Prince of Wales (later King Edward VIII), who rode in the 1924 hunt. The view from the piazza at the Baldpate Inn was breathtaking. With open fields gently descending from the slope of the hill, the panorama of surrounding hills and countryside was superb. The *Georgetown Advocate* said on July 12, 1890, that "the view from [the piazza] is grand and embraces the city of Haverhill, the Saddleback mountains in N.H., Agamentleus [*sic*] in Me. On the north, the Atlantic ocean and the hills of old Rowley and Ipswich on the east; those of Hamilton, Topsfield and Boxford on the south, while immediately in front of the house and in full sight is a pretty lake."

In 1939, the old inn was sold to a consortium of doctors from Boston. The Baldpate Hospital was opened for the treatment of patients with neuroses, personality disorders, alcohol and drug addictions, and psychoses. The basic premise was to offer an attractive, homelike setting for 40 patients in an old New England inn, with severe psychotics being confined to an independent hospital unit. With 100 acres of land, the attractiveness of the natural scenery was as evident in the mid-20th century as it had been in the late 19th century. Ellsworth Tidd once said, "It seems appropriate . . . that having started out as the home of a doctor, it has, in a way, returned to its original station still a house of healing."

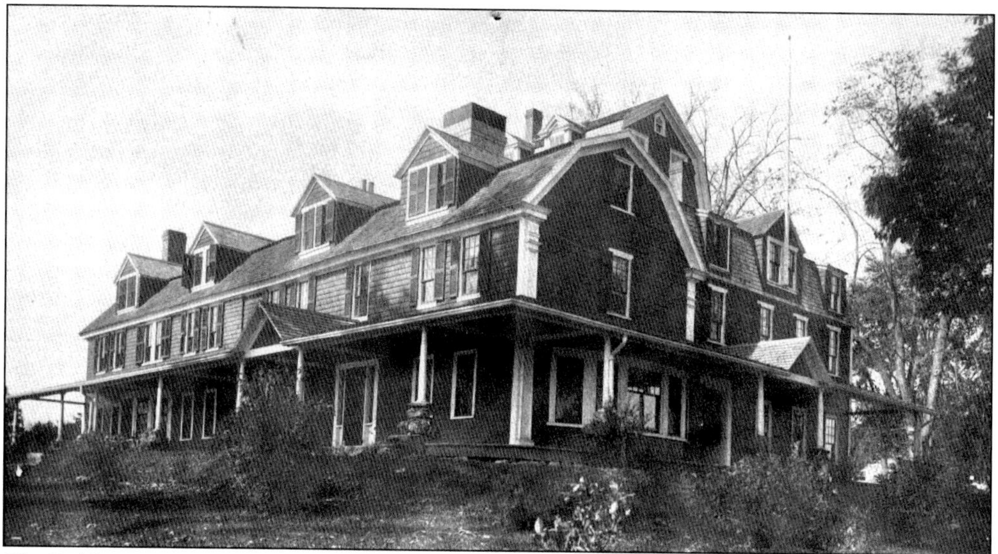

The Baldpate Inn was originally built in 1724 by Nathaniel Mighill as his home. It was enlarged *c.* 1734 by his son, Dea. Stephen Mighill. A wealthy family of aristocratic pretensions, the Mighills kept slaves, who catered to their every need and built many of the extant stone walls on the property. In 1889, the house was purchased from John and Elizabeth Bridges Mighill by Paul Nelson Spofford and became known as the Baldpate Inn. For the next five decades, the inn offered country retreats for visitors to Georgetown. The old house had numerous additions made for guestrooms, many of which were occupied by families who returned every summer. (Courtesy of Louise A. Richardson.)

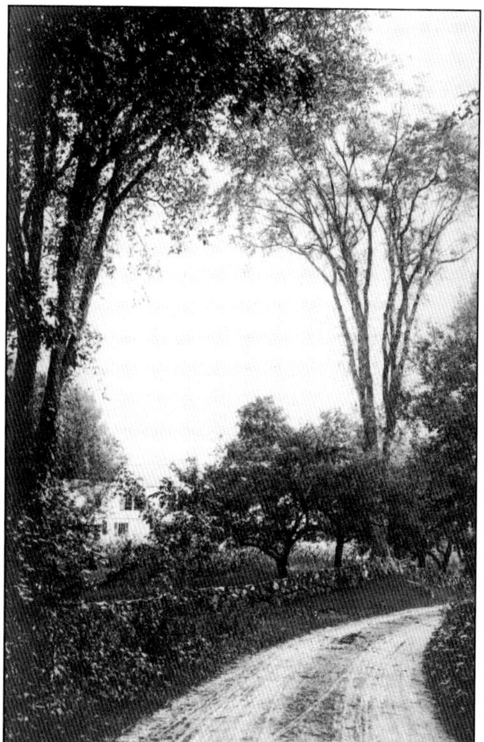

The charming rural drive from the railroad station to the Baldpate Inn, described in *We Visit Old Inns* (1925) as "a rambling, picturesque old farmhouse painted red," had idyllic views of low stone walls, open fields, and tall shade trees. The drive created a sense of pleasurable relaxation for guests even before their arrival at the inn. The "four-in-hands pulling the Tally-Ho always took the curve onto Baldpate Road at a run for the uphill drive to the inn's entrance and into the curving and steep inn yard." (Courtesy of the Georgetown Historical Society.)

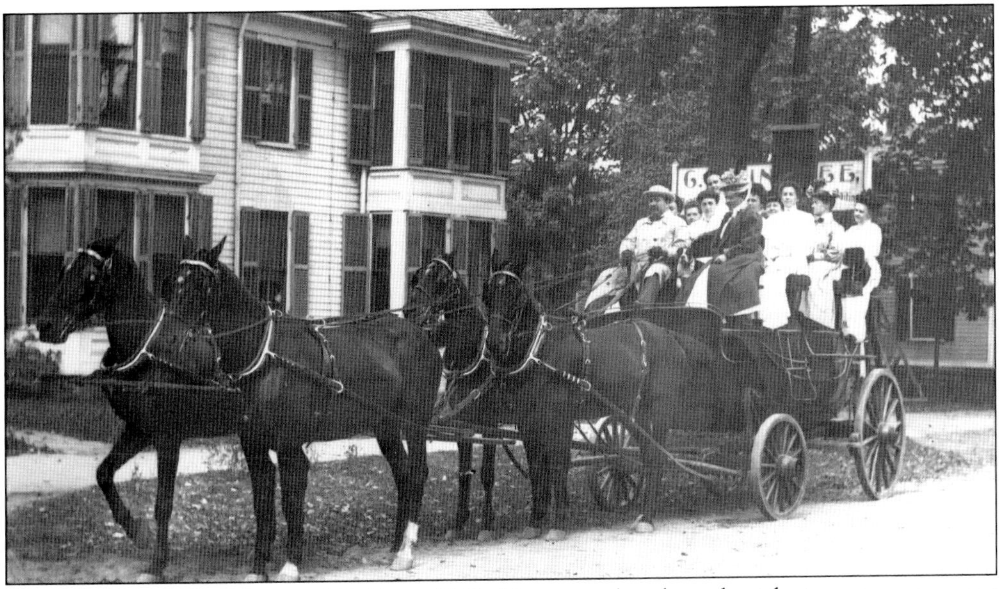

The yellow-and-black-trimmed Baldpate Tally-Ho, an enclosed coach with six seats on top, was a popular attraction for guests arriving at the South Georgetown depot of the Boston & Maine Railroad. The four-horse team (named Duke, Duncan, Frank, and Fred) is pictured *c.* 1907 passing 20 North Street. The driver is William Bray, holding the reins. Harriet Olive Harriman (Mrs. Calvin Pingree), the first Georgetown telephone operator and aunt of his son-in-law, is seated beside him on the right. The Tally-Ho attracted as much attention as it passed through town as the excitement it gave its riders. A contemporary newspaper account said that Bray would entertain his guests by driving the Tally-Ho "at a spanking pace all around our part of the world, passing Stanley Steamers, which ran all of twenty-five miles an hour." (From the collection of Albert E. Meader.)

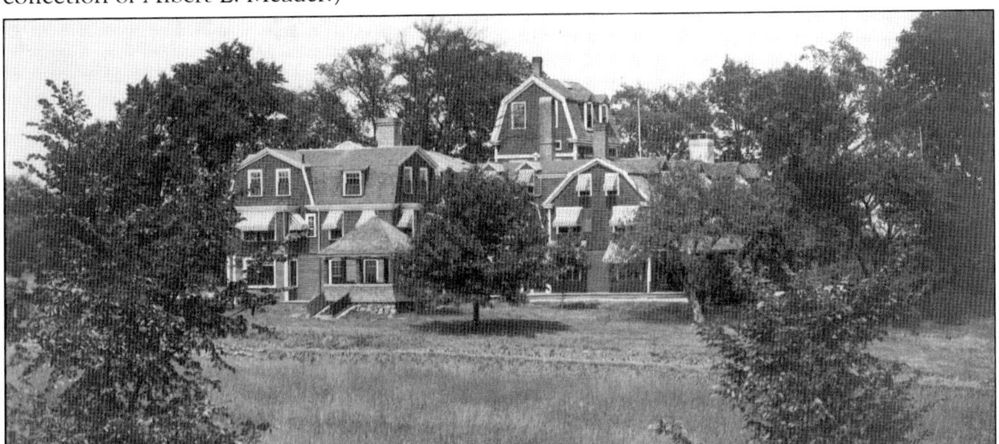

By the early 20th century, so many Colonial Revival gambrel-roofed extensions had been added to the Baldpate Inn that it seemed one gambrel roof had been built upon another. According to a newspaper of the time, Paul Nelson Spofford had "the gambrel-roofed tower-like structure added in 1895 as his personal quarters during his visits to the inn so he could enjoy an unobstructed view of Baldpate Pond and the surrounding countryside while in residence" during the summer months. This gambrel-roofed addition can be seen in the center, rising high above the other roofs. (Courtesy of the Georgetown Historical Society.)

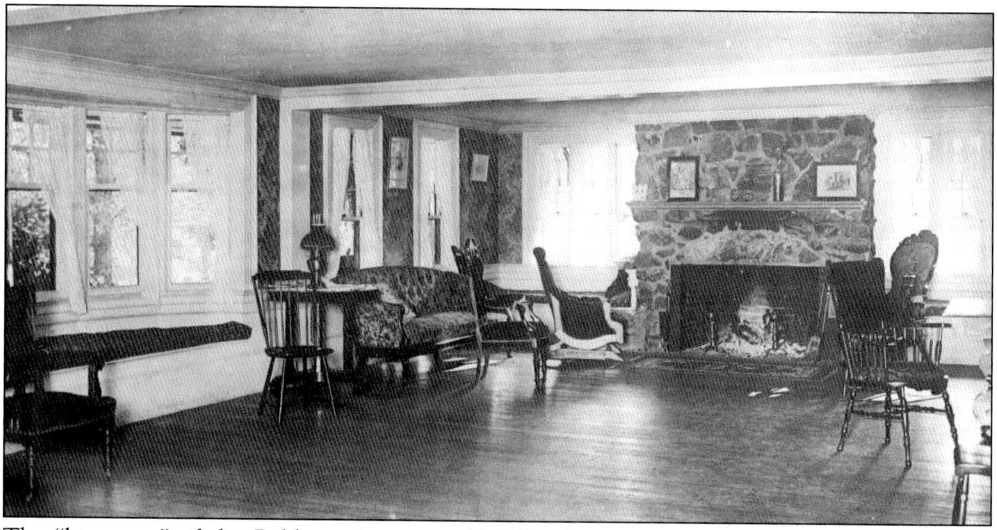

The "big room" of the Baldpate Inn was added by the Brays soon after their arrival. It was where guests often congregated around a blazing fire in the stone fireplace or had impromptu dances. With a wide assortment of furniture from elegant Empire sofas to Victorian upholstered parlor chairs, the room was comfortable without being pretentious. Mary Northend, in her 1925 book *We Visit Old Inns*, described her visit to the inn as an enchanting time: "Alluring quaint nooks come upon us as we turn corners, each one showing an individuality that is charming." (Courtesy of the Georgetown Historical Society.)

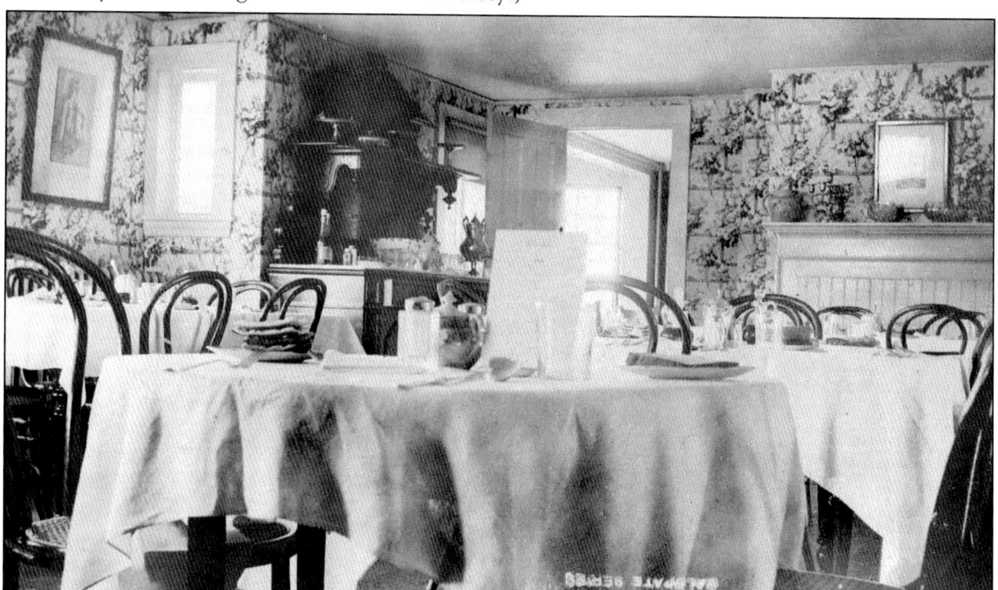

The dining room had linen-covered tables with simple Bentwood side chairs for the guests. Guests were summoned to dinner by the banging of a brass gong in the front hall. Ellsworth Tidd wrote that "food was appetizing and abundant. The specialties were broiled chicken, golden bantam corn in season and Mrs. Bray's delicious cinnamon cake. Many an afternoon the local ladies would drive to the inn for cinnamon cakes and tea." It is no wonder that so many guests returned year after year and that the inn retained its popularity with Georgetown residents. (Courtesy of the Georgetown Historical Society.)

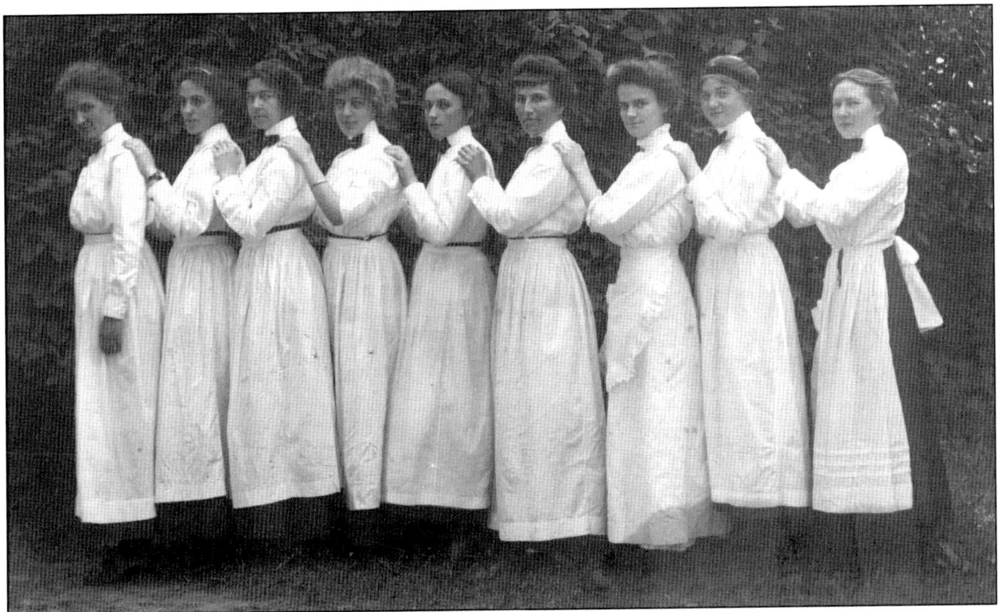

The waitresses of the Baldpate Inn and Mrs. William Bray (on the far right) line up for a group photograph in the early 20th century. An evening in a rocking chair on the piazza of the inn after one of Mrs. Bray's dinners must have been sheer pleasure a century ago. The Brays' daughter Wilhelmine and her husband, William A. Harriman, continued the exceptional hospitality offered by her parents after her father's death in 1922. (From the collection of Albert E. Meader.)

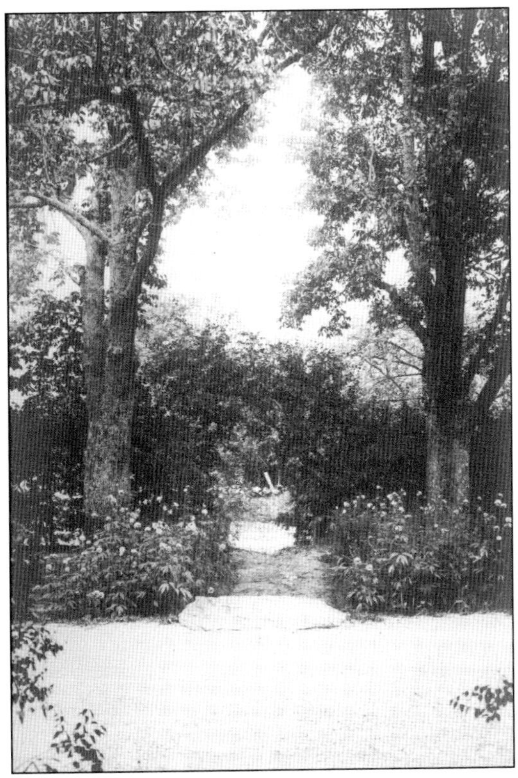

In this view, looking from the entrance to the Baldpate Inn, two trees flank a walkway that is lined with flowers and shrubs. The Baldpate Tally-Ho would pull up in front of the inn, and excited guests would descend from their seats at this spot. Their first view would be of massive trees and extensive grounds of 100 acres and then of the extensive piazza lined with armchairs, rocking chairs, and benches. The *Georgetown Advocate* once said, "From the heat and dust of cities and towns to this cool, sequestered retreat the change is delightful, and opens to life new springs of joy. Come and rest." (Courtesy of the Georgetown Historical Society.)

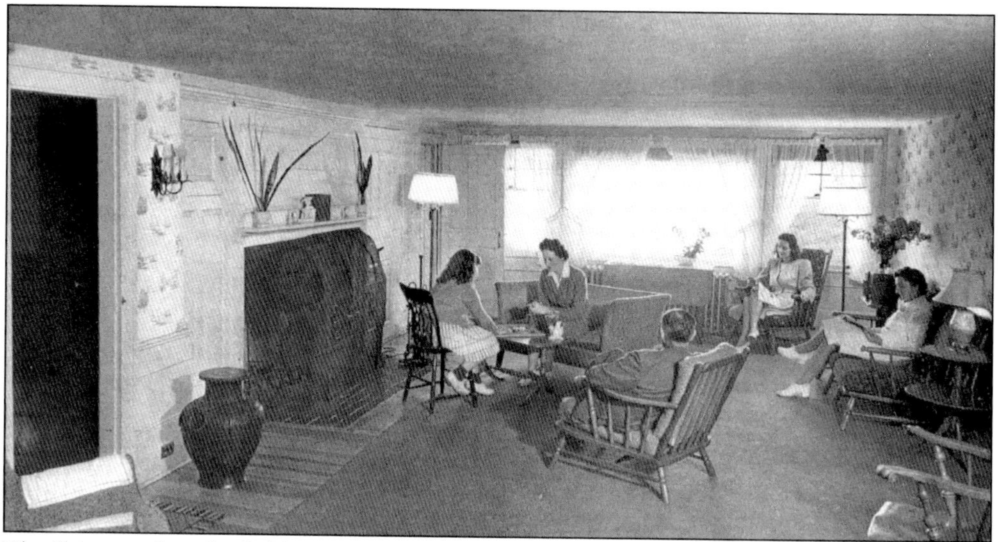

The "big room" at the Baldpate Inn was easily adapted in 1939 for the new living room of the Baldpate Hospital. In this c. 1950 view, residents and staff relax in a comfortably furnished room with the 18th-century paneling intact on the fireplace wall. One of the aspects of the prescribed treatment at the hospital was a strict avoidance of any form of institutional atmosphere with a homelike social environment. The man in the center, with his back to the camera, is Dr. Harry Solomon, the consultant psychiatrist and neurologist. On the far right is Nurse Dillon. (Courtesy of the Georgetown Historical Society.)

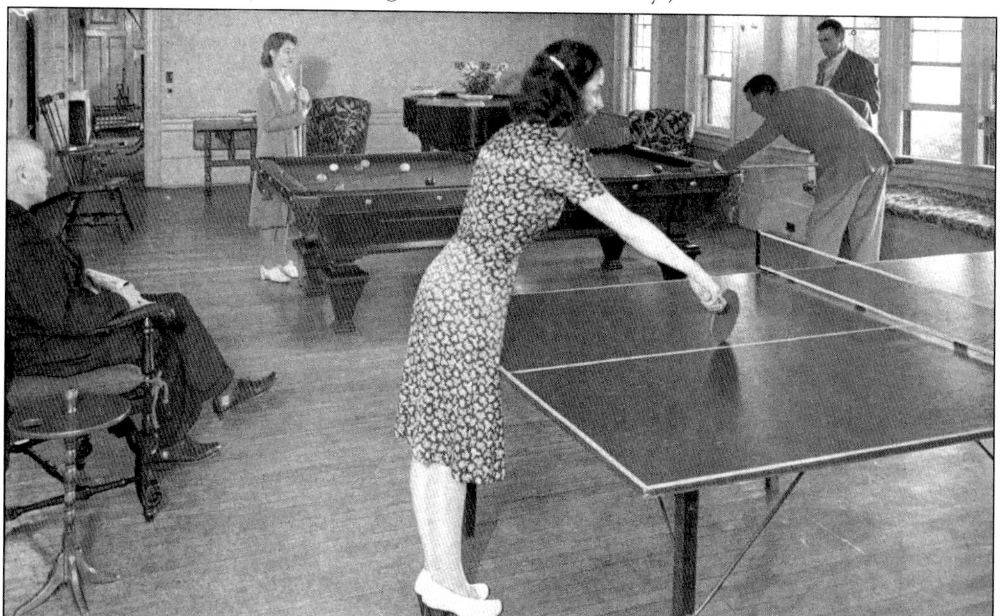

The game room at the Baldpate Hospital had such diversions as billiards, table tennis, and darts, as well as a baby grand piano for musically inclined residents. Seated on the left is Dr. George Schlomer, the resident medical director. These diversions for residents also included swimming and boating on Baldpate Pond, picnics in the surrounding woods and the beach, and excursions to neighboring towns for bowling, dancing, and movies. (Courtesy of the Georgetown Historical Society.)

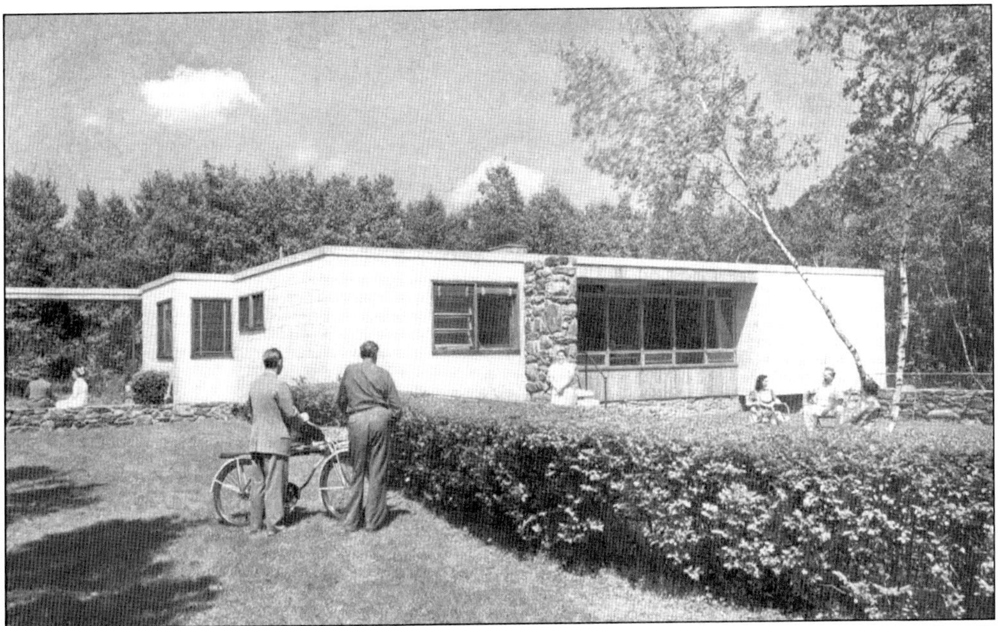

A new building on the grounds of the Baldpate Hospital was built as a one-story hospital with modern rooms and private baths for severely psychotic residents. Dr. Harry Solomon is on the left, holding the handgrips of a bicycle while he and a patient speak with a nurse across a low hedge. (Courtesy of the Georgetown Historical Society.)

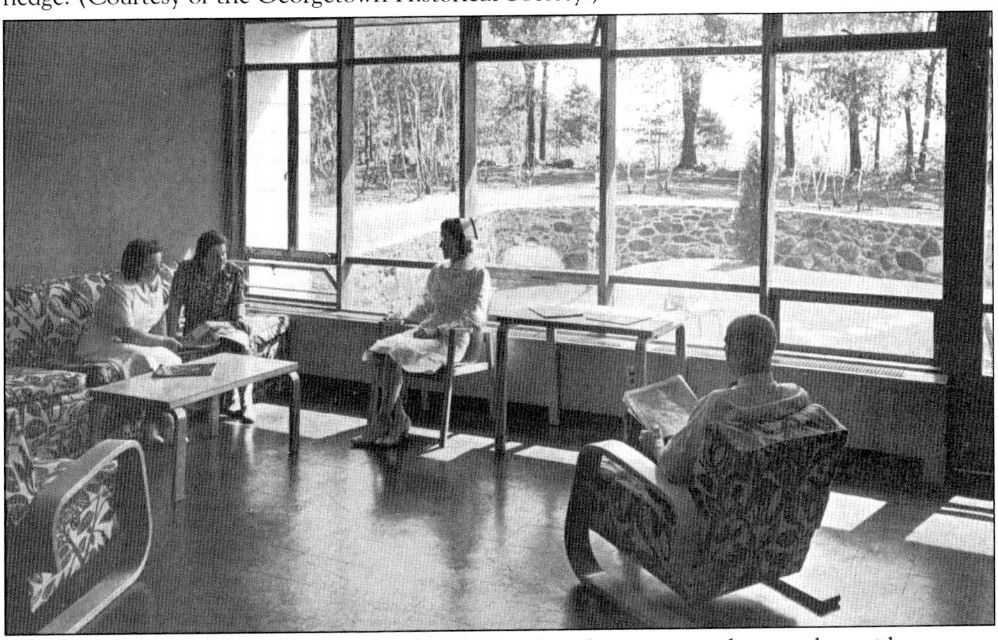

The dayroom at the Baldpate Hospital had a bright, cheery atmosphere with a wide expanse of windows overlooking the scenic grounds. Seen in the center, speaking with two residents, is Nurse Hogan. On the right is Dr. George Schlomer. The hospital was immortalized in the book *Seven Keys to Baldpate*, a mystery thriller written by Earl Derr Biggers and set in the Baldpate Inn during the winter, with seven guests holding an equal number of keys. (Courtesy of the Georgetown Historical Society.)

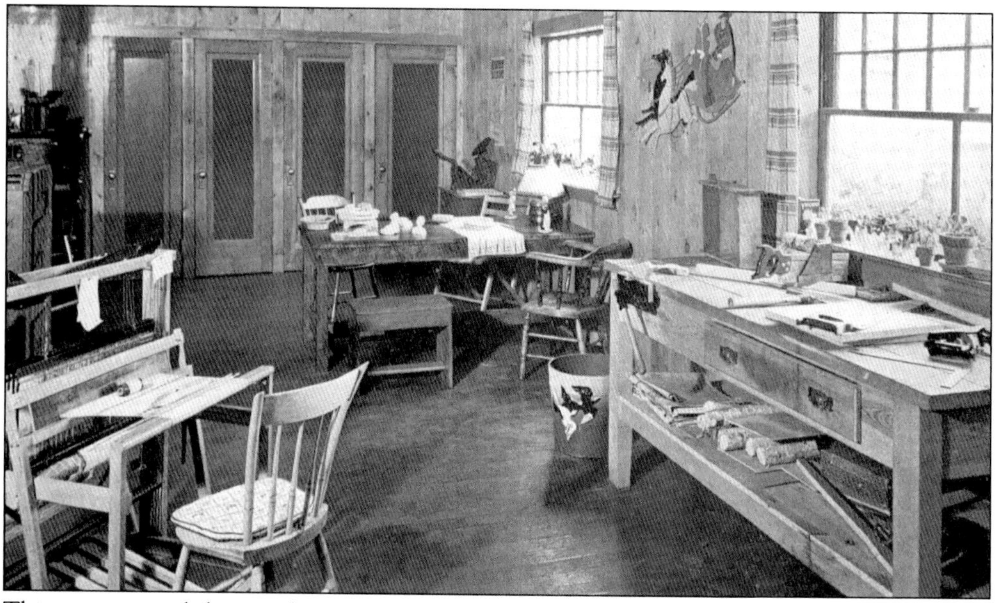

This occupational therapy shop at the Baldpate Hospital had been converted from the stables. It had a weaving loom, a woodworking bench, pottery wheels, and handcraft classes that were under the direction of a well-trained therapist. Mental disorders were usually treated by a combination of medicine and physical activity, rather than operations, to effect a lasting cure. (Courtesy of the Georgetown Historical Society.)

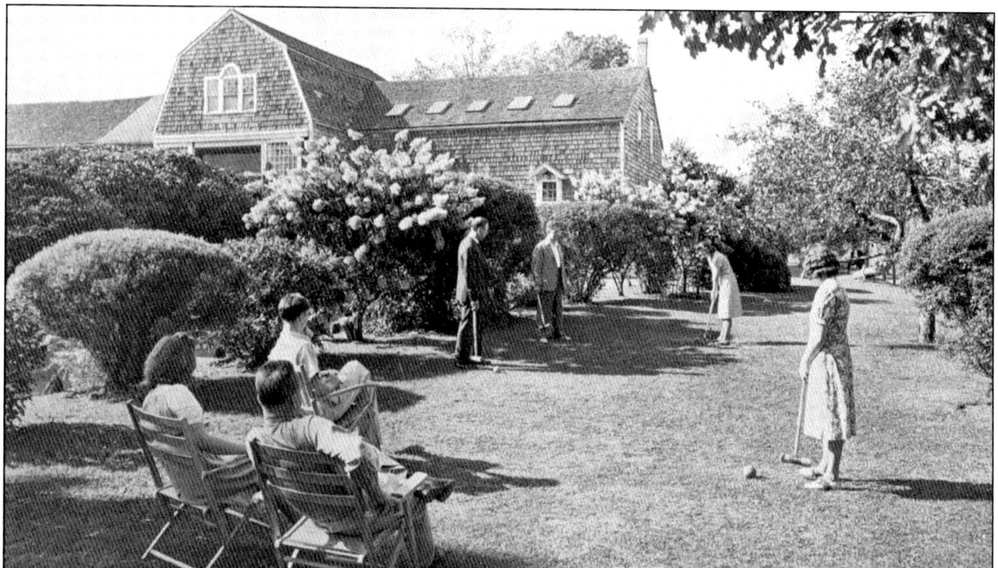

Residents and staff members of the Baldpate Hospital enjoy a game of croquet on a side lawn. The large gambrel-roofed building in the distance originally housed the stables of the Baldpate Inn and were remodeled for the occupational therapy shop. Nurses at the Baldpate Hospital lived in a large mansard-roofed Italianate house at 169 Central Street (once the home of Thurston Hardy) or the Nurses' Home on Baldpate Road. Dr. George Schlomer and Dr. Harry Solomon (both of whom were Jews who fled Germany prior to World War II) lived with their families in houses on the hospital property. (Courtesy of the Georgetown Historical Society.)

Ten

Scenic Georgetown

Georgetown's natural scenery includes dells and valleys; meadowlands; Baldpate, Spofford, and Long Hills; and Scrag, Rock, and Pentucket Ponds. Called in 1875 by the *Boston Traveler* "one of the prettiest and pleasantest of all New England towns," Georgetown retained its undeveloped and countrylike aspect well into the 20th century. The Parker River, Wheeler Brook, Rock Pond, and Pen Brook added to the arable lands, and it was thought that the Pentucket Indians had once cleared the land of trees and brush by slashing and burning, as it was so open in the mid-17th century when first seen by the Puritans. *The History of Essex County* notes that in 1888 the two lakes "of water are very pure. Rock nestles at the foot of gravelly and grassy knolls, and Pentucket for nearly one-fourth of a mile, has on Pond Street a pebbly beach, as its eastern limit." One stretch of open flatland was referred to as Elder's Plain, in honor of Elder Humphrey Rainer, and later as Marlborough, a southeastern section of town. Much of the early development centered on what is now Georgetown Square, and the outlying areas were used for farms and timber forests. In the 19th century, Georgetown was noted for its forests of white oak. Oak was cut on Bald Pate Hill and was used to repair and reside parts of the famous USS *Constitution* (known as Old Ironsides due to the strength of its oak hull) when it was in dry dock in Portsmouth, New Hampshire, in 1858.

In the late 19th century, the bucolic quality of Georgetown attracted people to the ponds and nature trails that created a feeling of rural tranquility. At this time, noted conservationists such as Beltran de la Casas, Charles Eliot, and Elishur Wright began to agitate for the conservation of undeveloped land. In this period (1885–1910), numerous communities around Boston began to designate areas as conservation districts, and the result locally was the 1,112-acre Georgetown-Rowley State Forest in the southwest corner of town.

Charles Eliot, father of the Metropolitan Park System, once said, "[In order for people to] live in health and happiness, they must have space for air, for light, for exercise, for rest, and for the enjoyment of that peaceful beauty of nature, which . . . is so refreshing to the tired souls of the townspeople."

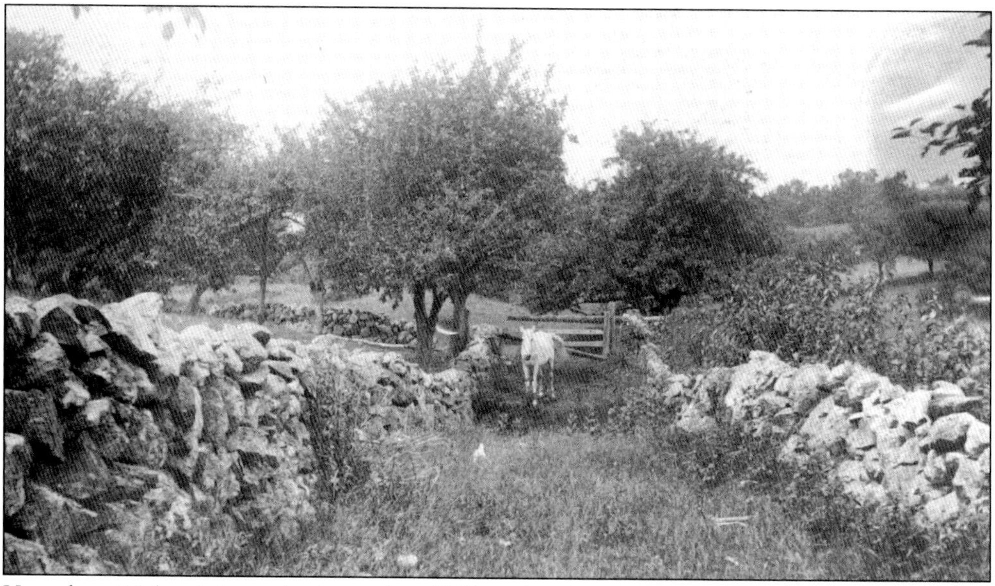

Humphrey Nelson's Lane is pictured *c.* 1890 with a horse trotting between stone walls that mark the edge of open fields. Humphrey Nelson was a lineal descendant of Stephen Nelson, who had settled New Rowley. Through the clearing of fields, farmers since the 17th century stacked scattered stones, creating stone walls that marked the borders of their land and left the fields open for cultivation of crops. Today, the lane is known as Nelson Street and runs from Central Street to the Boxford line just east of Bald Pate Pond. (Courtesy of the Georgetown Historical Society.)

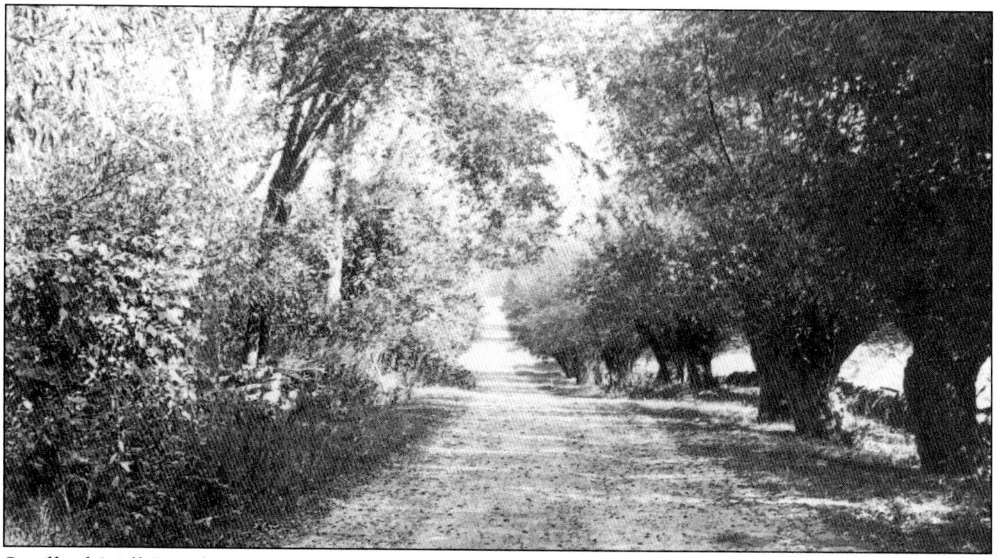

Spofford Mill Road is shown *c.* 1890 as a dirt road, with trees of massive trunk girth on the right. Named for John Spofford (the first permanent resident of the western section of New Rowley that in 1838 became Georgetown), this bucolic setting was typical of how rural Georgetown would remain well into the 20th century. John Spofford lived on Andover Street near West Street. Once the area of numerous members of the extended Spofford family, the road is now known as Spofford Street, near Bald Pate Hill. (Courtesy of the Georgetown Historical Society.)

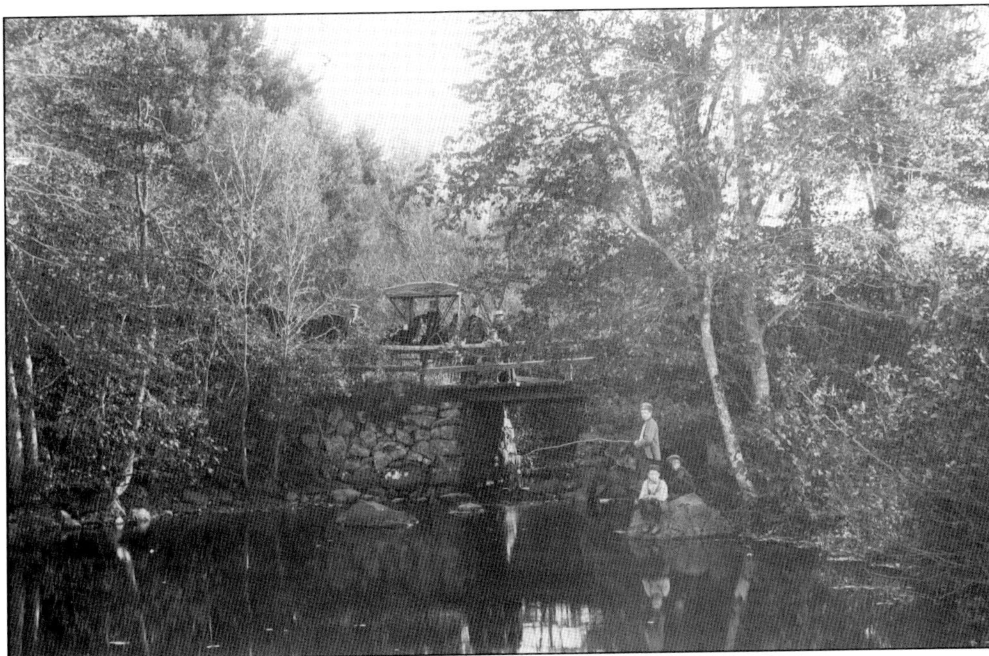

The Squirrel Street (now Thurlow Street) Bridge over the Parker River was built in a naturalistic manner of wood with railings fashioned from sapling trunks. Stones were collected along the brook's edge and stacked to create piers on either side of the brook to support the bridge. In this view, a shay stops on the bridge. Its passengers and three young boys who are fishing from a rock all look toward the photographer. (From the collection of Albert E. Meader.)

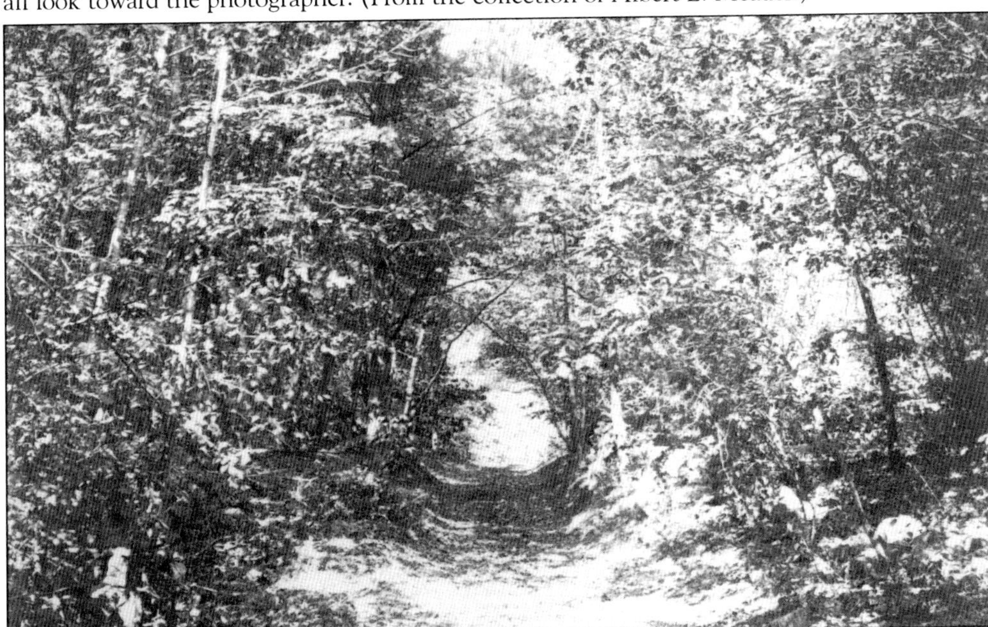

Bailey Lane is pictured *c.* 1890 with a narrow, grass- and moss-covered path shaded by trees and dense foliage on both sides. Bailey Lane (named for Asa Bailey, whose house was located on the lane) runs from West Main Street near the Groveland border to Andover Street, just west of Rock Pond. (Courtesy of the Georgetown Historical Society.)

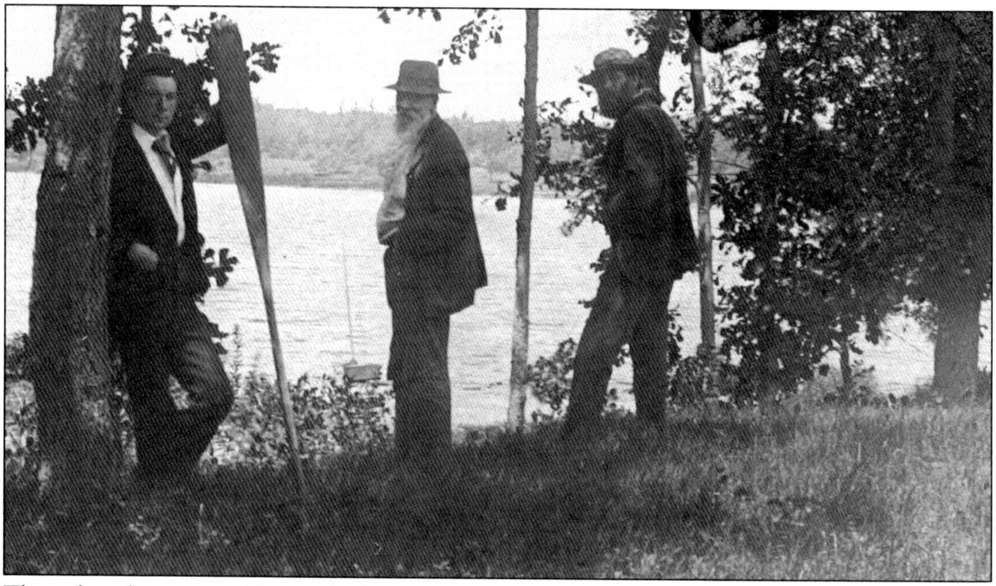

Three friends pose c. 1900 on the bank of Pentucket Pond. The man on the left holds an oar, so they are probably headed for an afternoon of rowing. Many rowboats were drawn up on the shore for lake excursions during the summer months. (Courtesy of the Georgetown Historical Society.)

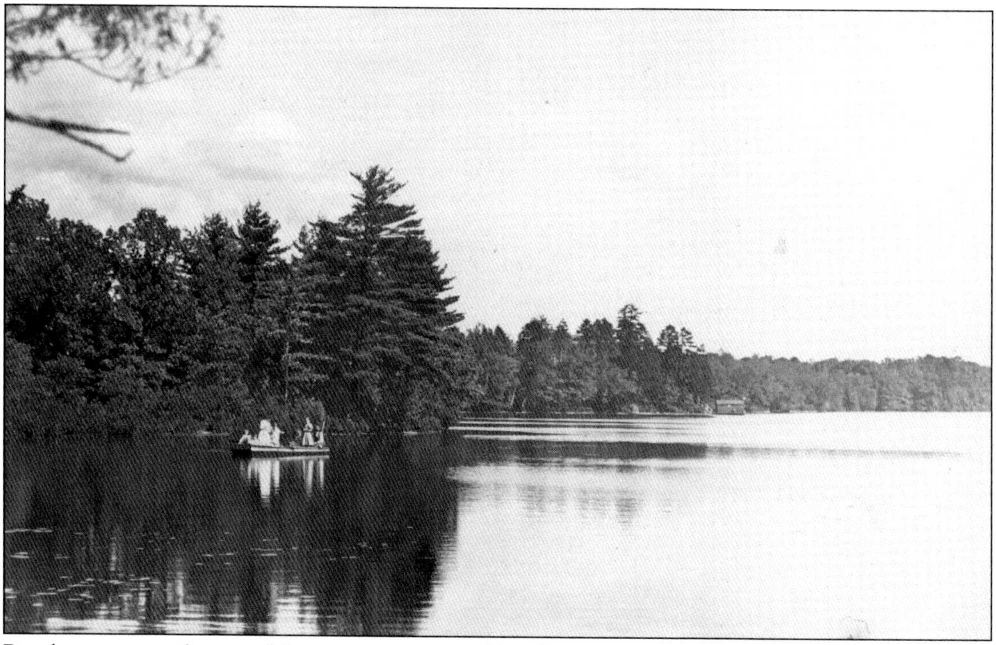

Rowboats were often used for recreation as well as for exercise on Pentucket Pond, referred to in a newspaper article a century ago as one of the "prettiest sheets of water in Essex County." In this view, a group of friends is shown in a rowboat on the south side of the pond. With densely set trees that in some cases came directly to the edge of the pond, the area has been an attractive one for picnics and summer activities that revolve around the picturesque lake. (Courtesy of the Georgetown Historical Society.)

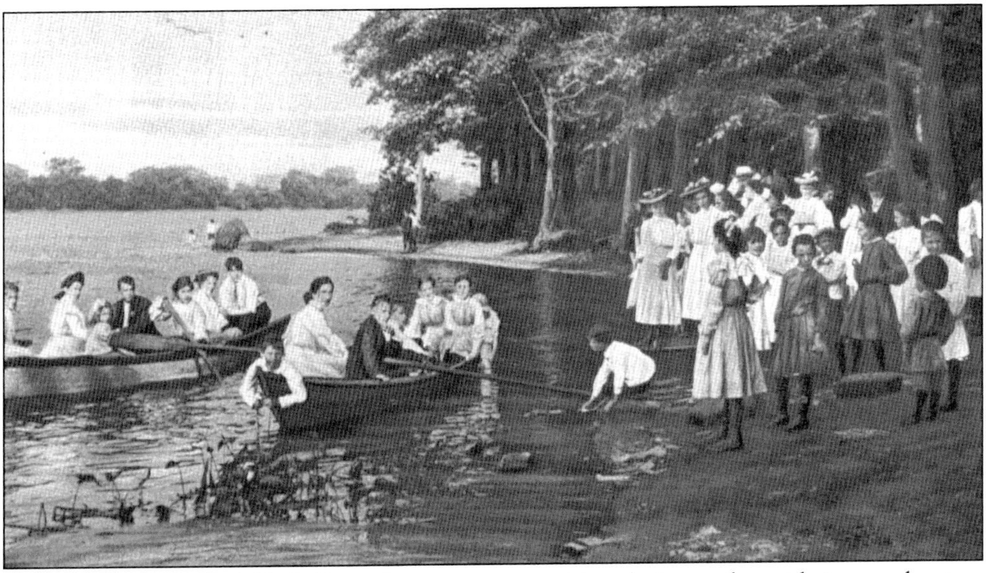

In this *c.* 1905 postcard, York Grove has youngsters waiting their turn for a ride in a rowboat on Pentucket Pond. They seem to be quite well dressed for a day at the lake. York Grove, named for Charles W. York, was a popular destination that once boasted a dance hall with a player piano. On the Fourth of July, a stunt man would parachute to earth from a hot-air balloon, much to the delight of both children and adults. In addition to York Grove, there was Oak Dell in South Georgetown and Little's Grove. (Courtesy of Louise A. Richardson.)

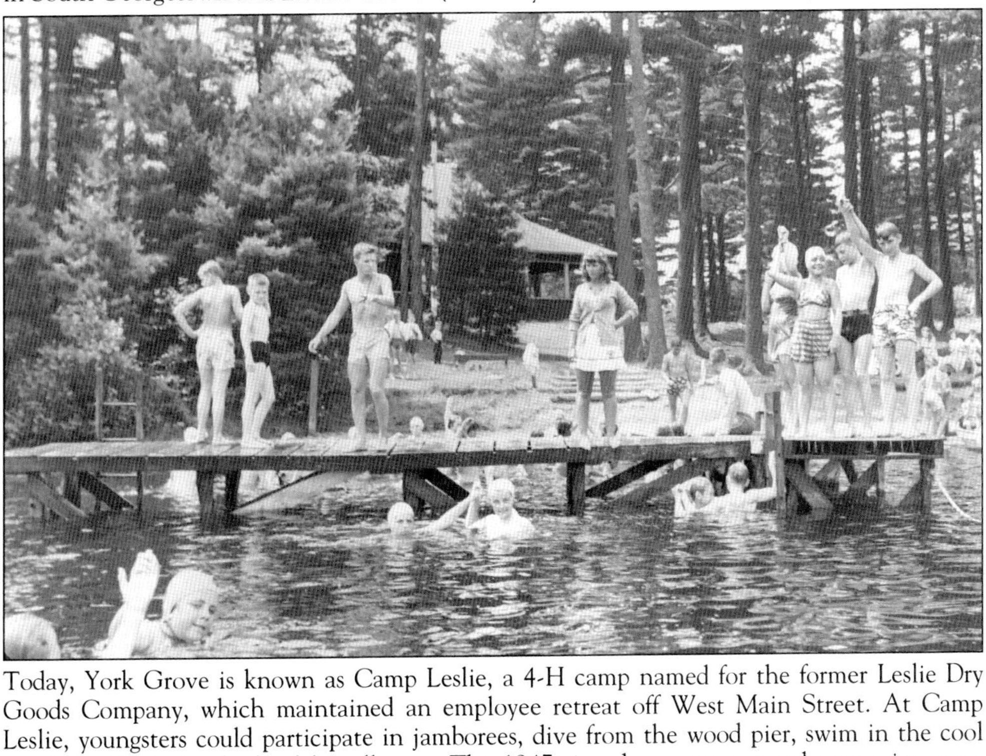

Today, York Grove is known as Camp Leslie, a 4-H camp named for the former Leslie Dry Goods Company, which maintained an employee retreat off West Main Street. At Camp Leslie, youngsters could participate in jamborees, dive from the wood pier, swim in the cool pond, or hike in the shade of the tall pines. This 1947 view shows campers and a gesturing camp councilor enjoying a summer afternoon. (Courtesy of James H. Boynton.)

Acknowledgments

I wish to extend my sincere thanks to Louise A. Richardson, who spearheaded the compilation of this photographic history and who generously loaned many of her family photographs for this book. I also wish to thank the officers and board members of the Georgetown Historical Society for their support, encouragement, and generosity in the use of their photographic archives for this book: Clif Morse, president; Gregg LaBrecque, first vice president; Sue Sprague, second vice president; Barbara Miller, secretary; Dick Elliott, treasurer; Steve Keene, curator; Beverly Knapp; Beth Kostura; Bruce Miller; Dick Thomas; and Sylvia West.

I would also like to thank the following: Sally Applegate of the *Georgetown Record;* James H. Boynton; Jamie Carter; the Central Fire Company—Mike Anderson, Deputy Chief John Durkee, Capt. Jay Barta, and Lt. Rusty Ricker; Dexter; Megan Dumm, my editor; Erie Fire Association No. 4—Chief Herbert T. McDonald, Secretary Brad Legere, Steward Rick Palardy, and Mike Legere; Jane Field, author of *A Brief History of Georgetown (1838–1963)*; Charles E. Flanders, author of *Old Legends of Georgetown, Massachusetts;* Michael P. Franciscovich; Nicole C. Franciscovich; Winifred Holt Gatchell; the Georgetown Historical Commission—Gladys Kneeland (chair), Richard Elliott, Harriett Kneeland, Gloria Maina, Arthur Paquette, and associate Charles Brett; trustees and staff of the Georgetown Peabody Library and Nanci Milone Hill, library director; Forrest P. Hull, author of *Georgetown: The Story of One Hundred Years (1838–1938)*; Robert Johnson Lally, archivist of the Archdiocese of Boston; Bainbridge Morse Larkin Jr.; Daniel Cooper Larkin; David Morse Larkin; Janet Adams Larkin; Albert E. Meader; Daniel E. Meader; Henry M. Nelson, author of "Georgetown" in *The History of Essex County;* Kay Ogden; Arthur Paquette; Peter Pratt; Merton Roberts; Harold C. Roeder; Natalie Severance; Eleanor Spaulding; Claire Spirito; Eleanor Stetson, author of *Tales and Reminiscences of Georgetown;* Homer K. Tapin; Hazel Thompson; Wayland Thompson; Ruth Flanders Tyrie; Gretchen Wilmarth; and Paul Wilmarth.

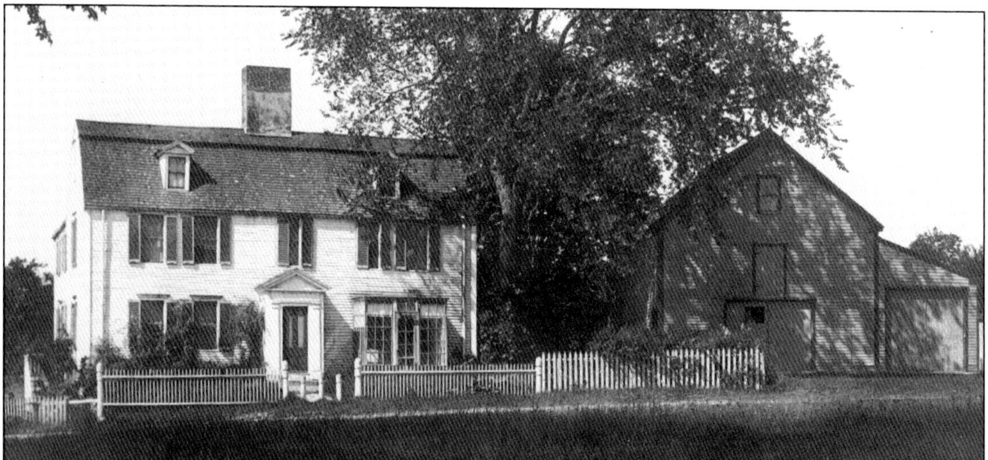

The Georgetown Historical Society purchased the Brocklebank House in 1975 and opened it as the Brocklebank Museum, which is maintained as a house museum with artifacts and furnishings representing the various families that occupied the house. Built c. 1660 by Samuel Brocklebank (1628–1676), the house was located in the West Parish section of Rowley. Brocklebank led the local militia during the Indian Wars. He and his militiamen were killed in 1676 in Sudbury while fighting King Philip and his warriors. In 1858, the house became the parsonage of the Old South Church, with Rev. Charles Beecher occupying the house. The house was sold in 1931 to Everett Spaulding, a descendant of the builder. He and his family lived here until they sold it to the Georgetown Historical Society. (Courtesy of the Georgetown Historical Society.)